Representing Middle-earth

Representing Middle-earth
Tolkien, Form, and Ideology

ROBERT T. TALLY JR.

McFarland & Company, Inc., Publishers
Jefferson, North Carolina

This book has undergone peer review.

LIBRARY OF CONGRESS CATALOGUING-IN-PUBLICATION DATA

Names: Tally, Robert T., Jr., author.
Title: Representing Middle-Earth : Tolkien, form, and ideology / Robert T. Tally Jr.
Description: Jefferson, North Carolina : McFarland & Company, Inc., Publishers, 2024. | Includes bibliographical references and index.
Identifiers: LCCN 2023051266 | ISBN 9780786470372 (paperback : acid free paper) ∞
    ISBN 9781476651927 (ebook)
Subjects: LCSH: Tolkien, J. R. R. (John Ronald Reuel), 1892-1973—Criticism and interpretation. | Tolkien, J. R. R. (John Ronald Reuel), 1892-1973—Literary style. | Narration (Rhetoric) | BISAC: LITERARY CRITICISM / Science Fiction & Fantasy | LITERARY CRITICISM / General | LCGFT: Literary criticism.
Classification: LCC PR6039.O32 Z8346 2023 | DDC 823/.912—dc23/eng/20231103
LC record available at https://lccn.loc.gov/2023051266

BRITISH LIBRARY CATALOGUING DATA ARE AVAILABLE

ISBN (print) 978-0-7864-7037-2
ISBN (ebook) 978-1-4766-5192-7

© 2024 Robert T. Tally Jr. All rights reserved

No part of this book may be reproduced or transmitted in any form or by any means, electronic or mechanical, including photocopying or recording, or by any information storage and retrieval system, without permission in writing from the publisher.

Front cover images © 2024 Shutterstock

Printed in the United States of America

McFarland & Company, Inc., Publishers
   Box 611, Jefferson, North Carolina 28640
   www.mcfarlandpub.com

For Reiko

Table of Contents

Preface and Acknowledgments	1
Introduction: The Perilous Realm in an Era of Multinational Capitalism	11
Strange Bedfellows: Tolkien and Marxist Literary Criticism	13
Towards a Literary Cartography of Middle-earth	17
On the Shadowy Marches of Faërie	19
1. **"Almost it seemed that the words took shape": Narrative, History, and the Desire Called Marx**	23
"The theatre of my tale is this earth"	25
In the Hall of Fire	29
"Endless untold stories"	35
2. **Formulae of Power: Generic Discontinuities in the Saga of the Jewels and the Rings**	40
Harmonizing Heterogeneous Narrative Paradigms	41
Modern Epics	45
"The starry sky is a map of all possible paths"	47
The Red Book of Westmarch	52
"A more or less mediocre, average English gentleman"	55
The Cauldron of Story	60
3. **Three Rings for the Elven Kings: Trilogizing Tolkien in Print and Film**	64
"There is no real division into 3": Defining Trilogy	65
"The rhythm or ordering of the narrative": Trilogizing The Lord of the Rings	70
"Too much hobbitry": The Hobbit *as a Film Trilogy*	74
An Artificially Ordered World	77

Table of Contents

4. **The Geopolitical Aesthetic of Middle-earth: Space, Cinema, and the World System in *The Lord of the Rings*** — 79
   - *"I wisely started with a map"* — 82
   - *The Eye of Sauron* — 85
   - *The Conspiracy of the Ring* — 90
   - *Geopolitical Fantasy* — 95

5. **The Politics of Character: The Dark Lord, the Witch-Queen, and the White Wizard** — 98
   - *Sauron, Healer of Middle-earth* — 99
   - *Galadriel, Witch-Queen of Lórien* — 105
   - *Song of Saruman* — 110
   - *"Satan fell": Ethics as False Consciousness* — 116

6. **Let Us Now Praise Famous Orcs: Simple Humanity in Middle-earth's Inhuman Creatures** — 118
   - *"Whence they came or what they were"* — 119
   - *No More Big Bosses!* — 123
   - *Human, All-Too-Human* — 126
   - *Orcs' Untold Stories* — 128

7. **Demonizing the Enemy: Monstrosity, Ethics, and the Sense of the World Wars** — 131
   - *Manufacturing Monsters* — 134
   - *Sympathy for the Devils* — 138
   - *After the Wars* — 141

8. **"Places where the stars are strange": Fantasy, Utopia, and Critique** — 145
   - *Surveying the Great Schism* — 146
   - *"The world as it appears under the sun"* — 148
   - *Reflections on Magic* — 151
   - *Beyond Good and Evil* — 155
   - *The Fantastic Is Good to Think With* — 161

Conclusion: "We should not neglect the red dragons" — 163

Notes — 167

Bibliography — 183

Index — 189

Preface
and Acknowledgments

Like so many readers, I discovered the work of J.R.R. Tolkien when I was a child, and in my case it likely had to do with the release of the Arthur Rankin, Jr., and Jules Bass animated television-film adaptation of *The Hobbit*, released in November 1977. I read the novel at about the same time, and then went on to *The Lord of the Rings* and, later, *The Silmarillion*. Even as a young reader, I believe I was most taken with the world of Middle-earth itself, rather than with Bilbo or Gandalf or their adventures together (although I liked them too, of course), and thus the more expansive history, geography, and mythology, as well as what might be seen as a sort of cultural anthropology in detailing the languages, customs, and mores of various groups in Middle-earth, to be found in the legendarium as a whole intrigued me all the more. Perversely, perhaps, I found in Tolkien's fiction a crucial way of seeing our own world through the representation of his imaginary otherworld, or as I have expressed it in my book on *The Hobbit*, a way of realizing history through fantasy.

By establishing, shaping, elaborating, and populating an alternative world system in the manner he did, Tolkien opened up spaces for further literary and philosophical exploration. Tolkien's realism, if one can call it that, enabled a kind of critical thinking that I found exhilarating, even as I realized that my view of this led me in divergent directions and to rather different conclusions than those found in most readers' experience. In particular, I found that Tolkien's presentation of Middle-earth led me to sympathize with orcs and with others considered by most to be "evil" in these narratives, and this was due, not just to my own perversely revisionist tendencies, but largely to Tolkien's own words, characterizations, and histories. Contrary to how some of Tolkien's detractors would have it, Tolkien's legendarium was not about escapism, but rather functioned as a means by which to engage critically with our own times and places. Critique, to put it bluntly, is an inherent aspect of fantasy. Along those lines, as I continued thinking about Tolkien's work while pursuing my academic career in literature, literary history, criticism, and theory, I found that Marxist criticism was particularly well suited for reading fantasy, inasmuch as its dialectical approach urges the critic to consider the totality of relations, paying attention always to both form and content, the individual and the collective, psychological and social forces, and so on. Middle-earth as represented in Tolkien's writings offers an especially productive territory for such critical explorations.

Representing Middle-earth: Tolkien, Form, and Ideology is one of my contributions to such exploratory endeavors, and it is in many ways the result of my lifelong interest in Tolkien, going back to that cartoonish Rankin/Bass version in all its weirdness. For the most part, the chapters in *Representing Middle-earth* are semi-autonomous, insofar as they can probably be read as individual essays, but I view them as parts of a single, continuous project. Read as such and in order, I hope they serve to enlarge and refine the critical perspectives on Tolkien's major works, their twenty-first-century film adaptations, and their place in contemporary culture more generally.

I discuss some of these matters more fully and lay out my argument as a whole in the Introduction. Then, in Chapter 1, "'Almost it seemed that the words took shape,'" I examine what I take to be Tolkien's motivation for creating his saga in the context of his implicit critique of modernity. Tolkien's desire to create a new mythology for England, which is well known, is itself a rather modern if not *modernist* response to the shifting ground upon which he stood, in reaction to what Marx and Engels in the *Communist Manifesto* had called the "constant revolutionizing" and the "cosmopolitan character" of bourgeois society, industrial civilization, imperialism, and the rise of monopoly capital. Tolkien's yearning for a mythic past, despite its clear nationalism and chauvinism at first, reflected a deep desire to connect his modern world with an august, barely accessible past through forms of historical narrative. This is not an escape into a mythical, premodern realm as is frequently imagined. Rather, it is an attempt to take the broken and disconnected fragments of culture and put them together into a meaningful history, evoking what Tolkien would call "the seamless web of story." What Fredric Jameson, following Jean-François Lyotard, has referred to as "the desire called Marx" is really this urgent need to connect up the various shreds in the fabric of history to form a continuous narrative. Tolkien's experiments with different genres and styles betray the difficulties he had in organizing this overall narrative project, but his impulse in producing a grand narrative involving myth, fairy story, romance, history, and the modern novelistic form reflects his ardent desire to give shape to a world that had, in his view, lost its sense or meaning. Tolkien's great legendarium provides a history for a world that had forgotten how to think historically.

Chapter 2 examines the "generic discontinuities" of Tolkien's Saga of the Jewels and the Ring (as he referred to the integrated project of his legendarium), looking especially at the ways in which *The Silmarillion*, *The Hobbit*, and *The Lord of the Rings* make use of and blend the mythic and historical modes. For example, *The Silmarillion* is poised to be an epic narrative written in support of a larger mythology, but in some ways, with respect to both the ideology of form and the thematic content of *The Silmarillion*, Tolkien's project there navigates this liminal space between the epic and the novel, between myth and history, and between the Perilous Realm of elves and the human, all-too-human condition in "the world as it appears under the sun." I take up the "intrusion" of *The Hobbit* upon this meticulously detailed, if incomplete and uncertain world. Hobbits appear nowhere in the "Silmarillion" materials, and the accidental or "chance" arrival of Bilbo Baggins on the scene of great events of world-historical importance characterized both the novel itself and its place in Tolkien's Saga of the Jewels and the Rings. *The Lord of the Rings*, Tolkien's *magnum opus*, is a modern epic that figures forth an entire world system while maintaining its character as a heroic romance. The adventures of the hobbit companions, along with the enormous cast of characters, all of whom have different and conflicting aims, delineate so many trajectories across the map of the geopolitical relations of Middle-earth at the end of the Third Age. The situation of the various heroes in the midst of everything going on, with the perceived threat of social disintegration coming from nearly all sides, provides a sort of allegory, not the crude version regarding the world wars that Tolkien definitively dismissed, but one in which the contradictions of an age are made visible to all and a great social revolution is at hand. Tolkien's quasi-religious vision of a eucatastrophe is analogous to the dialectical reversal at the heart of the historical narrative, where "even the very wise cannot see all ends."

In Chapter 3, "Three Rings for the Elven Kings: Trilogizing Tolkien in Print and Film," I address the effects of the trilogy format on *The Lord of the Rings*, first as it appeared in print, then as it shaped the blockbuster movie franchise. In general, the predominance of the trilogy format in medieval-styled, "sword-and-sorcery" fantasy today is the result of a historical accident. The genre's foundational work, *The Lord of the Rings* was published as a trilogy for economic, rather than aesthetic, reasons, owing especially to postwar paper shortages and high costs of paper in Great Britain. Hence, the irony of the decision of the filmmakers to turn *The Hobbit*, which in print was most definitely *not* a trilogy, into three films. The dynamics of publishing and filmmaking have changed dramatically since the mid-twentieth century, and these changes to the economic base have had radical superstructural effects. What Jameson, following Ernest Mandel, calls "late capitalism" is understood to be the third stage of capitalism, after market and monopoly capitalisms, and, according to Giovanni Arrighi, the third phase of twentieth-century capitalism, a phase of "financialization," governs the present moment, as thirds-within-thirds have come to dominate the scene in the twenty-first century. In this chapter, I examine this curious generic "thirding" or trilogizing as a side-effect of late capitalism, arguing that the accidental reification of the trilogy in Tolkien becomes symbolic of the need to imagine a triangulated ordering in our own postmodern condition.

Chapter 4 looks at the geopolitical aesthetic of Middle-earth as it is made apparent through the cartographic plot of *The Lord of the Rings*. Whereas *The Hobbit* had sketched a much narrower vision, the expansive geography and distinctive *topoi* of *The Lord of the Rings* elaborates an entire geopolitical world-system in which the narrative elements unfold. Indeed, I would go so far as to say that the literary cartography of Middle-earth is the principal aim of the narrative. Starting from Tolkien's own text, we can see the ways in which the Peter Jackson film trilogy adapts, translates, and in some ways enacts the geopolitical aesthetic of *The Lord of the Rings*. Drawing upon Jameson's call for a "cognitive mapping on a global scale," along with his reading of cinema and space in *The Geopolitical Aesthetic*, I argue that the overlapping narrative spaces of the novel and the films enable readers or viewers to envision a kind of global totality that might not always be available to them in narratives produced in a more strictly mimetic mode. Geopolitical fantasy provides a map in which the system's other spaces—those liminal and hybrid zones in which the strange, seemingly fantastic, but possibly liberating elements of this world make themselves visible—may be discerned. As Tolkien suggested in "On Fairy-stories," this is the vocation of fantasy: to produce imaginative cartographies of a world (that is, an otherworld) that can allow us to conceptually grapple with our own world system. Looking at *The Lord of the Rings* films in particular, I argue that the fantastic literary cartography makes possible a rethinking of our own all-too-real world today.

Chapter 5, "The Politics of Character: The Dark Lord, the Witch-Queen, and the White Wizard," examines what might be called the moral geography of Middle-earth as allegorized through the persons of three key characters in *The Lord of the Rings*, each of whom I believe has been misunderstood by most Tolkien fans and many scholars. My reassessment of these characters does not imply a simple reversal (for example, arguing that a "bad guy" is really good and the "good" really bad), but an attempt through these character studies to explode the "good guy *versus* bad guy" opposition, in favor of a more nuanced assessment that can illuminate the geopolitical condition of Middle-earth at the time of the War of the Ring. Galadriel, for instance, has far more in common with the great enemy Sauron than is normally recognized, whereas Saruman is one of the most complex, interesting, and tragic figures in *The Lord of the Rings*. Placing these characters in a cultural context, I argue that a revisionary reading of their roles makes possible a whole new understanding of Tolkien's universe.

Following up on this critical reinterpretation of these supposedly "good" and "bad" characters, in Chapter 6, "Let Us Now Praise Famous Orcs," I address one of the most troubling problems in Tolkien's legendarium: the existence of sentient, rational beings for whom no sympathy or moral feeling is shown whatsoever. Investigating the various origin stories of the orc, which changed over time according to Tolkien's own worries about whether orcs could be "redeemable" and, moreover, worthy of their very existence, I demonstrate that even by Tolkien's own considerations these "inhuman" creatures are, in fact, among the most human to be found in *The Lord of the Rings*. Focusing especially on two key chapters from that novel, my reading illuminates the richly diverse cultures, as well as the distinctive personalities of various orcs, who turn out to be far more like members of distinctive, demonized ethnicities among humans than the demonic monsters they are taken to be in the popular imagination. As a notorious orc-sympathizer, I argue that a revised understanding of the orcs as a people results in a different way of seeing Middle-earth's history more generally.

Chapter 7 builds upon this by examining how this creation and characterization of the orcs engenders serious problems in the so-called real world, while at the same time serving a purpose within a broader narrative by figuring forth an imaginary solution to the most salient contradiction of warfare, thereby helping to make sense of the twentieth-century's devastating world wars. By literally "demonizing the enemy," Tolkien helped to shape the way in which modern warfare could be represented and made meaningful amid the absurd carnage that typified the experience of war, including his own. A seemingly inescapable feature of military conflict is the demonization of the enemy, who becomes somehow less human and more deserving of death in times of military strife, which unsurprisingly helps to justify the violence against them. This chapter looks at the development, character, and role of the orcs—who are not only demonized but also clearly racialized in such a way to promote and reinforce white supremacist bigotry—in connection with the ideological desire to demonize the enemy in World Wars I and II. Yet even in creating an enemy whom the heroes could kill without compunction, Tolkien also betrayed his own sympathy for the devils, perhaps owing to his own experiences as a soldier. This ambiguity pervades Tolkien's writings, even as his demonized race of orcs are dispatched by the thousands, thus shaping the sense or meaning of warfare and our experience of it according to the desire to simplify, and make more comprehensible, the martial narrative of the world wars. This, in turn, has lasting ramifications that shape the way we understand the world system in an era of globalization now.

Chapter 8, "'Places where the stars are strange,'" explores the elements of Tolkien's literary cartography that have troubled a number of Marxist critics, most especially the putatively simplistic ethics of a distinctive good versus an equally identifiable evil, as well as the problems related to magic and to a fantastic or otherworldly setting. Drawing upon Jameson's discussion of the "great schism" between fantasy and science fiction in *Archaeologies of the Future*, I argue that the critique of Tolkien along these lines is both incorrect and wrongheaded, insofar as it oversimplifies the narratives and the philosophies on display. I find in Tolkien's Saga of the Jewels and the Rings, along with his reflections on otherworldly literature in letters and essays, a discernibly critical and utopian strand, which resonates more generally with the Marxist critique of ideology and false consciousness in our own era. Tolkien's legendarium is thus less of an escape from the real world and more of a vista into unfamiliar domains in which new spaces are possible.

Finally, in my conclusion, I briefly discuss China Miéville's call for a properly Marxist appreciation for fantasy as both a literary genre and a critical mode. Although he himself has notoriously been critical of Tolkien, Miéville has also expressed his admiration, and in admonishing critics for their neglect of "red dragons," Miéville urges socialists and others on the political left to recognize the potential of fantasy literature to fire the imagination and to undermine hegemonic and uncritical "realisms" in ideological service of the powers that be. Notwithstanding his own personal political and religious views, Tolkien establishes a fantastic mode of historical and critical alterity, and his writings enable readers to see our world from fresh vantages, making available new vistas, and with unexpected and possibly perverse interpretations. In representing Middle-earth, an otherworldly space that illuminates and transfigures our own worldly world, Tolkien helps us to imagine still other worlds to inhabit.

* * *

A note on the texts and citations: For ease of reference, I have chosen to use the trade paperback editions of his novels wherever possible, as most readers probably have these editions. I also trust that professional Tolkien scholars, along with many devoted fans, will have no trouble finding my references regardless of the edition. Unless otherwise noted, my references to *The Hobbit* are to the revised, finalized version, featuring the Gollum most of us know so well. When citing *The Lord of the Rings*, I list the individual volume name, the book and chapter numbers using Roman numerals, and the page number using Arabic numerals: hence, for example, *The Fellowship of the Ring*, II.iv.346. This convention is intended to make it easier for people whose editions have different page numbers to find the cited passage, following a Tolkien Studies convention. Also, following another convention in Tolkien Studies, I use the term "Silmarillion" (in quotation marks) with reference to the wide-ranging, heterogenous materials of Tolkien's larger *legendarium*, in order to distinguish it from *The Silmarillion*, curated, "regularized," and made coherent by Christopher Tolkien, but published as a singular work *by* J.R.R. Tolkien alone in 1977.

* * *

This book has been in progress over many years, ultimately going all the way back to my childhood reading of Tolkien. I dedicated *J.R.R. Tolkien's* The Hobbit: *Realizing History Through Fantasy* to my brothers, who have shared my love of Tolkien and who are great explorers of Middle-earth in their own rights. I dedicate this book to Reiko Graham for all her love and support, as well as for putting up with me during most of the time I have been writing. While working on this book we lost the company of Dusty Britches, sadly, but I am happy to have the feline encouragement of Windy Britches, Steve French, and Nigel Tuffnail, who are probably nothing at all like the cats of Queen Berúthiel.

I have been fortunate to be able to teach Tolkien in classes at Texas State University, and I would like to thank my students who have walked alongside me on those journeys, often illuminating paths and features I might have otherwise missed. Among them, I will mention two, Bianca L. Beronio and Joyana Richer, whose enthusiasm and insight have made teaching and mentoring such a pleasure. My indebtedness to the generous community of Tolkien scholars cannot be measured, and I am grateful to the many friends, colleagues, and critics who have helped me along the way, including but not limited to Suparno Banerjee, Gerry Canavan, Jane Chance, Janet Brennan Croft, Dimitra Fimi, Katrina Goudey, Sean Guynes, Michael Hennessy, Matt Hudson, Fredric Jameson, Katie Kapurch, Whitney May, Susan Morrison, Amanda North, Keren Omry, Benjamin Reed, Robin Anne Reid, Teya Rosenburg, Norbert Schürer, Leah Schwebel, Victoria Smith, Robert Stuart, Christopher Vaccaro, and Phillip E. Wegner.

Some of the ideas that went into this book were first presented at conferences, in person or online, including numerous sessions of the Tolkien Studies Area organized by Robin Anne Reid for the Popular Culture Association in 2011, 2014, 2021, and 2023; Mythcon, the annual conference of the Mythopoeic Society, in 2016 and 2021; the 19th Annual University of Vermont Tolkien Conference in 2023; the Theoretical Aspects of Fantasy Studies: Representations of Magic Across Media conference, sponsored by the Centre for Fantasy Literature Studies, Taras Shevchanko Institute of Literature and the National Academy of Sciences of Ukraine, Kyiv, in 2023; the Texas Medieval Association conference in 2015; and the South Central Modern Language Convention in 2012. I would like to thank the organizers, chairs, fellow panelists, and audience members for their support and feedback throughout.

I have also had the good fortune to present invited talks or keynote lectures in which I discussed aspects of this project. These include the Zeit und Raum in Tolkiens Werk / Time and Space in Tolkien's Work, the 18th Tolkien Konferenz, Deutsche Tolkien Gesellschaft e.V. and the Institut für Anglistik / Amerikanistik, Friedrich Schiller Universität, Jena, in 2022; the U.S. Studies Online "Book Hour," sponsored by British Association of American Studies, University of York, in 2020; and local events at the San Marcos Public Library in 2019 and 2022. I am very grateful to the organizers, organizations, participants, and attendees, especially Thomas Honegger, Jun Qiang, and Pamela Carlile.

Representing Middle-earth includes material that, in one form or another, appeared elsewhere and is used with permission of the respective publishers. Earlier versions of Chapters 1 and 2 appeared as "'Don't the great tales never end?' Tolkien, History, and the Desire Called Marx," *Journal of English Language and Literature* 67.3 (2021), 529–549, and "Tolkien and Form: Generic Discontinuities in *The Hobbit* and *The Lord of the Rings*," *Journal of English Language and Literature* 68.1 (2022), 167–192, respectively. Chapters 3 and 6 reprint and expand upon essays previously published in *Mythlore*, "Three Rings for the Elven Kings: Trilogizing Tolkien in Print and Film," *Mythlore* 131 (Fall/Winter 2017): 175–190, and "Let Us Now Praise Famous Orcs: Simple Humanity in Tolkien's Inhuman Creatures," *Mythlore* 111/112 (Fall/Winter 2010), 17–28, respectively. A somewhat different version of Chapter 4 appeared previously as "The Geopolitical Aesthetic of Middle-earth: Tolkien, Cinema, and Literary Cartography" in *Topographies of Popular Culture*, edited by Maarit Piipponen and Markku Salmela (Cambridge Scholars, 2016), 11–34. Parts of Chapter 5 were first published in the *Los Angeles Review of Books* as "Song of Saruman" (December 27, 2014: http://lareviewofbooks.org/essay/song-saruman) and "Galadriel, Witch-Queen of Lórien" (May 7, 2015: https://lareviewofbooks.org/essay/galadriel-witch-queen-of-lorien). An earlier version of Chapter 7 was published as "Demonizing the Enemy, Literally: Tolkien, Orcs, and the Sense of the World Wars," *Humanities* 8.1 (2019): 1–10. Much of the substance of Chapter 8 appeared in an earlier version of my "Places Where the Stars Are Strange," in *Tolkien in the New Century: Essays in Honor of Tom Shippey*, edited by John Wm. Houghton, Janet Brennan Croft, Nancy Martsch, John D. Rateliff, and Robin Anne Reid (McFarland, 2014), 41–56. I am grateful to the editors and publishers for permission to reprint these works, and especially to Janet Brennan Croft, a brilliant Tolkien scholar and editor of *Mythlore*, for her indefatigable assistance and support over the years.

Any errors and omissions are my own responsibility, although I would not rule out the possibility that tricksy elves may have played a part.

Introduction

The Perilous Realm in an Era of Multinational Capitalism

J.R.R. Tolkien's legendarium depicts a vast, complex world-system in Middle-earth, complete with intensely detailed historical, geographical, and multicultural content and presented through an array of poetic forms that combine elements of myth, epic, romance, fairy tale, history, and the modern novel.[1] In their form and content, works such as *The Hobbit* and *The Lord of the Rings*, as well as *The Silmarillion* somewhat differently, evoke a global, geopolitical framework that exceeds the boundaries of the adventure genre. This makes them appear extravagant, both in ways many readers admire and in others that some do not. Understandably, for fans of his work, these stories enchant and delight in their own right, but for many, the enjoyment is enhanced by the remarkably broad sweep and minute detail used in the representation of the world in which they take place. Tolkien's work thus invites readers to speculate upon deeper meanings and extended trajectories that indicate socially symbolic aspects of the narratives of Middle-earth. Tolkien's elaborate world-building in his works has been much discussed, and this textual abundance stands out all the more when fairly basic elements of character, story, setting, and plot are transformed into extensive spatiotemporal archives of languages, cultures, social hierarchies, histories, and geographical formations, along with an extraordinarily vast and complex world system in which Tolkien's memorable people, places, and things exist.

The mode of representation of Middle-earth is also arguably excessive, inasmuch as it involves an array of narrative forms and techniques, combining comic and tragic elements, with richly ekphrastic description alongside dramatic dialogues and action scenes, chronologies disrupted and mingled via *entrelacement*, heteroglossia at multiple levels, historical contradictions, and generic discontinuities, among many other pertinent features. Drawing on the work of the Marxist literary theorist and critic Fredric Jameson, among others, I would suggest that the development of the world system of Middle-earth involves a correspondent form of "cognitive mapping," in which the system can be grasped and made meaningful through a sort of literary cartography that unfolds in the texts themselves.[2] Reading Tolkien's work dialectically discloses a sort of "political unconscious," which operates simultaneously through the form and the content of Tolkien's narratives. *Representing Middle-earth: Tolkien, Form, and Ideology* analyzes Tolkien's novels *The Hobbit* and *The Lord of the Rings*, along with *The Silmarillion* and other posthumously published material,[3] while exploring Tolkien's broader philosophical and political aims of reviving a sense of history and historical consciousness in a modern age that had increasingly lost its ability or will to think historically. In the process, I also examine the ways that Tolkien's world has been depicted in film and other media, which have shaped the contemporary understanding of Middle-earth and the uses of fantasy more generally.

Representing Middle-earth is thus a study of Tolkien's overall literary project, paying close attention to narrative form and style, while also examining the social content, which in turn opens up broader discussions of philosophy, religion, politics, and history. Mine is not so much a matter of reading "against the grain" here as it is a close reading mixed with theoretical speculation, paying meticulous attention to Tolkien's use of detail in such a way as to evoke the rich complexities of his world system. This will be perhaps most apparent in my discussion of orcs, the "enemy" foot soldiers of Tolkien's world, who along with other key figures in Tolkien's legendarium are revealed to be far more nuanced and sympathetic than most readers or filmgoers would think. But this "revisionist" reading itself comes almost entirely from Tolkien's own depictions of these characters. In his insistence on creating a fantastic narrative that is nevertheless part of a "real world," even if that is still a somewhat otherworldly place, Tolkien could not help but make even his "bad guys"—but also his "good guys," in fact—complex and ambiguous, much like the world they inhabit.

Representing Middle-earth supplements and greatly expands upon the argument made in my more limited 2022 study, *J.R.R. Tolkien's* The Hobbit: *Realizing History Through Fantasy (A Critical Companion)*, in which I argued that Tolkien's 1937 fantasy tale constituted a historical novel in the sense given in Georg Lukács's monumental treatise on that genre, and that Tolkien's vision of Middle-earth as a "real" space in which imaginary historical events take place serves to educate the imagination of his readers, allowing them to experience, and to make *real*, the historical register in a forgetful, modern society obsessed with the "new."[4] This helps to establish a broader sense of awareness of history and of the world system of which one is a part, thus corresponding to a sense of class consciousness or cognitive mapping in Jameson's sense. *Representing Middle-earth* not only extends this analytical approach to *The Lord of the Rings*, *The Silmarillion*, and other texts (including films), but also delves deeper into the interrelations of narrative form and social content, evoking aspects of the political unconscious of Tolkien's world-building.

Strange Bedfellows: Tolkien and Marxist Literary Criticism

Marxist literary criticism, along with other modes of narrative criticism and theory of the novel, provides the foundation for my reading of Tolkien's work in *Representing Middle-earth*. In some respects, that may be controversial, as many members of both "camps" as it were—that is, Tolkien fans and scholars on the one hand and Marxist critics or socialists more generally on the other—might object to being placed together in the same space. (I discuss the still-prevalent Marxist antipathy toward both Tolkien and fantasy genre more generally in Chapter 8 and in the Conclusion, especially.) Tolkien himself is certainly not a socialist or communist, but then neither were Honoré de Balzac, George Gissing, or Joseph Conrad, socially conservative writers to whom Jameson devotes chapters in *The Political Unconscious*, not to mention the fascist Wyndham Lewis, to whom Jameson devoted a superb book-length study, *Fables of Aggression*. Rather, Marxist criticism of the sort Jameson has spent more than sixty years practicing and theorizing can offer the most insightful and expansive readings of Tolkien's text, capaciously including elements of other critical traditions (such as myth-criticism, historicism, semiotics, psychological analysis, and so on), while also maintaining a sense of the big picture, the social totality as a whole. With *Representing Middle-earth*, I thereby hope to contribute to the field of Tolkien Studies, offering new interpretations and revisionary readings of the familiar texts, while also bringing Tolkien's work into conversation with narrative criticism, theory and history of the novel, social theory, and Marxist cultural critique.

Underlying the argument is a desire to help emancipate the idea of fantasy from its ideologically circumscribed characterizations by both the political left and the right, where it is associated with the idle wish-fulfillments and perverse cathexes of a psychoanalytic tradition, or it is subjugated by some reality principle that can imagine fantasy only in terms of escapism. (Far worse still, particularly in Tolkien Studies and fandom, the active fascist appropriation of Tolkien's work as inherently and celebratorily white supremacist has only increased in recent years.) From perspectives like these, fantasy finds itself dismissed as immoral or politically retrograde and at the same time as impractical, these two registers overlapping in a crudely utilitarian model of literary value. Notwithstanding Tolkien's own defense of the idea of "escape," fantasy always presupposes an intense if figurative engagement with this world. The "allure of alterity," as I have referred to it elsewhere,[5] undoubtedly accounts for the immense popularity of fantasy fiction and works in other related genres, but this has less to do with the obstinate refusal to countenance the world that we inhabit and far more to do with those Brechtian estrangements that force us to look upon and engage with the world in new ways. To see and to think differently by means of the literary imagination are themselves politically enabling, for any radical alternatives to the status quo must first be imagined, and speculative fiction and theory are crucial for developing an empowered imagination. This might be characterized as the utopian dimension of fantasy.

Hence, Marxist criticism is valuable for fantasy literature both in its more narrowly conceived role as a literary genre and in its broader conceptualization as a discursive mode or way of seeing. *Representing Middle-earth*, in addition to its main theses, maintains a two-pronged polemic, which has a dialectical counterpart in a dual *apologia*. On the one hand, I want to argue for the value of Tolkien's work in particular and fantasy writing in general for Marxist cultural criticism, and this argument requires me to oppose the prevailing and cogent Marxist critiques of fantasy to be found in the work of such eminent critics as Jameson himself, Darko Suvin, Carl Freedman, and many others. This involves recovering the power of Tolkien's fantasy *for* Marxism. On the other hand, I also want to impress on Tolkien scholars and critics, those doing excellent work in the field of fantasy studies, that Marxist literary criticism and theory are supremely valuable to their enterprise. Indeed, I would affirm that, because its proper conceptual territory is coterminous with the social totality itself, including those ways in which individual and collective subjects conceive of and navigate the tortuous relays and relations that make up that totality, Marxism is an indispensable theoretical practice and body of critical thought for effectively analyzing and understanding the legendarium of Tolkien and the worlds made available by the fantastic genre or mode. Given the mystifications and alienation of life in societies organized under the capitalist mode of production, the "real world" is itself mostly occluding or masking the underlying truths of the conditions of human existence and social relations. As such, as China Miéville has asserted, "[t]he fantastic might be a mode peculiarly suited to and resonant with the forms of modernity."[6] Although this matter is explicitly addressed in only a few places, particularly in Chapter 8 and in the Conclusion, this implicit defense of the value of fantasy animates the project of this book as a whole.

Perhaps it goes without saying that I am in no way arguing that Tolkien himself is a Marxist or even the lesser claim that Tolkien would endorse a Marxist interpretation of his work. Tolkien's own political views, which appear to have been far more varied and nuanced than many of his fans and most of his detractors assume, are largely irrelevant for the purposes of my argument and my explorations of his works, although I will find occasion to cite his comments on current events here and there. I confess, it has always surprised me that some Marxist or otherwise leftist, politically oriented readers have been dismissive of Tolkien based on the "fact" of his conservatism, as if that somehow made him less worthy of study. If nothing else, such people manage to forget that Karl Marx's favorite novelist was Balzac, a conservative bourgeois and royalist; according to Marx's son-in-law Paul Lefargue, "[h]e admired Balzac so much that he wished to write a review of his great work *La Comédie Humaine* as soon as he had finished his book on economics."[7] Alas for world literature, Marx never completed his work on economics—*Capital*, which likely could never be completed so long as the dynamic system of which it was the critique remained in motion—and so the study of Balzac was never undertaken. Mikhail Bakhtin's great book on Fyodor Dostoevsky's poetics, while not always viewed as being itself a work of Marxist criticism, is nevertheless the work of a Marxist critic on a rather conservative, religious, and "right-wing" writer. Lukács, of course, in *The Historical Novel*, had no trouble writing about, and praising, the romances of Sir Walter Scott, notwithstanding the latter's Tory politics. And, more recently, one of Jameson's most underrated single-author studies, *Fables of Aggression*, is devoted to the writings of Wyndham Lewis, "the modernist as fascist" as the subtitle to Jameson's book would have it.[8] These are merely a few famous examples. I suspect that much of the antipathy toward Tolkien on the part of many Marxist critics can be chalked up to matters of personal taste, more than of politics, for even where Tolkien's views may seem odious from a modern leftist perspective, they are hardly more objectionable than the views of many of these other, apparently more worthy authors.

Moreover, the fact is that it may not be so easy to label Tolkien's views as "conservative," even if he was no socialist or liberal either. Famously, in a wartime letter to his son Christopher, Tolkien revealed that his "political opinions lean more and more toward Anarchy (philosophically understood, meaning abolition of control not whiskered men with bombs)—or to 'unconstitutional' Monarchy"; in the same paragraph, ironically perhaps, he complains about incipient globalization, and observes that the only "bright spot" of late is "the growing habit of disgruntled men of dynamiting factories and power-stations."[9] Most readers probably expect that the social formation and political system Tolkien idealizes here, and elsewhere, is something like the Shire in times of peace and plenty, such as in the early years of the Fourth Age, when King Elessar could officially rule, benignly but at a distance, and the internal affairs of the Shire were handled without much hierarchy or need for State bureaucracy. This seemingly natural but well nigh utopian state of things is perhaps why so many fans from across the political spectrum have been charmed by the life of the hobbits. The problems with this vision are manifold, and some of them will be addressed in my reading of Tolkien's works, but the author's personal opinions on statecraft and governance are not the main aspects of even a political interpretation. As an exploration of a political unconscious in Tolkien's work, this study pays closer attention to the ideology of the form—the content of the form, as well as the form and content separately—of these literary works, an operation that does not require, or even make it desirable, that one dwell at length on the author's personal beliefs.[10]

Indeed, as Verlyn Flieger, Robin Anne Reid, and other astute critics have noted, Tolkien's positions over a long life varied, and it is probably never a good idea to select this or that quotation only to discover another that contradicts it before or after. Referring to the inconsistencies to be found in Tolkien's views as seen through his letters, lectures, and published or unpublished writings over many years, for instance, Flieger has written that "[t]here are many such turnabouts in Tolkien's writings, reversals of direction that not only make him appear contradictory but invite contradictory interpretations of his work, permitting advocates with opposite views to cherry-pick the statements that best support their positions."[11] Because I do quote from Tolkien's letters somewhat frequently in this book, I am aware of this potential pitfall, and I mention this as a caveat to the reader. Scholarly habit, as well as a desire to touch on the author's stated ideas, requires that I frequently refer to Tolkien the person, to *his* views and *his* words, but it should also be understood that much of what I discuss in this book is not based on the man's personal or biographical authority. This is not so much my way of invoking some Barthesian "death of the author" or Foucauldian "author-effect," as it is an allusion to the sort of unconscious or structural assemblage of associations that emerges from the dynamic complex of author, text, and reader, combined with the supra-individual forces of language, genre, and history. Tolkien is a person, a writer, an Englishman, and many other things as well, but *Tolkien* is also a sign with its own range of meanings. If, in this study, I frequently use this sign in ways that implicate the man also, that is largely unavoidable and, one hopes, potentially productive.

Towards a Literary Cartography of Middle-earth

Uncontroversially, I take *The Lord of the Rings* to be Tolkien's *magnum opus*, and a little more controversially, perhaps, I see it as a major work of late modernism.[12] Of course, this complex literary masterpiece would not have existed were it not for the far more humble offering, *The Hobbit*, to which *The Lord of the Rings* was an unexpected and unplanned-for sequel. As Tolkien informed his publisher in 1937, when asked about the possibility of a sequel, "I cannot think of anything more to say about *hobbits*"; he much preferred to continue his labors on "this private and beloved nonsense,"[13] that is, the materials that would serve as the basis for the posthumously published work, *The Silmarillion*. Even though that book did not appear in print until 1977, a full forty years after *The Hobbit* and more than twenty years after *The Lord of the Rings*, its ideas, myths, histories, and, in the case of Elrond and Galadriel, two of its characters, were crucial to the overall realization of the other novels. As such, and for other reasons I will discuss in more detail later, I have chosen to read these three "complete" books: *The Silmarillion*, with its epic structure and mythic world; *The Hobbit*, with its starkly anachronistic hero "intruding" into the grand historical narrative and wide world of Tolkien's legendarium; and *The Lord of the Rings*, with its dazzling blend of styles, genres, and discourses comprising a vast, multiformal, and heteroglossic world system.

My choice of treating *The Silmarillion* as a complete work deserves another word or two. *The Silmarillion* was published as a single work *by J.R.R. Tolkien*, "edited by Christopher Tolkien," in 1977, and it became the year's most popular work of fiction, topping the *New York Times* bestseller list for a remarkable twenty-three consecutive weeks from October 1977 to March 1978. However, as Christopher Tolkien lamented later, *The Silmarillion* gave an artificial and misleading sense of continuity and even completion; in reality, it had been compiled by Christopher from materials written by his father across many decades, with numerous inconsistencies and revisions, as one might expect of such a vast assemblage of notes and drafts. Some of the difficulties associated with *The Silmarillion* can be attributed to this illusory coherence, as many of the texts included may not have been originally written for inclusion, in those forms, or with the exact ordering of things in the way that they are presented in the published volume. Starting with the publication of *Unfinished Tales of Númenor and Middle-earth* in 1980, and then extending to the monumental, 12-volume *History of Middle-earth* series, published between 1983 and 1996, Christopher attempted to rectify matters by revealing his father's original drafts in all their sketchiness, along with Christopher's own commentary which tended to situate those drafts in relation to his father's biography and to his other writings.

More recently, Christopher and the Tolkien Estate have come out with additional books, including three extended versions of major tales from *The Silmarillion* (or the "Silmarillion"): that is, the story of Húrin and his children, the adventures of Beren and Lúthien, and the narrative of the events leading to the fall of Gondolin. To these have been added a steady stream of other previously unpublished writings by Tolkien, including his translation of *Beowulf* and his juvenile retelling of the story of Kullervo, a character from the Finnish epic, the *Kalevala*, which is also a source for Tolkien's story of Túrin Turambar in *The Silmarillion*. Although I have benefited from my perusal of these works, and some are occasionally cited in this book, I decided to focus on *The Silmarillion* itself precisely because it was organized into a seemingly coherent whole, thus being presented to the public as Tolkien's long-awaited body of legends which provided the deep history and underlying mythology that had so enlivened the narratives of *The Hobbit* and *The Lord of the Rings*.

Moreover, that *The Silmarillion* was such a bestseller, far more so than any of the *History of Middle-earth* volumes, suggests that Tolkien's fans—including me, of course—were likely more influenced by its stories, and the decision by Christopher to include in a single volume the cosmogonic myths and descriptions of the Valar alongside the story of the Silmarils, plus a narrative of the rise and fall of Númenor and a section on the Rings of Power in the Third Age of Middle-earth, makes *The Silmarillion* even more visibly a companion to the earlier novels than the far larger, less coherent, but more accurately presented *History of Middle-earth* in all its fragmentarity and incompleteness, could possibly be. Using his father's materials and restrained by the publisher's demands, Christopher forged in *The Silmarillion* the sort of "prequel" to those other novels that works rather effectively at depicting the historical and geopolitical terrain upon which sprouted the better known adventures of Bilbo, Gandalf, Frodo, Sam, Aragorn, and the others. As such, *The Silmarillion* is integral to the narrative mapping of Middle-earth that is developed in the earlier, published novels. Under these circumstances, even as I acknowledge that this involves a sort of working fiction, I have opted to read *The Silmarillion* as part of the overall story of *The Hobbit* and *The Lord of the Rings*, an approximation perhaps of what Tolkien himself had in mind as he urged his publishers include the "Silmarillion" materials in what he insisted was the unified "Saga of the Jewels and the Rings."[14]

The saga as a whole constitutes what might be called the *literary cartography of Middle-earth*. I employ this term somewhat metaphorically to refer to the way that the narratives themselves project a figurative representation of the social spaces in their apparent totality in order to figure forth an entire world.[15] Literary cartography thus operates somewhat in the manner of Jameson's *cognitive mapping*, only here understood in connection to poetics as well as aesthetics. That is, mapping is not merely a way of seeing the spatial form of the world but of producing a representation of it through narrative, and thus the poet—"the maker of plots," as Aristotle would have it—fabricates the world in all its depth and detail. The reference to geography is not meant to preclude or downplay the significance of history. On the contrary, the literary cartography of Middle-earth is itself a profoundly historical project, as social spaces themselves are historically produced and developed over time, as Henri Lefebvre's *The Production of Space* has made clear. To be sure, Tolkien's work is well known for its use of actual maps, hand drawn by Tolkien or by Christopher Tolkien, and maps play an important role in the narratives. In *The Hobbit*, for example, the artifact that motivates the quest itself is Thrór's Map, which also includes the hidden instructions on how to find the secret door on the Lonely Mountain. Outside of his own uses, Tolkien's work has inspired mapmakers to create their own, as with Karen Wynn Fonstad's magnificent *Atlas of Middle-earth*.[16] Moreover, *The Lord of the Rings* is arguably itself more map-like than many other works of its kind; in a lengthy chapter devoted to its form, Tom Shippey has maintained that the novel exhibits a "cartographic plot," for instance.[17] Apart from maps themselves, therefore, the overall narrative project comprising *The Silmarillion*, *The Hobbit*, and *The Lord of the Rings* may be considered a grand attempt to map this world, or otherworld, in all its diversity and splendor. Through the representation of Middle-earth in these narratives, readers have a powerful sense of the reality of the place, with its deep historical foundations and its vivid topography.

On the Shadowy Marches of Faërie

In his famous lecture "On Fairy-Stories," Tolkien insists that the genre by that name be defined not as stories about fairies or elves, but as stories about *Faërie*, "the realm or state in which fairies have their being." Moreover, he notes that such tales rarely feature or even include those creatures; rather, "[m]ost good 'fairy-stories' are about the *aventures* of men in the Perilous Realm or upon its shadowy marches." Any definition of the genre should therefore ignore fairies themselves and focus on "the Perilous Realm itself, and the air that blows in that country."[18] This is a somewhat geographical or even geopolitical assessment, and without now getting into Tolkien's much more elaborate argument concerning the relationship between the Primary and Secondary Worlds we could say that Tolkien's vision of literature carries with it some of these literary cartographic tropes, images, and allegories. In his representation of Middle-earth in *The Hobbit*, *The Lord of the Rings*, and other writings, Tolkien combines form and content, style and history, psychology and social theory, among others, in order to create "maps" worthy of the spaces they figure forth.

The "shadowy marches" of the Perilous Realm refers to those liminal or boundary spaces between domains, which can operate simultaneously as limits that separate, thresholds inviting one to cross over, or indeterminate spaces whose affective geography may not readily be apparent in advance of one's experiences there. Although Tolkien may also be thinking of the medieval world, as indicated by his use of the French word for adventure (as in the *chancon d'aventure* genre), the essay published in 1947 is all too timely in its postwar moment in which "shadowy marches" between nations had been subject to dramatic, violent transgression and transcription, with national and cultural borders drawn, redrawn, erased, or obliterated all within a few years. In our own time, in an era of globalization in which many apparently postnational forces, the multinational corporation and transnational financial institutions preeminent among them, seem to be redrawing our own social if not also geographical maps daily. Tolkien's contemporary and fellow philologist Erich Auerbach had expressed hope that this could lead to a more cosmopolitan and postnational world in which one could affirm with Hugh of Saint Victor that *mundus totus exilium est* ("the whole world is a foreign land"),[19] but Tolkien in his profound adherence to a sort of English nationalism lamented that prospect bitterly. Tolkien's great fear of "Americo-cosmopolitanism," which is as effective a precursor to the term *globalization* as any at the time, expressed in an 1943 letter to Christopher,[20] undoubtedly registered his unease with the world system as it was then developing, and the idea of forging and mapping fictional spaces that offered an alternative order of things, an "otherworldly" art to make sense of the world, must have been compelling. That Tolkien's imaginary world, the one we know as *Middle-earth*, is so detailed and heterogeneous is at once a recognition of our own world's complexity and diversity and a tribute to the artist who constructed it. The world, *our world*, is itself a perilous realm, complicated, dynamic, and subject to unforeseen reversals. Hence, our ways of making sense of it, our stories and our maps, must be supple and polysemic, open to numerous interpretations and revisionary visions.

Given my now well established sympathy for the devils—signaled expressly by my title of my essay, "Let Us Now Praise Famous Orcs" (the basis for Chapter 6), a phrase used with a tip of the hat to James Agee and

Walker Evans's monumental Depression-era, photojournalistic chronicle of the lives of impoverished working-class laborers in the United States, *Let Us Now Praise Famous Men*—one might reasonably expect my version of a Marxist take on Tolkien to involve a simple, hierarchical reversal. That is, following somewhat along the lines of the revisionist narrative of Kirill Yeskov's *The Last Ringbearer*, one could merely invert the good-versus-evil narrative, making the orcs, along with Saruman and Sauron, the heroes, and interpreting the hobbits as dupes of an elvish and Númenorean strategy for world domination orchestrated by Gandalf with the aid of hereditary monarchs, Elrond, Galadriel, and Aragorn, for example. Such a reversal might make for an amusing exercise, but even when writing a "history from below" (to cite E.P. Thompson's marvelous phrase), it is never enough to merely invert the hierarchies. More crucial is to recognize the greater complexities of the texts and events; in launching a critique of the dominant or received interpretations, one normally discovers that *they* are themselves oversimplified and in need of critical complication. To the extent that my own interpretations present views that sympathize with the "enemies" and trouble the easy acceptance of or identification with the "heroes," I hope to show that such perspectives are already and always present in Tolkien's writings, which I find generally more nuanced and ambiguous than most detractors, and some enthusiasts, would admit. Tolkien would likely disagree with some of these interpretations, but his work readily makes them available and, perhaps, convincing. In any event, it is a sign of the strength and richness of Tolkien's storytelling that multiple perspectives and disparate readings are not only possible, but also inevitable.

Representing Middle-earth is imagined as a contribution to the critical discussion of Tolkien and of fantasy in the present, a moment when fantasy, broadly conceived, has arguably become the dominant genre in literary and popular culture.[21] The fantastic has also influenced critical theory, as students attempt to make sense of the bizarreries of the post-postmodern condition and to attempt to imagine alternatives. As old-fashioned or foundational (depending on one's predilections) as Tolkien may seem, *The Hobbit* and *The Lord of the Rings* remain salient. What does *Faërie* hold for us today, in the twenty-first century? As a literary genre or a generic mode, fantasy is so much broader and deeper than it was during Tolkien's lifetime, and it has become all the more influential, both in the popular marketplace and in various forms of "high" culture. And while some may argue that the demand for the fantastic reflects a desire for escape, or worse, for mere escapism, the critical edge of fantastic works of the imagination remains a commitment to the idea of radical alterity, what Herbert Marcuse called "the scandal of qualitative difference."[22]

Empowering the imagination, such literature opens and maintains spaces in which other realities, other worlds, are possible. Some of these worlds may contain dragons, the very symbol of the otherworldly, and in a global system that seems ever more interconnected and inescapable, we must not neglect the red ones,[23] those whose fires and flights can make visible alternative vistas and vantages from which to interpret, and perhaps also change, the world we live in.

Chapter 1

"Almost it seemed that the words took shape"

Narrative, History, and the Desire Called Marx

Among the many significant and memorable moments in J.R.R. Tolkien's *The Lord of the Rings*, a novel filled with multiple protagonists, diverse settings, intertwining storylines, and, arguably, several distinct climaxes, one seemingly inauspicious scene embodies the spirit of the entire Tolkienian project. I am thinking of the moment in which Samwise Gamgee suddenly realizes his own place in a grander historical narrative that extends back thousands of years while also directly affecting his present situation. Making reference to the legendary adventures of Beren and Lúthien, the full story of which would not emerge for Tolkien's readers until the publication of *The Silmarillion* in 1977 and of subsequent posthumous writings later, Sam recounts that

> Beren now, he never thought he was going to get that Silmaril from the Iron Crown in Thangorodrim, and yet he did, and that was a worse place and a blacker danger than ours. But that's a long tale, of course, and goes on past the happiness and into grief and beyond it—and the Silmaril went on and came to Eärendil. And why, sir, I never thought of that before! We've got—you've got some of the light of it in that star-glass that the Lady gave you! Why, to think of it, we're in the same tale still! It's going on. Don't the great tales never end?[1]

Sam's reference to "the great tales," which may well be figured forth and not merely translated as *les grand récits* (as in Jean-François Lyotard's famous formulation from *The Postmodern Condition*), implicates the great metanarrative of History, into the midst of which these hobbits find themselves thrust.

It is a memorable, if brief scene. With the full weight of "the terrible" pressing down on the protagonists, Sam recognizes in a sudden epiphany the full extent of history and its direct effect on him in his own present. Not insignificantly, Sam is also the least worldly of the hobbit protagonists, also belonging to a lower social class than they, which makes his sudden insight all the more striking, insofar as it shows how the legendary and heroic are bound up in the quotidian, and vice versa. Sam knew of these tales from hearing Bilbo tell them, but he would hardly have been considered learned, even by hobbit standards.[2] Comparing his and Frodo's circumstances to those found in the grand narratives he is already familiar with, Sam wonders aloud "what sort of tale we've fallen into," and attempts—like so many others before him—to use a story he had heard to help make sense of their current situation. In recalling the story of Beren and Lúthien, Sam stumbles across the unforeseen links between it and his own adventures; in this case, an artifact, the Phial of Galadriel, which is a sort of *mythic* element ensconced within the *historical* narrative, provides a point of reference to connect the distant, mist-enveloped domains of the legendary past with the all-too-real exigencies of the present. This scene functions as a somewhat metafictional instance, in which the fictional character recognizes himself to be a character in a story, only to then remind the readers that they too are part of this story, since the narrative in question is really History itself.

A brief moment of epiphany, Sam's *realization* of history—in a quite literal sense, inasmuch a history at once becomes for him both recognized and real—not only connects the different parts of Tolkien's overall project in the Saga of the Jewels and the Rings but reveals a key theme and goal of the work itself: to make History visible and knowable. Sam's shock of recognition may also provoke in the reader a similar sense of historical consciousness. Functioning almost in the way of a Brechtian *Verfremdungseffect*, Sam's reminder that we are living in the same "story" that we also tell ourselves at bedtime constitutes a moment of radical estrangement, a bewildering jolt to the system, and one which in turn recalls us to the material reality of our place in the world system, broadly conceived.

Occurring as it does in the middle of a lengthy modern novel, Sam's realization of his place in a larger historical narrative also exposes the omnipresence of history in the palimpsest of generic forms that make up both *The Lord of the Rings* and Tolkien's larger legendarium.[3] Beren's story, which itself begins long before Beren was born, of course, is still happening, many millennia after Beren's death. What had seemed the stuff of myth or legend, as told in "lays" or through epic poetry, taking the forms of romantic adventures and heroic quests, is suddenly shown to be connected to the most prosaic moments of everyday life in the present. That Sam, who himself proves to be a heroic figure in his own right, notwithstanding his humble origins and modest ambitions, is the one to enunciate this idea of historical interconnectedness helps to underscore Tolkien's larger point. As an intermediary who can most ably connect the modern readers to this imaginary and mostly unknown history, Sam also allows us to see the deep connections between things otherwise assumed to be unrelated in their own "real" worlds. In making those connections, we find others that disclose our own historical and social situatedness in a grander scheme of things. Or, to put it somewhat differently, through the use of this fantasy we are better able to form cognitive maps of use for making sense of our own vast historical and geographical system. Multiformal and polyphonous, Tolkien's layers of text in *The Silmarillion*, *The Hobbit*, and *The Lord of the Rings* can help us figuratively map a Faërie which is very much part of this world. In so doing, we gain a more vibrant understanding of our own place in the almost impossibly complex system that is our "real" world and its history.

"The theatre of my tale is this earth"

Tolkien's apparent nostalgia for the premodern and especially the pre-industrial age is frequently taken to be a sign of his native cultural conservatism or reactionary political views. (To be sure, a nostalgia for a pre-industrial epoch can be found in putatively leftist thinkers as well, as in as William Morris, for example.) But Tolkien does not long to escape into the distant past so much as he wants to recover it. That is, like others across the political spectrum, Tolkien was concerned with the ways that Englishmen in particular, and people more generally, were losing touch with and even knowledge of history. One sees this concern in his scholarship as well as in his fiction. For example, in his famous 1936 essay "*Beowulf*: The Monsters and the Critics," Tolkien insists on the basic connection between this seemingly ancient, inaccessible epic and those living in present-day England. Acknowledging its antiquity, and noting the fact that even *Beowulf*'s author would have been treating of matters already ancient at that point, Tolkien observes that "it is in fact written in a language that after many centuries has still essential kinship with our own, it was made in this land, and moves in our northern world beneath our northern sky, and for those who are native to that tongue and land, it must ever call with a profound appeal."[4] Tolkien's nationalism aside, this desire to make the seemingly archaic *real* for his contemporary audience is part of his broader mythopoeic project, and it bears greater similarity to Marxist understandings of history than many would expect.

Of course, Tolkien does maintain a rather nostalgic view of the past, clearly favoring the pre-industrial social formations to the modern world in which he finds himself. Famously, he once declared "I am a *Hobbit* (in all but size)," and Tolkien's hobbit-like love of peace, comfort, and stability is understandable enough.⁵ The famous lines from Marx and Engels in *The Communist Manifesto* concerning the radical transformations of all aspects of society during the relatively recent reign of the bourgeoisie reflect the situation that Tolkien, coming from a very different political perspective, laments as well. As Marx and Engels put it,

> [t]he bourgeoisie cannot exist without constantly revolutionising the instruments of production, and thereby the relations of production, and with them the whole relations of society. Conservation of the old modes of production in unaltered form, was, on the contrary, the first condition of existence for all earlier industrial classes. Constant revolutionising of production, uninterrupted disturbance of all social conditions, everlasting uncertainty and agitation distinguish the bourgeois epoch from all earlier ones.⁶

At a basic level, this sort of revolutionizing would be most directly seen by Tolkien as the bulldozing of the natural landscape, the replacement of artisans and their crafts with factory-workers and assembly lines, and so forth.⁷ But as Marx and Engels observe, this is not simply a matter of increasing efficiency or productivity through the use of machinery, thus affecting the overall supplies and demands for goods. Rather, it extends to every sector of social and intellectual life: "All fixed, fast-frozen relations, with their train of ancient and venerable prejudices and opinions, are swept away, all new-formed ones become antiquated before they can ossify. All that is solid melts into air, all that is holy is profaned, and man is at last compelled to face with sober senses his real conditions of life, and his relations with his kind."⁸ This is the condition of modernity itself, which Marshall Berman has likened to "a maelstrom,"⁹ and the critical response of writers as different as Marx and Tolkien to this modern condition is part of that modernity as well.

Tolkien's interests in fairy tales, myth, ancient epic traditions, and heroic romances are undoubtedly a bit antiquarian, in both a professional and amateur sense, but they are also related to his profound desire to bring such distant elements of the past to bear on the present world, to retrieve and recover them for the modern world.¹⁰ In this way, the myth-making project of the "Silmarillion" (Tolkien's vast, lifelong, and unfinished work), along with the more distinctively historical romances of *The Hobbit* and *The Lord of the Rings*, are part of an arguably modernist project intended to address and to rectify that waning of historicity figured forth in an image like "all that is solid melts into air." Tolkien includes all these disparate elements of the past, both mythic and historic, in order to preserve them, yes, but also to extend them into the present moment, which, for Tolkien, has such great need and desire for them.

Tolkien's work as a whole thus partakes of mythology, fairy stories, and history, and it unfolds across narratives whose generic conventions include elements of the epic, the romance, the historical narrative, and the modern novel, with noticeable aspects of what would be understood to be modernist and even postmodernist narrative techniques.[11] Most crucial for Tolkien himself was the powerful sense of *history*, and this is where his geopolitical fantasy might be most closely connected to the Marxist project delineated by such critics as Fredric Jameson, who has argued that history can only be made truly cognizable through narrative. *The Lord of the Rings*, among Tolkien's other works, mobilizes a variety of historical and literary forms in its attempt to give vivid meaning to history itself.

Tolkien's well known comment from the 1966 Foreword to the second edition of *The Lord of the Rings* regarding his cordial "dislike" of allegory offers a telling example of how he viewed his project of bringing history to life in the mind of the reader. But the sort of allegory in question is the reductive, strictly one-to-one matrix of symbol-to-referent or crude metaphorics, a system that essentially replaces the narrative on the page with another, ostensibly more significant one, and in so doing denies the value of the text itself in favor of a more highly valued alternative, "hidden" text. However, a broader notion of allegory, such as that found Jameson's work, in which almost all discrete narratives also become figuratively associated with a larger narrative of human history, does not require any such reduction or retreat from the formal text. On the contrary, close attention to the formal features of the text (including the diction, the formation of sentences, the organization of the materials, their presentation, the genre, and so forth) lies at the core of Jameson's method. In Jameson's reckoning, the allegorical is not a reduction of the narrative so much as an expansion of its interpretative possibilities.

In that "Foreword," Tolkien takes a moment to respond to those who have tried to identify in the narrative of *The Lord of the Rings* a facile allegory for the events of World War II, presumably imagining Sauron as a Hitler-like figure, Saruman as Stalin, the One Ring as nuclear weapons, and so on. Tolkien indulges this allegorical fancy only far enough to dispute it. He explains how differently things would have occurred and then turned out in his story if they had been modeled on topical references to real world events during the war. Tolkien then contrasts this type of allegory with history: "I much prefer history, true or feigned, with its varied applicability to the thought and experience of readers. I think that many confuse 'applicability' with 'allegory,' but the one resides in the freedom of the reader, and the other in the purposed domination of the author."[12] Tolkien asserts that the novel be understood as a work of imaginative history, which is not to be considered entirely at odds with works of fantasy, to name its more familiar generic label.

Elsewhere, in another correction of readerly misperceptions, Tolkien explained that Middle-earth ought not be conceived of as a fantasy-land, such as a Narnia or a Never-Never-Land, but as our own real world, only one with a slightly different or "feigned" history (and geography). Responding to a largely favorable review of *The Return of the King*, written by W.H. Auden in 1956, Tolkien wrote that

> I am historically minded. Middle-earth is not an imaginary world. The name is the modern form (appearing in the 13th century and still in use) of *midden-erd* > *middel-erd*, an ancient name for the *oikoumenē*, the abiding place of Men, the objectively real world, in use specifically opposed to imaginary worlds (as Fairyland) or unseen worlds (as Heaven or Hell). The theatre of my tale is this earth, the one in which we now live, but the historical period is imaginary. The essentials of that abiding place are all there (at any rate for inhabitants of N.W. Europe), so naturally it feels familiar, even if a little glorified by the enchantment of distance in time.[13]

As if to underscore this point more definitively, Tolkien ends the long note by repeating it: "Mine is not an 'imaginary' world, but an imaginary historical moment on 'Middle-earth'—which is our habitation."[14]

Needless to say, Tolkien's position on this matter ought not be taken too literally. For instance, the maps included in *The Hobbit*, *The Lord of the Rings*, and *The Silmarillion* are not expected to align with the geography of Europe, even if some readers have tried to make it do so.[15] The *oikounemē* that is Middle-earth is the world we live in, but that does not mean that the physical geography, any more than the political geography, need be aligned with that of actually existing Europe or of other parts of the planet. Tolkien's point is not to make readers seek out the "real places" in which his fictional tales are set, like the attempt to find Leopold Bloom's house from Joyce's *Ulysses* on the actual Eccles Street in Dublin; although enthusiasts may be tempted to engage in this sort of literary geographical fandom,[16] to do this would be merely a spatial form of the allegory that he insists is not part of the work. Rather, Tolkien grounds the fantastic narratives in the reality of the world. The "verisimilitude" of a story like *The Hobbit* and the setting in which it takes place, as he had observed in a 1937 letter to his publisher Stanley Unwin, is based very much on the presence of the terrible, which is to say the experience of history, and this is in part what makes it seem "real."[17]

Strange bedfellowship notwithstanding, Tolkien's project ultimately coincides with certain aims of Marxist criticism, inasmuch as the goal is to disclose the operations of history itself, which in turn is prerequisite to a certain conception of class consciousness.[18] Among other things, this involves making connections across space and time, connections between places and events that others, in their ideologically inflected blindness or limitations, would insist are and remain separate and distinct.

In the Hall of Fire

"Men make their own history," writes Marx in *The Eighteenth Brumaire*, "but they do not make it as they please; they do not make it under self-selected circumstances, but under circumstances existing already, given and transmitted from the past. The tradition of all dead generations weighs like a nightmare on the brains of the living."[19] This characteristically poetic formulation gets at the heart of a historical truth equally valid for Tolkien as for the Marxist tradition, to wit: we as individual and collective subjects do indeed "make" history, yet we are also subject to a vast array of social and historical forces beyond our control.

In a January 30, 1945, letter to Christopher, Tolkien mentions the (draft) scene referenced at the beginning of this chapter above, citing "Sam's disquisition on the seamless web of story."[20] The mixed metaphor is both striking and apt. Sam at first thinks he is talking about a distinct story, the legendary tale of Beren and Lúthien in their quest to recover a Silmaril (a jewel) from the iron crown of Morgoth, but even as he imagines its successful conclusion (they did manage to wrest the jewel from him and escape the various monsters), Sam realizes that the tale "goes on past the happiness an into grief and beyond it," becoming the tale of Eärendil and of the Fall of Gondolin, which directly led to the First-Age-ending War of Wrath, continuing into the long history of the Second Age as well as that of the ongoing Third, and—with a sudden shock of recognition—eventually becoming part of the tale of Frodo and Sam himself. Where these stories might have been thought of as discrete patchwork to be stitched together into a larger narrative, the *seamless web* discloses that the "great tales" never end. But the metaphor of the *web* is even more telling, since we are clearly not dealing with a more simple, linear, or teleological narrative proceeding from some distinctive *alpha* to a predetermined *omega*, but rather, we are caught up in the sticky and diverse strands of narrative, some forming more or less dense sections, others long and sinewy. The "accident" by which Bilbo discovers the One Ring in the tunnels beneath the Misty Mountains is the link that will eventually make Frodo and Sam the heroes of the most recent events in the story of Beren and Lúthian, which itself was already the long tale going back to before Fëanor and the crafting of the jewels, the destruction of the trees of Valinor by Morgoth, the Flight of the Noldor, and so on. But such accidents are themselves very much part of history, and what is called *chance* may also be understood as *necessity* or *fate* or even just as History itself, here understood in connection with a sort of *grand récit* by which it can become cognizable and realized. As Gandalf famously insists, "even the very wise cannot see all ends," for what had seemed to be a matter of historical contingency nevertheless may turn out to have repercussions that "rule the fate of many."[21]

Bilbo's role in *The Hobbit* provides a nice example of the way in which this philosophy of history is conceived in Tolkien's world. In the final scene of *The Hobbit*, which takes place many years after Bilbo's adventures with Gandalf, Thorin, and the dwarves, the dragon, and the Battle of the Five Armies, Bilbo relaxes in his comfortable home at Bag End, catching up with Gandalf and Balin who have stopped by for a visit. When Balin relates the news that, in Laketown, people are already singing about the rivers running with gold, Bilbo declares, "Then the prophecies of the old songs have turned out to be true," to which Gandalf responds:

> "Of course [...]. And why should not they prove true? Surely you don't disbelieve prophecies, because you had a hand in bringing them about yourself? You don't really suppose, do you, that all your adventures and escapes were managed for mere luck, just for your sole benefit? You are a very fine person, Mr. Baggins, and I am very fond of you; but you are only quite a little fellow in a wide world after all."[22]

"Quite a little fellow in a wide world" is a nice phrase for describing Bilbo, but also for referring to any individual whose lifespan is measured against the tides of history.

Bilbo Baggins is a most unlikely hero of an epic quest, and throughout much of *The Hobbit* his sense of being out-of-place elicits both humor and *pathos*. His situation also fits well with the idea that the protagonist of the historical novel who, in Georg Lukács's analysis, cannot be the "world-historical individual" (such as Thorin Oakenshield or Bard the Dragon-Slayer, for instance), but rather a "mediocre, prosaic hero."[23] At the beginning, Bilbo knows very little of the "wide world," and is for the most part pleased to remain apart from it. What we witness in Bilbo's adventure is not only the expansion of the self-satisfied hobbit's geographical experience of his world (that is, by leaving the Shire and seeing new, exotic parts of Middle-earth), but also the awakening of a kind of historical consciousness, as Bilbo becomes aware of his *situatedness* in world history and makes his own contributions to that history. In a formal sense, *The Hobbit* might be thought of as a kind of historical novel, and within Tolkien's overall legendarium, this novel registers an entry into History with a capital "H" (and into the "grand narrative" of history). Unwittingly intruding into the mythic and epic world in which ancient elves fought in "the Goblin Wars" and dragons terrorized the land, Bilbo the burglar reluctantly assumes a role within that world, and his presence signals the movement from myth to history in Middle-earth.[24]

This vision of history as "the seamless web of story" also comports well with Tolkien's sense of the need for telling these stories. Creative writers or poets—indeed, we might call them *mythmakers*, knowing that *mythos* in Greek can also mean *account*, *plot*, or *story*—give form to the world by representing it and by allowing ourselves to experience a version of it.[25] As Frank Kermode has put it, "[m]en, like poets, rush 'into the middest,' *in medias res*, when they are born; they also die *in mediis rebus*, and to make sense of their span they need fictive concords with origins and ends, such as give meaning to lives and poems."[26] Situated as we are, "in the middle of things," in this *Middle-earth* as well as in the midst of a history extending backwards beyond memory and projecting itself forwards beyond our ability to descry its as yet unimaginable future features, we must make sense of the world and our place in it through narrative. This is also associated with what Jameson has referred to as the "desire called Marx," which is really nothing other than the desire for narrative.

In a rare moment of autobiographical reflection, Jameson mentions that his attraction to a Marxian worldview stemmed, in part, from Sartrean existentialism, which contrary to stereotypes, "did not have the subjectivizing or psychologizing consequences often attributed to it. On the contrary," he says, "it has always seemed to me that an intense awareness of one's individual existence serves to provoke and to exacerbate an equally strong and painful sense of what transcends it, in particular of what we call History."[27] Jameson then explains this more fully, borrowing a "wonderful phrase" from Lyotard's *Libidinal Economy*, by invoking the "desire called Marx":

> The time of individual human biology is radically incommensurable with the time of nature or the time of social history (or indeed, in capitalism, the time of the great economic cycles); nor is this some easily adjustable matter of *durées*, but rather a vision of interlocking, yet somehow also alternate, worlds, in which beings of brief life spans are also components of enormous and properly unimaginable totalities which develop according to vast and inhuman rhythms, and in a different temporality altogether. The units of individual life, whatever meaning we try to give them, are never the same as those of history, even when in rare and punctual convulsions—what we call revolutions—they briefly coincide. The "desire called Marx," then, is not the will to reduce one of these dimensions to the other (in any case an impossible matter), but rather the effort to develop organs of perception capable of enabling us fitfully to position ourselves in that other temporality, that other story, over which we also hope—but now as groups and collectives, rather than as individuals—to assert some influence and control. The "desire for Marx" can therefore also be called the desire for *narrative*, if by this we understand, not some vacuous notion of "linearity" or even *telos*, but rather the impossible attempt to give representation to the multiple and incommensurable temporalities in which each of us exists.[28]

In Tolkien's fantasy, in particular in *The Lord of the Rings*, which has the deep historical as well as mythic underpinnings of the "Silmarillion" materials to give it color and texture, these multiple temporalities are given form in multiple ways, including through prefatory background material (in the Prologue), "lore" disseminated at various times on the story, the interlacing narrative threads, discrete individual characters, and the well nigh encyclopedic trove of information to be found in the Appendices.

It ought to go without saying that Tolkien's is not a Marxist philosophy of history. Given his devout religious beliefs, his idea of the movement of historical development, the fatal Necessity behind the appearance of mere Chance, is closer to what we would associate with Divine Providence, whereas Marx insisted that the motor of history involved human agency, namely class struggle, even as its larger epochal movements—in particular, transitions between modes of production—could be apprehended according to "objective" or impersonal laws of historical development. But one could argue that Divine Providence, like fate, is itself a figure for understanding History writ large, and as such, religious belief is grounded in an ideology which is not altogether inconsistent with Marxist theory. Religion becomes an allegorical form, a sort of "cognitive mapping" (to use Jameson's famous term), by which people make sense of the larger world system, which is beyond any individual's perception even as the individual subject is always part of it. Indeed, as Jameson has observed, the comparison of Marxism with religion, far from discrediting the one with the other, "may function to rewrite certain religious concepts—most notably Christian historicism and the 'concept' of providence, but also the pretheological systems of primitive magic—as anticipatory foreshadowings of historical materialism within precapitalist social formations."[29] If, for believers like Tolkien, the ineffable will of the Almighty, moving in mysterious ways, accounts for the grand mobile trajectories of time, then we could see how that can still stand as but another figure for what those operating in a Marxist tradition understand as the movement of history itself.

The "desire for Marx is really the desire for *narrative*." Jameson's comment resonates well with Tolkien's project, as Tolkien attempts to register these multiple temporalities that give shape both to our own personal experience and to our broader sense of history. Working in the fantasy genre, in fact, Tolkien is able to expand and complicate the scope of what we think of as personal history, for he has sentient beings whose own experiences and memories come to function allegorically as vast historical epochs in their own right. The brief lifespan of a Sam Gamgee (who is 36 when the One Ring is destroyed and who left Middle-earth at age 102) or even a King Elessar (a.k.a. Aragorn, who died at age 207) is hardly a season when compared to that of Arwen Undómiel, who would be almost 3,000 years old when she first appears in the story, and she cannot be considered anything but young when compared with her father Elrond Half-elven, who was born in the First Age, at least 7,000 years earlier. Elrond is himself young compared to some others characters in *The Lord of the Rings*. For example, Galadriel's youth predates the formation of the sun and moon, and thus before the count of years, so she is quite literally prehistoric, while Tom Bombadil and Treebeard are each referred to as "the Eldest," with the suggestion that they are as old as the earth itself.[30] Even older, however, are Gandalf, Saruman, and Sauron, for each is a member of the Maiar, which is to say also of the *Ainur*, would have participated in the cosmogonic "Music of the Ainur" at the uttermost beginning of time and space; it is not clear that, in their current incarnations, these characters do have memory of such an ancient event, but they are undoubtedly beings who existed before the creation of Arda itself. An advantage of myth and fantasy, but also with other genres or discourses that Tolkien here exploits, is the ability to personify these disparate historical perspectives. With immortal or near-immortal characters, the visible traces of history as memory can be brought to light more easily, although one could argue that "lore" itself serves as similar purpose.

Take Elrond, for example, who is the great master of lore in Tolkien's tales. That Elrond is heroic, not for his valor in battle, but for his role as a lore-master, is Tolkien's way of emphasizing this aspect of historical consciousness. True, Elrond was *there* in great cataclysms, in the sense that he fought alongside Isildur and Elendil against Sauron's forces at the end of the Second Age, but Elrond's wisdom, like Gandalf's, goes far beyond his personal experience. In fact, Elrond's kingdom in Rivendell is primarily a place of learning, which is for Tolkien also a place of healing and rest. Like other elven enclaves, it is almost removed from the flow of history, serving as a hospitable island—the Last Homely House east of the Sea—amid the turbulent onrush of historical developments. The elves, as I have discussed elsewhere, pose problems for this larger historical narrative, in part because they tend to resist if not actively oppose historical change, seeking an everlasting present that is itself the preservation of an immutable, antiquarian past.[31] As such, they become cautionary examples for men and hobbits, who must not only appreciate history, but also live in its tumultuous unfoldings.

Rivendell is a key locale in the Tolkien's world, both for its location on the map and for its role in the narratives. As Tolkien himself points out, it is a place of healing and reflection, a repository or "lore" that gives sustenance at once to both the storyteller and the adventurer. "Elrond the Half-elven, son of Eärendil, maintains a kind of enchanted sanctuary at *Imladris* (in English *Rivendell*) on the extreme eastern margin of the western lands," and as Tolkien explains,

Elrond symbolizes throughout the ancient wisdom, and his House represents Lore—the preservation and reverent memory of all tradition concerning the good, wise, and beautiful. It is not a scene of *action* but of *reflection*. Thus it is a place visited on the way to all deeds, or "adventures." It may prove to be on the direct road (as in *The Hobbit*); but it may be necessary to go from there in a totally unexpected course.[32]

Elrond himself serves as an advisor, and his racial or ethnic character, being an elf who is also "half-elven," contributes to his wisdom, perhaps even suggesting that he has greater insights into the geopolitical order, if not the natural order, than even Galadriel or others who have more exalted lineages. Elrond, along with his realm, operates a figure for both deep historical knowledge and practical counsel with respect to the present situation.

In the Hall of Fire, located in Elrond's Last Homely House at Rivendell, songs are sung and stories are told that inform the myth and the history of Middle-earth, thus helping to *realize* that world, making it real by incorporating its apparent otherworldliness in a more coherent grand narrative in which the fantastic and the everyday commingle effortlessly. In the scene in *The Lord of the Rings* in which Frodo listens to the elvish tales being told in the Hall of Fire, Tolkien provides a vivid example of how storytelling can enchant us while at the same time bringing the historical register to life. After his reunion with Bilbo, during which they exchange many stories between themselves, Frodo is left alone in the Hall to listen to the elvish bards, and Tolkien writes: "Almost it seemed that the words took shape, and visions of far lands and bright things that he had never yet imagined opened out before him; and the firelit hall became like a golden mist above seas of foam that sighed upon the margins of the world."[33] Like Sam later, but here in a moment of calm and rest, Frodo is surprised to find his place in history and in a world that had seemed foreign and remote.

In writing *The Lord of the Rings*, along with his other materials comprising what he called "the Saga of the Jewels and the Rings," Tolkien's words "took shape" as well. The content of those tales is well known, but in creating this immense work Tolkien took care to fashion the appropriate form for the narratives. In so doing, he drew upon a variety of familiar genres, only to create something relatively new, if also rather old in spirit: a modernist epic in which myth and fairy story provide the foundations for a heroic and historical romance that is also a realist novel in a fantastic mode, as I discuss further in Chapter 2. Within the narrative, individuals like Frodo and Sam "make history," of course, but they do so only as they increasingly recognize the degree to which "the tradition of all the dead generations" weighs upon them, for good or for ill, and their agency is bound up in a complex, dynamic, and structural network of relations known as history itself.

"Endless untold stories"

In an essay on Brian Aldiss's *Starship*, included in *Archaeologies of the Future*, Jameson distinguishes between the sort of formal narrative unity achieved by reference to existing mythology as a kind of organizing principle, as in James Joyce's *Ulysses*, and what he refers to as *collage*:

> the bringing into precarious coexistence of elements drawn from very different sources and contexts, elements which derive for the most part from older literary models and which amount to broken fragments of the outworn older genres or of the newer productions of media (for example, comic strips). At its worst, collage results in a kind of desperate pasting together of whatever lies to hand; at its best, however, it operates as a kind of foregrounding of the older generic models themselves, a kind of estrangement effect practiced on our own generic receptivity.[34]

Although I would not necessarily characterize Tolkien's method as collage, I do think that this description aptly characterizes the sort of thing going on in Tolkien's major texts, especially given their seemingly accidental and sometimes adventitious manner of production, as I discuss further in subsequent chapters. In letters, Tolkien not infrequently distinguishes between myth and history, even as he admits to blending the two in his narratives. Thus, for example, he notes that the One Ring is a mythic element embedded within a historical narrative.[35] Naturally, Tolkien recognizes the different generic forms and registers he is employing, but he is able to overlay one upon another in such a manner as to more effectively represent the history and geography of Middle-earth.

Jameson's "at worst" scenario, for instance, might well bring to mind the inclusion of materials by Tolkien that do not always seem to belong to the narrative, such as the appearance of Tom Bombadil in *The Lord of the Rings*. Tom Bombadil has been originally created quite separately from both Tolkien's "Silmarillion" materials and *The Hobbit*, appearing in his own free-standing poem "The Adventures of Tom Bombadil," published in *Oxford Magazine* in 1934. Tolkien himself later questioned whether he ought to have included Tom Bombadil in *The Lord of the Rings*, telling one correspondent that "I put him in because I had already 'invented' him independently (he first appeared in the Oxford Magazine) and wanted an adventure on the way"; in another letter, Tolkien conceded that "Tom Bombadil is not an important person," at least as far as "the narrative" was concerned, though the character might have value as a "comment" related to a sort of benign lack of all interest in power or control which appears as a sort of "natural pacificist view."[36] Although many readers have been enchanted with the character and found his brief scenes to be favorites in the novel, Tolkien acknowledges the ways that Tom Bombadil does not really "fit" in the narrative as well as he might. In terms of Jameson's sense of collage, therefore, this inclusion might seem jarring.

But, similarly, Jameson's "at its best" scenario likely helps to explain why Tolkien's work, especially *The Hobbit* and *The Lord of the Rings*, were initially so popular and have remained so in the decades since. For Tolkien, this was a ratification of his view that this sort of material, fairy-stories and heroic romances of a medieval spirit, had a large and devoted audience, or put more simply, that there were many others like him out there. However, it may also be that the generic discontinuities themselves have helped to make this sort of narrative all the more popular. After all, it is not necessarily the case that the medieval source material is more popular, although it is true that Tolkien and other fantasy writers have probably led many readers and students to become enamored with medieval history and literature. But *modern* fantasy, of the type that *The Lord of the Rings* represents, also brings the modern novel and its conventions to bear on the medieval and otherworldly raw materials, in such a way as to draw readers in and keep them entertained. The lack of some of these elements, and of hobbits in particular, may have cost *The Silmarillion* in the long run. Tolkien himself acknowledged that the lack of hobbits would affect the "appeal" of the "Silmarillion."[37] But the existence of the unpublished and still-in-progress "Silmarillion," with its discordant mythic or epic aspects, makes published, complete, and *modern* novels *The Hobbit* and *The Lord of the Rings* all the more powerful and effective.

Published as a standalone book in 1977, *The Silmarillion* was a bestseller, but it has generally been regarded as difficult to read and less enjoyable than Tolkien's other novels. It was likely quite well received by those readers interested in an almost nonfiction, historical and geographical account of events prior to those of *The Hobbit* that could provide background, detail, and elaboration of the world of *The Lord of the Rings*, and some undoubtedly embraced the work almost as a reference book, like a dictionary or encyclopedia. Understandably, however, many readers just "could not get into it," finding its prose turgid and its narrative less than compelling. Along those lines, Tom Shippey has identified two key problems that *The Silmarillion* presents, which may help to explain why Tolkien never satisfactorily completed the "Silmarillion" materials' sixty-year project and why a number of readers find the book more difficult and less enjoyable than *The Lord of the Rings*. First, without the hobbits, there is a lack of a mediator—for example, "Bilbo acts as the link between modern times and the archaic world of dwarves and dragons"—which makes exploring the world, but also experiencing it in its full verisimilitude, more difficult for the reader. Second, by filling in the historical lacunae implied but not expressed in *The Hobbit*

1. "Almost it seemed that the words took shape" 37

and *The Lord of the Rings*, the "Silmarillion" materials lacked the desirable silences or omissions that provided the "impression of depth" or the "illusion of historical truth" which makes the fantasy world so enchanted, precisely because it also makes it so seemingly "real."[38]

Shippey amplifies this second point by citing a 1963 letter in which Tolkien expresses doubt as to whether a sequel to *The Lord of the Rings* would be possible, or more to the point, desirable. As Tolkien explained, "Part of the attraction of The L.R. is, I think, due to the glimpses of a large history in the background: an attraction like that of viewing far off an unvisited island, or seeing the towers of a distant city gleaming in a sunlit mist. To go there is to destroy the magic, unless new unattainable vistas are again revealed."[39] *The Silmarillion*, along with the richly multifarious documents included in *Unfinished Tales* and Christopher Tolkien's vast 12-volume assemblage, *The History of Middle-earth*, does not really eliminate all of the "unattained vistas" only distantly glimpsed in *The Hobbit* and *The Lord of the Rings*. But, according to Tolkien's own sense of things, the lack of a properly unwritten history and distinctively distant sights render the composition of the "Silmarillion" and other such works somewhat less than fully three-dimensional. The reader, accordingly, may find the characters, places, and events to be less vivid and compelling by comparison.

The Lord of the Rings, and to a lesser extent *The Hobbit*, benefits mightily from the deep history undergirding its narrative thanks to the extensive foundations provided by Tolkien's "private and beloved nonsense." When Gandalf battles the balrog and announces that he is "the servant of the Secret Fire, wielder of the flame of Anor," or when Aragorn assures the company that Gandalf "is surer of finding the way home in a blind night than the cats of Queen Berúthiel,"[40] readers may not know—and may never know—what these names are referring to exactly, but such discourse lends weight and substance to the happenings that are depicted in the text. It is a sort of detail without detail, fine points in the architecture that are never featured fully, that make the main narrative all the more salient, and all the more part of a greater historical picture. *The Silmarillion* lacks such background, precisely because it provides the background for *The Lord of the Rings*.

Moreover, even in what could arguably be taken for the "main" narrative of *The Hobbit* or *The Lord of the Rings*, much is left, as it were, "off camera." Notoriously, in *The Hobbit*, for example—and this even before Tolkien revised it in order to make its plot fit more neatly with that of *The Lord of the Rings*—Gandalf leaves the party of Thorin and Company to deal with a pressing matter of the Necromancer, a key scene never depicted and only somewhat vaguely described subsequently during the Council of Elrond. Moreover, much of what would seem to be the action in The Battle of Five Armies in *The Hobbit* is not even shown, since the focalized character (Bilbo) is unconscious during it and learns the details only later. Toward the end of *The Lord of the Rings*, in Appendix B, in fact, readers interested in witnessing more battle scenes are teased with the knowledge that, while the battles depicted in the novel occurred, Galadriel and Celeborn had led an army from Lothlórien to do battle with the forces of Dol Guldur in Mirkwood, that Thranduil (also known as Elvenking) to the north repelled attacks upon his kingdom, and that King Brand and the men of Dale fought alongside the dwarves of the Lonely Mountain and were besieged by the Easterlings at the very gates of Erebor, without ever seeing any more of these glorious battles.[41] Nor do readers see how other parts of the figured spaces on the map of Middle-earth were affected by the far-reaching ramifications of the War of the Ring. Yet, as with the deep history only alluded to and provided by the "Silmarillion" materials, these unseen "scenes" make the novels' actual narratives all the more compelling, largely by making them richly historical in form and in spirit. Thus the simpler tales of four hobbits are set within the global War of the Ring, which in turn is set within a universal history that extends indefinitely into the past.

In a wartime letter to Christopher—the same one in which he referenced "Sam's disquisition on the seamless web of story," in fact—Tolkien mentions the need for "untold stories," as well as the dilemma such a need presents to those who, understandably enough, have stories to tell. Referring to Celebrimbor, the elf craftsmen who had fashioned the three rings for the elven kings, but also a very distant and arguably minor figure who plays no direct part in the events of the novel, Tolkien writes: "A story must be told or there'll be no story, yet it is the untold stories that are most moving. I think you are moved by *Celebrimbor* because it conveys a sudden sense of endless *untold* stories: mountains seen far away, never to be climbed, distant trees (like Niggle's) never to be approached."[42] Tolkien refers here to his "Leaf by Niggle," first published in *The Dublin Review* in 1945, a tale of an artist who spends most of his like attempting to paint a tree, but manages to paint just one leaf beautifully; it is understandably taken as an allegorical representation of Tolkien's own struggles to complete the "Silmarillion" or the Saga of the Jewels and the Rings, of which, perhaps, *The Lord of the Rings* stands as itself merely a marvelously realized "leaf."

In this sense, telling the story, say, of a not-terribly-remarkable person like Bilbo Baggins, thus also becomes, by dint of the many "untold stories" embedded in it, if not by some more properly allegorical association, a way of seeing and understanding the "big picture," which is ultimately History itself. Bilbo intrudes upon the grand historical narratives whose points of departure lie in the immemorial past, but in so doing becomes part of that history. Likewise Sam becomes a hero in a modern epic, a heroic romance that is itself merely an episode in a much larger narrative. As the revolutionary Marxist Victor Serge once put it, "the only meaning of life lies in conscious participation in the making of history."[43] Sam, like Bilbo before him, becomes "conscious" of making history, which endows his experience with additional and supra-individual significance.

Storytelling is thus the way in which history reveals itself to be, not merely a chronological succession of discrete or random moments, like Henry Ford's infamous and apocryphal characterization of history as just "one damned thing after another," but the mythopoeic or storytelling activity that actually gives meaning to the world. Here I am following the basic Aristotelian understanding of the poet as "a maker of plots," where plot-making is understood as the artful combination of the incidents, the poetic choice to tell some stories in some ways while leaving others untold. History itself is made cognizable through narrative, which in turn allows us to see our place in its disparate, overlapping temporalities, as Jameson had suggested. Tolkien's work gives us a profound example of the way this operates, even within the genre of fantasy fiction. Given the well-nigh infinite untold stories available to enrich the stories that we do tell, and that we are necessarily a part of, it is no wonder that, as Sam Gamgee imagines, the great tales never end.

Chapter 2

Formulae of Power

Generic Discontinuities in the Saga of the Jewels and the Rings

One of the more curious aspects of Tolkien's career and legacy is that his *magnum opus* was largely the result of an accident. The novel for which he is best known and which is one of the most influential literary works of its era was, up until the moment he began writing it, something that he did not really want to write at all. Tolkien's true passion throughout his life was for what he referred to as his "private and beloved nonsense," a large body of interconnected stories that in the aggregate made up the "Silmarillion" and related materials, from which *The Silmarillion*, published posthumously in 1977, was derived.[1] *The Hobbit*, a popular novel originally intended for children and published in 1937, was not really a part of that larger project, and Tolkien even referred to *the* hobbit, Bilbo Baggins, as having "intruded" upon the latter; elsewhere, Tolkien puts it more strongly, asserting that the hobbit had been "dragged against my original will" into the legendarium of the "Silmarillion."[2] Tolkien mentions this "intrusion" in order to explain to his publisher why he had no interest in writing a sequel to *The Hobbit*, but he then relented, saying "if it is true that *The Hobbit* has come to stay and more will be wanted, I will start the process of thought, and try to get some idea of a theme drawn from this material for treatment in a similar style and for a similar audience—possibly including actual hobbits."[3] Thus, with this sentence, we find the inauspicious beginnings of *The Lord of the Rings*, a novel that would go on to be voted "the greatest book of the century."[4]

Tolkien's language, as usual, is quite precise, and by referring to "a theme," "treatment," "style," and "audience," he is obviously thinking in terms of *genre*. That is, he is asking, what *kind* of work can I produce? One thing that seemed clear at the time, at least to the publisher Stanley Unwin, was that the materials he had produced so far in his "Silmarillion" were of a rather different sort than what would be required for a sequel to *The Hobbit*. Whatever generic characteristics those various writings by Tolkien shared—today, all might be easily subsumed under the popular marketing label of *fantasy*—*The Silmarillion* (not to mention the far more heterogenous and inconsistent "Silmarillion" texts), *The Hobbit*, and *The Lord of the Rings* clearly represent three rather different kinds of literary works. Tolkien later attempted to imagine and to reconstruct these three texts as part of a single, unified story, which he had referred to as the "Saga of the Jewels and the Rings," but in attempting to give shape to this story, he had to experiment with multiple narrative forms.[5] Ultimately, the project is marked by what Fredric Jameson has called "generic discontinuities," as Tolkien's writings integrate and mobilize aspects of the epic, romance, the historical novel, and other genres in order to build his vast, otherworldly world system.

It is not just that Tolkien writes using multiple genres or narrative forms, which is fairly obvious, but that Tolkien's writing manifestly (but perhaps even unconsciously) puts into play multiple generic characteristics in order to develop a different sort of narrative form. Tolkien's writings establish a hybrid form that can function as a palimpsest, whereby differing layers of mythic, epic, romantic, realist, and modernist forms coexist and infuse one another, as the overall historical and geographical world of Middle-earth unfolds itself before the reader's eyes. In particular, the interplay between myth and history typifies Tolkien's discourse as his project moved from the epic mode of the "Silmarillion" (some of which remains in *The Silmarillion*, which also does other things) to a much more historical and novelistic mode in *The Hobbit* and then *The Lord of the Rings*. These modes contribute to the generic frameworks by which these literary works are experienced, as the genre functions as a sort of formula of power, shaping both the text and the world represented in the text.

Harmonizing Heterogeneous Narrative Paradigms

As a professional philologist, a scholar of both languages and literatures, Tolkien was particularly attuned to the varieties and development of narrative forms or genres over the centuries. Thanks to the success of *The Hobbit*, he was becoming more familiar with the demands and protocols of contemporary children's literature or, more generally, popular fiction.[6] Tolkien's sometimes querulous tone in several of these letters reflects the degree to which he understood these general domains to be in conflict. For example, in the same letter cited above, he acknowledges that the backstory involving character of the Necromancer (i.e., Sauron) was "too dark," citing a complaint by one reviewer that *The Hobbit* as it stands might include material that many parents would find "too terrifying for bedside reading," but Tolkien then avers that "the presence (if only on the borders) of the terrible is, I believe, what gives this imagined world its verisimilitude. A safe fairyland is untrue to all worlds."[7]

This desire to remain "true" to "all worlds," including the otherworldly realms of fairyland as well as to our own all too real world, goes to the heart of the Tolkienian project. For all the talk of escapism that comes with fantasy, even where Tolkien himself seems to embrace the idea of escape (as in "On Fairy-Stories," for instance), Tolkien is most interested in the ways that stories deliver the truth, and the truth delivered is that of *our* world and *our* possible worlds. Tolkien's is a geopolitical fantasy, in part, because of this altogether worldly frame of reference.

With *The Lord of the Rings*, the unexpected sequel to a rather different kind of novel, Tolkien depicts a world and a narrative that rings "true" in the sense that he had in mind. The adventure story there is matched by a sort of historical, geographical, psychological, and social richness not to be found in its predecessor, and part of this has to do with the multiple genres embedded within the work. Indeed, it is difficult to pinpoint the genre of *The Lord of the Rings*, except in the most expansive terms, such as "fantasy," a categorical label that could contain any number of other genres associated with ostensible non-realism or radical alterity. Never mind the fact that even literary realism might also find itself circumscribed by different forms of the fantastic or strange, particularly in an era in which such "literary" writers as Thomas Pynchon, Toni Morrison, Cormac McCarthy, or Kazuo Ishiguro have produced novels that might have earlier been understood to be "merely" genre fiction. Tolkien himself identified the genre of *The Lord of the Rings* as "heroic romance,"[8] but even this seems to apply more directly to only one or more of its storylines than to the overall work; consider, for instance, that Tolkien maintained that the appendices, with all the variety of materials in them, were *necessarily* part of the whole, which in turn could not be fully understood without them. Hence, the novel not only embodies the form of the heroic romance, but also includes such apparently non-literary forms as genealogies and family trees, chronicles ("The Tale of Years"), guides to foreign languages and pronunciation, and so on. Add to this elements of the ancient epic, mythology, lyric poetry, the fairy tale, the realist novel, and other literary genres, which are in turn *integrated* into a singular work of what might even be considered modernism. *The Lord of the Rings* is arguably a sort of "modern epic" in the sense used by Franco Moretti, who included in that category such diverse works as Goethe's *Faust*, Melville's *Moby-Dick*, Wagner's *The Ring*, Joyce's *Ulysses*, and García Márquez's *One Hundred Years of Solitude*.

As Moretti explains the term, "'Epic,' because of the many structural similarities binding it to a distant past [...] But 'modern' epic, because there are certainly quite a few discontinuities."[9] The generic discontinuities that typify the form of *The Lord of the Rings* help to make the work's literary cartography of Middle-earth all the more richly significant.

Of course, literary forms such as the epic or the novel are themselves frequently made up of, or at least include, other forms. Embedded within any particular work of fiction one may also find lyric poems, tragic or comedic drama, regional humor, letters, nonfiction history, philosophy, or geography, and so on. Mikhail Bakhtin famously defines novelistic discourse itself as heteroglossic (i.e., involving many different kinds of language), in addition to being typically multiformal, which is to say, the novel is a form-giving form that is itself made up of a variety of distinctive forms or genres. As Bakhtin writes in "The Discourse of the Novel,"

> the stylistic uniqueness of the novel as a genre consists precisely in the combination of these subordinated, yet still relatively autonomous, unities (even at times comprised of different languages) into the higher unity of the work as a whole: the style of the novel is to be found in the combination of styles; the language of the novel is the system of its "languages."[10]

This conception of novelistic styles, moreover, does not even get at the various distinctive genres of fiction into which categories a particular text may be placed, such as detective fiction, fantasy, horror, romance, science fiction, or the Western, to name a few popular categories. A given novel will find itself awash in multiple generic formulae even as its own unity may be careful crafted by the author.

In *The Political Unconscious*, Jameson discusses the idea of generic discontinuities in connection to his reading of Alessandro Manzoni's 1827 historical novel, *I Promessi Sposi*, in which at least two distinct genres—a Gothic romance and a *roman d'aventures* or travel narrative—are present, thus (in Jameson's view) allowing for a new approach that combines the interior or psychological narrative with a larger, more sociological or historical one. Jameson argues that, in order to understand how this literary work of art operates in its own time and in our own, the reader must pay attention to this disparate and sometime conflicting genres that coexist in the text. As he puts it,

> [o]n this reading, then, the "novel" as an apparently unified form is subjected to a kind of x-ray technique to reveal the layered or marbled structure of the text according to what we will call *generic discontinuities*. The novel is then not so much an organic unity as a symbolic act that must reunite or harmonize heterogeneous narrative paradigms which have their own specific and contradictory ideological meaning. It is at any rate the systematic interweaving of

these two distinct generic modes [...] which lends Manzoni's book an appearance of breadth and variety, and a totalizing "completeness."[11]

Jameson is referring to what he elsewhere calls "the ideology of form," in connection to "the content of the form," and here he is focusing on a hermeneutic practice whereby such ideological messages may be discerned by the critic who is thus engaged in simultaneously formal and historical analysis. Hence, this is part of an *aesthetic*, a way of seeing, that in turn informs a hermeneutic practice designed to help lay bare the underlying political unconscious of the work in question. However, the idea of generic discontinuities also resonates well if we think of it in terms of *poetics*, properly speaking, inasmuch as the creative writer consciously or unconsciously draws upon and makes use of any number of generic conventions in order to give the fictional world some semblance of totalizing completeness.

In effect, genres represent so many formulae of power, each contributing to a certain way of shaping narrative representation of the world and of constraining the potential range of interpretation, not to say evaluation, by establishing sets of conventions or rules. For example, in famously asserting that the writer of a *romance* deserves more "latitude, both as to its fashion and material" than would be accorded the writer of a *novel*, Nathaniel Hawthorne in the Preface to *The House of the Seven Gables* (1851) invokes the power of genre both to determine the way story and its world appear in that text and to influence the manner in which the story's world is presented by the writer.[12] Genre is thus associated with power, and the coexistence of multiple generic conventions or styles within a given text may thus be likened to some alchemical experiments in which various formulae of power are combined in an efforts to see what their combinations might yield.

Along those lines, Tolkien's writings deploy genre strategically in ways that perhaps even Tolkien may not have intended. Tolkien's scrupulous attention to detail and his knowledge of languages and cultures frequently and ironically lead him to include elements that he knew were anachronistic or somehow inauthentic to the worlds and stories he was elaborating.[13] Indeed, as is well known among Tolkien fans and scholars, part of his failure to finish the "Silmarillion" or even to complete many of the major narratives within it—such as *The Children of Húrin*, *Beren and Lúthien*, and *The Fall of Gondolin*, which though unfinished have been published posthumously as discrete works—involved his desire to ensure that everything from his published writings would "fit" within the world represented in these writings. That is, Tolkien wanted to develop a fully integrated and consistent world system in which the "Saga of the Jewels and the Rings" would take place and unfold relatively coherently if not seamlessly. But his failures, as in the Hegelian ruse of history or dialectical reversal, turn out to be part of the strength of the overall work, for the generic discontinuities make for a richer, multiformal, and multilayered literary map of Middle-earth.

Modern Epics

As is well known, Tolkien's boyhood love of fairy stories, together with his passion for myths and for languages, blossomed into a lifelong devotion to the fantastic. In all of his writings, the fantastic plays a crucial part, as is most obvious from his best known works of fiction, *The Hobbit* and *The Lord of the Rings*. But even in his works of nonfiction, notably in such famous essays as "*Beowulf*: The Monsters and the Critics" and "On Fairy-Stories," Tolkien's enthusiasm for and defense of fantasy lies at the heart of his intellectual and creative mission. Understandably, then, Tolkien is primarily regarded as a fantasy writer, and his profound influence on others writing in the fantasy genre has quite appropriately turned Tolkien into a sort of founding father of the genre as it is practiced in the twentieth and twenty-first centuries. His presence, for better or worse (and many writers have alternately praised and lamented that presence), is almost inescapable for those working with the fantasy genre today. Fantasy is a genre, of course, and in its expansiveness as a generic category it serves well to name or characterize the broad range of writing to be found in the Tolkien corpus. However, it is also clear that many different things are going on with respect to the forms and structures of Tolkien's poetic and prose productions, such that the traditional label *fantasy* does not wholly capture the meaning of the texts. Or rather, as I would prefer to say, fantasy provides a larger, overarching categorical framework for discussing the various genres into which Tolkien's fantastic writings might be said to fit.

Tolkien's most detailed discussion of genre can be found in his lecture-turned-essay "On Fairy-Stories," which was originally presented as a public talk delivered at the University of St. Andrews in 1938, just as Tolkien was in the earliest stages of drafting his sequel to *The Hobbit*. It was published as a stand-alone essay in 1947, as part of a *Festschrift* in honor of Charles Williams, and subsequently paired with an exemplary tale, "Leaf by Niggle" (itself published in the *Dublin Review* in 1947), and published in book form as *Tree and Leaf* in 1964. "On Fairy-Stories," which is nominally a lecture defining the parameters and characteristics of a particular genre, actually serves as a complex meditation on the problem of genre itself. That is, while Tolkien is trying to explain what is known and what is misunderstood about the fairy-story genre, he cannot help but raise questions about various genres and their effects on narrative and form, which is also to say, their effects on the ways we both represent our world and imagine alternatives to it. Tolkien himself links the idea of this genre to a sort of geographical context, and in many respects, Tolkien's meditation on various genres contributes to a broader vision of literary cartography, as the forms in which a story is told shape the content as well.

Tolkien begins "On Fairy-Stories," naturally enough, by looking at the definition of the terms involved, in particular that of "fairy." But he quickly shows how standard definitions, including that to be found in the *Oxford English Dictionary*, are incorrect. First, Tolkien objects to the mistaken ideas about "fairies," in particular the image of them as being physically small or diminutive and the notion that they are supernatural rather than supremely natural. But more to the point, he notes that the defining feature of the fairy-story genre is not the presence of such creatures so much as the domain in which the narratives, characters, and events take place. As Tolkien asserts, "fairy-stories are not in normal English usage stories about fairies or elves, but stories about Fairy, that is *Faërie*, the realm or state in which fairies have their being."[14] As if to emphasize this point, he repeats it just a few lines later: "The definition of a fairy-story—what it is, or what it should be—does not, then, depend on any definition or historical account of elf or fairy, but upon the nature of *Faërie*, the Perilous Realm itself, and the air that blows in that country."[15]

The various narratives that in the aggregate constitute *The Silmarillion*, and less directly perhaps, *The Hobbit* and *The Lord of the Rings*, certainly partake in this nature and its air, but it is not entirely clear that they could be thought of as fairy-tales. As Tolkien himself noted, the "world" in which those stories occur, known as Middle-earth, is our own world, if only a version of it enchanted by alternative histories. What Tolkien manages to accomplish, possibly against his own better instincts, is a story or assemblage of stories in a hybrid or discontinuous genre that makes the Perilous Realm and the real world one and the same, at least as far as the stories go. Ultimately, Tolkien's experiments with fairy-stories, along with myth, romance, and realism, makes possible a thoroughly modernist aesthetic project, in which the disparate elements of multiple cultures and forms are rearranged and unified in the form of a largely coherent, self-contained world. The *modern epic*, as Moretti has dubbed it, becomes the novelistic form capable of containing an entire world system, and *The Lord of the Rings*, perhaps also *The Silmarillion*, might well be added to Moretti's list of such works. Indeed, notwithstanding Tolkien's famous youthful desire to create a distinctively English mythology,[16] his writings manifest something of a global, geopolitical quality, which is in line with Moretti's sense that modern epics are also *world texts*, deriving from "sites of combined development, where historically non-homogeneous social and symbolic forms, often originating in quite disparate places, coexist in a confined space." As Moretti says, modern epics are thus "*world* texts, whose geographical frame of reference is no longer the nation-state, but a broader entity—a continent, or the world-system as a whole."[17]

The Silmarillion, or at least the "Quenta Silmarillion" within it, is arguably an attempt to reconstruct or reconstitute an epic. Of course, the tales that together make up *The Silmarillion* derive from others, at times nearly to the point of plagiarism more than allusion or homage. For example, as Tolkien scholars know well, the tale of Túrin Tumanbar is almost directly taken from the story of Kullervo in the *Kalevala*, a story that Tolkien himself retold in a work of juvenilia posthumously published in 2015 as *The Story of Kullervo*, and Tolkien in a letter noted that Turin was "a figure that might be said (by people who like that sort of thing, though it is not very useful) to be derived from elements in Sigurd the Volsung, Oedipus, and the Finnish Kullervo."[18] But Tolkien's delving into the mythic past for examples to help populate and enrich his own invented mythology is not itself a sign of his lack of inventiveness, anymore than Joyce's invention of Stephen Daedalus or use of the *Odyssey* in *Ulysses* is an antiquarian, rather than modernist, convention. Indeed, the organizing and reattachment of various fragments into a new whole might be understood as the preeminently modernist practice, since it establishes on the one hand that an integrated totality can no longer been assumed or taken as a given, that things are already fragmented and heterogeneous, and on the other hand that the proper way of fashioning the semblance of a new totality is by means of the work of art. The artist shores these fragments upon the ruins of one's art, and then gives shape to and makes sense of the world by figuring forth a new totality in the form of the narrative.

"The starry sky is a map of all possible paths"

In terms of the theory of the novel, or perhaps more specifically Georg Lukács's *Theory of the Novel*, the sheer modernity of Tolkien's project in *The Silmarillion* precludes its being an *epic*, for the epic is impossible if the mythology imbuing it needs to be invented or modified for the reader. Homer and Virgil did not need to invent the gods or the heroes that were depicted in the *Iliad* or the *Aeneid*, no more than nameless authors of so much Norse mythology did. And, in such epics, as Aristotle points out in the *Poetics*, so much that is known of the characters may be purposively omitted from the epic poem itself, thus allowing the poet to craft a narrative according to the aims of poetic unity and totality, without having to list all details. For example, the Greeks knew various stories of Odysseus in addition to the specific representations and characterizations found in the *Odyssey*, but Tolkien's readers knew almost nothing of the sons of Fëanor prior to reading *The Silmarillion*. Those ancient epics and myths hail from an epoch when the gods very much part of the world. Or, as Lukács memorably put it in the opening lines of *The Theory of the Novel*, using language that almost sounds like something that could have come from Tolkien's pen,

> Happy are those ages when the starry sky is a map of all possible paths—ages whose paths are illuminated by the light of the stars. Everything in such ages is new and yet familiar, full of adventure and yet their own. The world is wide and yet it is like a home, for the fire that burns in the soul is that of the same essential nature as the stars; the world and the self, the light and the fire, are sharply distinct, yet they never become permanent strangers to one another, for fire is the soul of all light and all fire clothes itself in light. Thus each action of the soul becomes meaningful and rounded in this duality: complete in meaning—in *sense*—and complete for the senses; rounded because the soul rests within itself even while it acts; rounded because its action separates itself from it and, having become itself, finds a centre of its own and draws a closed circumference round itself. "Philosophy is really homesickness," says Novalis: "it is the urge to be at home everywhere."[19]

Not that the Hungarian Marxist critic would agree, but a Tolkienist so inclined could argue that this is a somewhat elvish perspective, one that characterizes the *Weltanschauung* and artistic temper of the elves in a way. (*Fëa*, after all, in Tolkien's universe is the Quenya word for "soul," but it is also connected to the Secret Fire and Flame Imperishable associated with divine *poiesis* itself.) Lukács is describing the world of the epic, which is the literary or narrative form proper to the sort of integrated or closed (*geschlossene*) civilizations that could have produced an *Iliad* or *Odyssey*. But the age of the novel, for Lukács, is one in which the world has been "abandoned by God," and the task of the novelist is to create through art the fictional totality no longer available to humankind in its day-to-day existence. Tolkien's longing for a properly English mythology, and his (failed) attempt to produce such a thing in the twentieth century, is itself a very *modern* phenomenon.

As it happens, at almost the exact moment when Lukács published this magnificent "historico-political essay on the forms of great epic literature" (as *The Theory of the Novel* is subtitled) in 1916, a young Tolkien was working on what would be the first drafts of his lifelong "Silmarillion" project. As Christopher Tolkien points out, *The Book of Lost Tales*, the unfinished project that served as the earliest drafts of what would later become *The Silmarillion*, "was begun by my father in 1916–17 during the First World War."[20] This project was part of the attempt to invent a mythological tradition for England that could be the equal to those he had admired from other cultures and national traditions. In other words, we might say that this was Tolkien's attempt to reverse-engineer, in his own imagination, an epic tradition that would establish a formerly non-existent English "integrated civilization" to match the *geschlossene Kulturen* that Lukács had envisioned. In this way, Tolkien's practice fits well into the system imagined by Lukács, in which "[t]he novel is the epic of a world that has been abandoned by God."[21]

Although I am mostly treating *The Silmarillion* as a complete work, it must of course be acknowledged that it became so only through the meticulous efforts of construction by Christopher Tolkien. In publishing the first volumes of what has now become the immense, 12-volume *History of Middle-earth*, Christopher acknowledged that "to publish in 1977 a version of the primary 'legendarium' standing on its own and claiming, as it were, to be self-explanatory" was "an error."[22] As he had begun with *Unfinished Tales of Númenor and Middle-earth*, published in 1980, Christopher endeavored to correct this error by presenting the materials as "a complex of divergent texts interlinked by commentary," as opposed to the apparently "completed and cohesive entity" that was *The Silmarillion*.[23]

With *Unfinished Tales*, whose very title abjures any notion of completion or coherence, Christopher delivered a book that is "no more than a collection of writings, disparate in form, intent, finish, and date of composition (and in my own treatment of them), concerned with Númenor and Middle-earth."[24] In *The Book of Lost Tales* and subsequent volumes, Christopher takes this practice one or more steps further. By introducing various fragments, incomplete tales, and other previously unpublished works in their original form, but with editorial commentary added that provides context for each, Christopher is able to preserve the uncertain and evolving nature of the work that makes up the "Silmarillion," in a way that *The Silmarillion* as published did not. However, by presenting these materials more or less chronologically (although not always), *The History of Middle-earth* becomes its own, far grander if less expressly literary, whole.[25]

The incompleteness and longitudinal complexity of its development mark the "Silmarillion" as a failed, and perhaps impossible, project. One aspect of its failure could be owing to the sense, as Karl Marx had suggested in the *Grundrisse*, that Achilles is not possible in an era of powder and lead.[26] Tolkien's project, as initially imagined, is too untimely. It is not that one could not write an *Iliad*-like epic in the twentieth century, but that such a work could only be considered pastiche relative to the original form. Homer or Dante can certainly be imitated, as could the anonymous or collective "author" of the *Kalevala*, but the resulting work could not have the same effect or do the same sort of cultural work.[27] However, the attempt to produce an epic suited to an entire mythology organized around a new vision of one's culture is precisely the sort of Quixotic project that a truly modernist aesthetic might conjure into being. A bard in ancient Greece may have cleverly stitched together fragments of a world in order to tell a particular story—to be a maker of plots (*mythoi*), as Aristotle put it—but no one would have imagined creating the entire world itself, complete with gods, heroes, places, and events. A great irony of Tolkien's seeming antiquarian sensibility is that its result required it to very nearly capitulate enthusiastically to Ezra Pound's notorious, modernist injunction to "make it new."

A sign of Tolkien's perverse, perhaps unintended, modernism in *The Silmarillion* is the fact that he felt the need to include a true genesis, complete with an actual cosmogony as well as a delineation of a pantheon, rather than allowing his epic to begin, as traditional epics always have, *in medias res*. The first two sections of *The Silmarillion*, the "Ainulindalë" and the "Valaquenta," properly lie outside of the main story of the "Quenta Silmarillion" and thus of the broader Saga of the Jewels and the Rings. And yet it makes sense that Tolkien should wish to include as part of these materials a cosmogony and a brief description of the Valar. In building a complete world—required of a more modernist project, as opposed to an ancient epic tradition that can assume this "world" as a given totality—a genesis story is desirable, and "The Music of the Ainur" enables Tolkien to elaborate an mythical beginning of the world alongside an entire mythology that can function as both a religion and a heroic *dramatis personae* for the tales to come. Given the greater length and detail of the "Quenta Silmarillion," it is tempting to see the "Ainulindelë" and "Valaquenta" as mere extras, something like appendices of *The Lord of the Rings*, only attached at the beginning rather than at the end. However, from the perspective of both a world builder and storytelling, the cosmogonic tale and the description of the major demigods (the "Powers" of Arda) are crucial. The "Quenta Silmarillion" does not work without these, for much of its own narrative depends on some knowledge of the background provided in these sections.

The "Quenta Silmarillion" differs greatly from most ancient epics and myths by attempting to tell a complete story, starting from the very beginnings of time to the cataclysmic end of the First Age, with the Fall of Gondolin and the War of Wrath, which resulted in the casting out of the original Satan figure, Melkor, "through the Door of Night beyond the

Walls of the World, into the Timeless Void."²⁸ As inconsistently detailed and fragmentary as much of the narrative is, the "Quenta Silmarillion" as published in *The Silmarillion* manages to tell a single, albeit complex, tale of the fashioning and rape of the Silmarils, the epic battles and heroic struggles to recover them, and the tragedy and eucatastrophe involved in their ultimate disposition in earth, sea, and air. In this way, the tale as put together by Christopher out of his father's heterogeneous writings across six decades does not so much resemble the "epic" form of mythological traditions as it does the very modern sense of the word *epic*, referring to any single, "big" story. That the story is assembled from various drafts, notes, and fragments, makes it something of a collage in the sense that Jameson understands with respect to generic discontinuities, and the heterogeneity of Tolkien's sources and influences makes *The Silmarillion* seem more like T.S. Eliot's *The Waste Land* than it does a series of "fairy-stories."

Moreover, given that *The Silmarillion* as a whole retroactively establishes the world in which *The Hobbit* and *The Lord of the Rings* takes place, the materials on the second and third ages are equally part of the whole. The "Akallabêth," chronicling the rise and fall of Númenor in the Second Age, establishes the historical foundation for the tales of Aragorn and of Gondor, which are crucial to so much of the plot in *The Lord of the Rings*. And, naturally, the section of *The Silmarillion* titled "Of the Rings of Power and the Third Age," offers a great deal of desirable background for the previously published novels whose stories are set at the end of that Age and in the aftermath of the rings' creation. Tolkien's mythology, to the extent it is on display in *The Silmarillion*, fleshes out the grand spatiotemporal reality, the geography and the history, of *The Hobbit* and *The Lord of the Rings*, effectively rendering *The Silmarillion* a "prequel" to these other works, even if the "Silmarillion" materials had never been imagined as such by their author.

The Silmarillion is, for the most part, *elvish* mythology and history; Tolkien's mythology is not, therefore, anthropocentric, but rather fairy-centered. In the guiding conceit of the Tolkien world, as he later developed this metafictional history of the tales of the Jewels and the Rings in *The Lord of the Rings*, all these stories are brought to us by Bilbo Baggins, who would have encountered many of the original manuscripts while in Rivendell, which was itself a repository for much of the history of Númenor as well as of the older tales from the first age, with Elrond himself having been born in Gondolin before its fall. As we are given to understand, Bilbo himself translated these tales and histories from the old elvish tongues, and as many readers are shocked to learn in the Appendices to *The Lord of the Rings*, Bilbo's own language is not our own. The "Red

Book of Westmarch," in which all of these stories (including Bilbo's and later Frodo's and Sam's tales) ultimately appear, had to be translated into English, and presumably one "John Ronald Reuel Tolkien" is that translator.[29] These various distancing maneuvers help to shape the fictive world of the tales and also highlight the artificiality of the end product: translations of translations of ancient versions of what would have been largely prehistoric oral traditions give worldly depth and breadth to the otherworldly realms and peoples described in it. But it also establishes the writer, Tolkien himself, as the chief artificer, and no passive reporter or observer.[30] In establishing that his tales of *Faërie* are translated and transcribed from the Red Book of Westmarch, Tolkien definitively transports his narratives from the realms of mythology to those of history, which is to say, of our own all-too-real world.

The Red Book of Westmarch

In her superb study *Tolkien, Race, and Cultural History: From Fairies to Hobbits*, Dimitra Fimi has explored the trajectory from Tolkien's earliest "Silmarillion" writings to his later published novels, and she has demonstrated the degree to which Tolkien's work evolved from a mythical to a historical mode. The interplay between myth and history inevitably involved potential conflicts between the purely fantastic presentation of the materials as wholly imaginary and the "realism" that compelled attention and lent the world a solidity and complexity worthy of the project. *The Hobbit* marks the turning point, but it is also clear that Tolkien's meticulous world-building would require a more historical (and geographical) approach than that employed in his earlier tales.[31]

Fimi argues that by the mid–1930s Tolkien's vast literary project, his "private and beloved nonsense" to which he was so devoted, began to move "from myth to history" with the advent and incorporation of hobbits, and especially with the enhanced role played by men as distinct from elves, who had dominated the "Silmarillion." The "accident" of *The Hobbit*, its intrusion into the mythic world of Tolkien's "Silmarillion" materials, transformed Tolkien's writing project profoundly. As Fimi observes, "[w]ith *The Hobbit*, some elements of his legendarium became fixed because they were published and therefore available to the public as authoritative facts from the author." This concerned Tolkien enough that he spent much of his later life making notes and revising drafts in an effort "to reconcile certain of these 'facts' with his original conception of the mythology or with its changing nature."[32] *The Hobbit* itself, as Fimi notes, is a "hybrid story," which started as an independent tale invented for his own children and only later become connected to the larger, mythic "Silmarillion" legendarium. As such, when published, the novel is "a mishmash of northern folkloric elements, Germanic nomenclature, and scripts as well as new original 'inventions,'" such as "[t]he 'newfangled' hobbits and Gollum," which "verged on the comic in comparison with the tragic and heroic characters of his mythology." *The Hobbit* is thus a major turning point in Tolkien's career, in many different respects, but it also marks what Fimi refers to as "the shift in his creative writing from a 'mythical' to a 'historical' mode."[33]

Tolkien had been (and continued to be) deeply committed to the project of "myth-making," as his poem "Mythopoeia" attests to with a passion. Written around 1931 in response to C.S. Lewis's assertion that all myths were "lies and therefore worthless, even though breathed through silver,"[34] and fashioned as a monologue in heroic couplets delivered by "Philomythus" (myth-lover) to "Misomythus" (myth-hater), "Mythopoeia" argues for man's well-nigh divine right to be a Sub-Creator, a term not used in the poem but familiar from Tolkien's later essay "On Fairy-Stories." That is, the true "Creator" (i.e., God) endowed human beings with the ability and the desire to create myths. As the poem's persona states:

> Though all the crannies of the world we filled
> with elves and goblins, though we dared to build
> gods and their houses out of dark and light,
> and sow the seed of dragons, 'twas our right
> (used or misused). The right has not decayed.
> We make still by the law in which we're made.[35]

Defiantly refusing to accept "your world immutable wherein no part / the little maker has with maker's art," the speaker concludes: "I bow not yet before the Iron Crown, / nor cast my own golden sceptre down."[36]

If the "Iron Crown" in this figuration represents the coldly rational, bloodless, and scientific "realism"—notably, the poem also registers an anti–Darwinian and anti-progressive animus in the lines, "I will not walk with your progressive apes, / erect and sentient. Before them gapes / the dark abyss to which their progress tends"—then Tolkien's God-given mythopoeic power (his "golden sceptre") makes possible an alternative vision of the world, which is also a vision of *this* world.[37] That is to say, for Tolkien, the making of myths is not an evasion from the scientific apperception of the ways this world works, but a necessary complement to it. In Tolkien's theory of Sub-Creation, for instance, the "secondary world" created by the human artist is an imitation of the "primary world" (i.e., God's own Creation), which means that all myth or fantasy partake of that "real" world.

The novel as a form also influenced Tolkien's project. As Fimi puts it, "*The Hobbit* gave birth to *The Lord of the Rings* and inaugurated a new way of writing. Tolkien was not writing mythology anymore, he was writing a novel."[38] Although Tolkien had begun to experiment with the novel as a means for telling his "Silmarillion" stories as early as *The Lost Road* in his drafts from the 1920s, it was not until *The Hobbit* that he wrote a complete novel. Earlier, he had been able to adjust, modify, revise, and generally tinker with his mythological elements in various ways, but *The Hobbit* and the demand for its sequel changed his approach, requiring Tolkien to set down a clearer history and arguably more "realistic" world for his narrative.[39] This also helps to account for the increasing prominence of humans or human-like hobbits, instead of elves, in the larger story that makes up the Saga of the Jewels and the Rings.

By the time he writes *The Lord of the Rings*, Tolkien had managed to square the circle of the myth-*versus*-history conundrum within his writings by using an ingenious device: the Red Book of Westmarch. Tolkien establishes as a regnant conceit within the world of the novels that Bilbo Baggins himself, while living in Rivendell, had translated the many stories and legends that are part of the "Silmarillion" from the original elvish languages, and we learn that the stories we had been reading are merely the translation into English of parts of the "Red Book," translations performed by Professor Tolkien himself. Moreover, as a means of explaining in part how such tales might differ in their mythic views of the world from our own understanding of what "really" happened, Tolkien suggests that the lore that Bilbo had been translating originates with the men of Númenor, the fallen kingdom whose works had been preserved in Rivendell by Elrond, whose brother Elros, after all, was the first Númenorean king. That is, men rather than elves are responsible for the creation and dissemination of these tales. As "natural" beings who are nearly as old as the Earth itself, the elves would presumably know—some would even be able personally to *remember*—the true history from its earliest days, so they would not be as likely as mortals to require "myths" to help them make sense of this incomprehensibly vast temporal span. Thus the myths regarding the initial creation of the world, the story of the Valar (or "Powers" of Arda), the epic tales revolving around Fëanor, his progeny, the Silmarils, the wars with Morgoth, and other events of the First Age would be presented as lore preserved from the Númenorians and stored at Rivendell. Additionally, the history of Númenor and its downfall, as well as the other events of the Second Age, would presumably have been safeguarded by the "faithful" Númenorians and by Elrond, so those stories as well could be preserved and translated by Bilbo, who eventually passes along the "Red Book" to Frodo and thence to Sam for further updating. As Fimi concludes,

[t]he choice of the "Red Book" as the method of transmission of the legendarium to the readers in modern times was a nearly perfect solution: Bilbo would have had access to the records of Rivendell where much material from Númenor was also preserved. The mythology would not reach us directly through the Elves, but through the Númenoreans and the subsequent "mediation" of the hobbits.[40]

Hobbits, already an anachronistic feature of Tolkien's world (hence their accidental status as "intruders" in this larger narrative), are thus superbly suited to help to bridge the extensive mythic and historical gap, bringing the story from a distant age into our own present.

Additionally, this marvelously effective "framing" device would allow a rather "realistic" transition from the mythical world of the "Silmarillion," the legends of which would have largely been set down in *lays*, ballads, lyric poetry, and especially in the form of the epic, to the more straightforwardly historical world of humans (i.e., *our* world), for whom the heteroglossic and multiformal novel becomes the predominant modern representative literary form. *The Hobbit* itself, in retrospect, exemplifies the process whereby Tolkien made the move from myth to history and from epic to novel, for Bilbo's "intrusion" represents the interventions of the most prosaic yet profound aspects of history into a grandly poetic and mythic fantasy world. In this way, *The Hobbit* helps to realize what will become Tolkien's larger political and philosophical project of making History (with a capital "H") meaningfully accessible to modern readers who are increasingly unconscious of it and its connections to themselves. *The Hobbit* thus also forms a kind of historical novel in its own right.

"A more or less mediocre, average English gentleman"

The modern fantasy novel, of which *The Hobbit* might be considered an exemplar, would appear to be nearly the opposite of the historical novel, a genre that developed through an admixture of romance and realism in order to establish a firm location, in time and space, visible in the historical events of the "real world." Fantasy, it is usually assumed, deals with an *otherworld* quite distant and distinct from the real one, and presents a place somewhat out of time, perhaps akin to a recognizably historical moment in our world (as with popular medievalism), but not really *of* that world. Perhaps unwittingly, in *The Hobbit*, Tolkien managed to establish many of the parameters of conventional fantasy, amounting to what Terry Pratchett has half-jokingly referred to as the "consensus fantasy universe" in which "Elves are tall and fair and use bows, dwarves are small and dark and vote Labour."⁴¹ But, at the same time, *The Hobbit* engenders a historical reality in a novel only apparently outside of history, depicting an otherworld that is altogether worldly.

In traditional literary history and theory, Sir Walter Scott is often credited as a founder of the historical novel genre, and his own critique of "the supernatural in fictitious composition" sets him on the side of an anticipatory realism over the fantastic in literature and the arts. Examining a tale by E.T.A. Hoffmann, Scott praises "the wildness of Hoffmann's fancy," but then complains that, "[u]nfortunately, his taste and temperament directed him too strongly to the grotesque and fantastic,—carried him too far 'extra mœnia flammantia mundi,' too much beyond the circle not only of probability but even of possibility, to admit of his composing much in the better style which he might easily have attained."⁴² But in hoping to rein in the extravagance of fantasy, Scott doth protest too much, and the divisions between the mimetic real and the imaginary fantasy are not so clearly drawn. Indeed, one of the main reasons that Scott's own novels, much like those of his American admirer James Fenimore Cooper, are not as highly valued today is thought to be because of their own romantic lack of "realism."

In fact, historical fiction and fantasy likely have more in common than many of their respective fans would allow. Even though Tolkien might be considered the *ur*-figure of the modern fantasy genre, Tolkien's mythic representational techniques become historical in a sense not unlike the historical aspects of the great so-called realist novels. To put it another way, with respect to literary form, as Tolkien's epic storytelling becomes distinctively novelistic in his attempt to tell Bilbo Baggins's story, a story rather different in form and content from Tolkien's earlier and later works, the work had to foreground and grapple with the problem of history. Indeed, *The Hobbit* could be read in the context of Lukács's magnificent and almost exactly contemporaneous study, *The Historical Novel* (first published in Russian in 1937, the exact year that *The Hobbit* appeared). Lukács's definition and characterization of the genre involves the sense in which, in the narrative, an ordinary or "maintaining" individual sustains a representation of world-historical events and individuals that discloses the emerging historical consciousness. The form of the novel, *The Hobbit*, incorporates and transcends the traditionally fantastic content, making its otherworldliness all the more critical to a figurative mapping of the "real" world.

As is fairly well known, Tolkien stumbled upon the idea for *The Hobbit* unexpectedly, and its story was only very loosely related to the "private and beloved nonsense" that would make of the materials in the "Silmarillion."⁴³ Fimi has observed that the pivotal moment of this gradual transformation of his *legendarium* was the "accidental" publication of *The Hobbit* and the demanded sequel, which became *The Lord of the Rings*. But writing *The Lord of the Rings* necessitated changes that transformed the whole mythology. Prior to 1937, during the first writing phase of the legendarium (represented by volumes I–V in the *History of Middle-earth* series), Tolkien was mainly writing in a "mythological mode." He imitated ancient as well as medieval myths and legends by writing creation myths. [...] Although he experimented with different narrative forms during that time, it was not until *The Hobbit* and *The Lord of the Rings* that Tolkien turned to a "novelistic mode," or more accurately, a "historical mode" for his mythology. He found himself writing in a completely different genre.[44]

In Fimi's view, "*The Lord of the Rings* was the point where myth became history," but clearly *The Hobbit* was the novel that forced Tolkien to take up the mode of the historical novel, abandoning but also reimagining the mythic substance of his "Otherworld" in relation to a global history and a geopolitical aesthetic. *The Hobbit* is an especially good point of entry into such a complicated world system, since the anachronistic intermediary that is Bilbo allows the reader to see that world from the perspective of one who is nearly as unfamiliar with it as we are.

Bilbo Baggins is an obvious anachronism, who seems almost to time-travel in his movement eastward from the comfortable and familiar landscape of the Shire toward not only Laketown and the Lonely Mountain, but to the historic events represented by those faraway places. Apart from certain distinctively "hobbitic" characteristics, like wooly toes and uncanny stealth, Bilbo is clearly an Edwardian bourgeois Englishman, a modern if still somewhat rustic inhabitant of a place not unlike those found in the West Midlands, presumably an inoffensive member of a *rentier* class who neither plies a trade or employs others to work for him (except, perhaps, a gardener or general handyman, Hamfast Gamgee [better known as the Gaffer], as we learn from *The Lord of the Rings* later), and so on. Although we learn that he has occasionally been interested in the "wide world," owing in large part to an adventurous streak inherited from his mother's side of the family, Bilbo knows quite little, practically or theoretically, about that world. To name but one of the almost innumerable examples of his ignorance or naïveté that readers encounter in the narrative, Bilbo "was not good at skinning rabbits or cutting up meat, being used to having it delivered by the butcher all ready to cook."[45] What could be more quotidian than purchasing food from a butcher? And yet, in that scene, Bilbo dines on rabbit-meat prepared by dwarves that had been delivered by giant eagles after being rescued from treetops while surrounded by wolves, which is already quite an adventure tale to tell.

Tolkien managed to sneak into the novel elements of his earlier mythological world, including references to Gondolin, the "Goblin Wars," and Sauron himself (as "the Necromancer"). However, particularly as he attempted to integrate the narrative of *The Hobbit* into the wide world of his imagined Middle-earth as he was writing his sequel, Tolkien repented and regretted some of the choices he had made. For example, Tolkien was not happy with his use of "conventional and inconsistent Grimm's fairy-tale dwarves" in the novel, who worked well for a comic tale of a hobbit, but did not fit neatly within a world containing a Nargothrond or Khazad-dûm.[46] The juxtapositions are a bit jarring, but it works well in terms of a "fish out of water" story; in Thorin's august company, Bilbo is most certainly and humorously an "out of water" fish. But even amid all the comedy, it is worth noting another observation made by Tolkien in a wartime letter to his son Christopher: "I imagine the fish out of water is the only fish to have an inkling of water."[47] This metaphor works effectively captures an individual's realization of his or her place in a larger history, whether that be Bilbo in the caverns beneath the Misty Mountains, Sam Gamgee on the outskirts of Mordor, or readers situated in their own place and time within a vast, spatiotemporal system of which they are a part but over which they have little control.

This is also an apt metaphor for history itself, of which Bilbo and we all are a part, but which brings itself into the open mostly as it becomes uncomfortable. As Jameson famously remarked, "History is what hurts, it is what refuses desire and sets inexorable limits to individual as well as collective praxis, which its 'ruses' turn into grisly and ironic reversals of their overt intention."[48] In its relative discomfort or unfamiliarity, history is (perhaps paradoxically) similar to fantasy. For instance, as Jerome de Groot has noted in his study of the historical novel, "History is other, and the present familiar. The historian's job is often to explain the transition between these states. The historical novelist similarly explores the dissonance and displacement between then and now, making the past recognizable but simultaneously authentically familiar."[49] The same might be said for fantasy, which often presents a world radically different from our own, and yet makes it seem not only possible, but actually real, at least within its sphere.

In *The Hobbit*, to be sure, dragons are remote, otherworldly, and the stuff of legend or myth; and yet, Smaug is all too real, and the experience of traveling alongside Bilbo, Gandalf, and the dwarves, is for the duration of the narrative an utterly real, perhaps historical, experience. In accompanying Bilbo especially, we discern his own awakening of historical perspective, moving from the good-natured but impatient hobbit who "Good mornings" Gandalf in the first chapter of *The Hobbit* to the "hero," as Gandalf names him in the Council of Elrond scene of *The Lord of the Rings*, whose accidental discovery of the One Ring will become quite possibly the most significant, or *historic*, event of the age.

In Lukács's analysis of the historical novel as a literary form, one of the key, defining characteristics of the genre is the foregrounded presence of the ordinary little guy, someone against whom the Hegelian "world-historical individual" (like a Cromwell or Napoleon) stands out in the distance. In *The Hobbit*, Bilbo's position is like that of an Edward Waverley in Scott's grand historical romance, *Waverley; or, 'Tis Sixty Years Since* (1814). That is to say, he is an utterly unremarkable, seemingly insignificant figure, who stumbles into the great world-historical events of the epoch. As Lukács writes of Scott's protagonists, and he could as just as easily be thinking of a Bilbo Baggins type of character, "[t]he 'hero' of a Scott novel is always a more or less mediocre, average English gentleman. He generally possesses a certain, though never outstanding, degree of practical intelligence, a certain moral fortitude and decency which even rises to a capacity for self-sacrifice, but which never grows into a sweeping human passion."⁵⁰ The fact that Bilbo's Middle-earth is not "real" in the same sense that Waverly's Scotland is real is beside the point, and in any case does not bear directly on the *form* of the literary work. Within the novel, each place is as real as the other.

As noted above, Tolkien's commitment to the creation, or "sub-creation," of a world apart does not necessarily mean that Tolkien turns away from an engagement with the "real" world. The imaginary projection of an alternate reality in Middle-earth, with its seemingly integrated *Lebenstotalität*—which, according to Lukács in *The Theory of the Novel* characterizes the age and the world of the epic—figures forth a kind of truth not seen in more crudely allegorical narratives. As Tolkien himself notes in "On Fairy-stories," "creative Fantasy is founded upon the hard recognition that things are so in the world as it appears under the sun; on a recognition of fact, but not a slavery to it."⁵¹ Moreover, as Tolkien points out, the "perilous realm" of Faërie "contains many things besides elves and fays, and besides dwarfs, witches, trolls, giants, or dragons: it holds the seas, the sun, the moon, the sky; and the earth, and all things that are in it: tree and bird, water and stone, wine and bread, and ourselves, mortal men, when we are enchanted."⁵² In other words, even in their apparent otherworldliness and amid the mythic elements included in their overall substance, these tales are worldly and historical, particularly when rendered in the form of the modern novel.

The Bilbo who returns to the Shire is, as Gandalf notes, not the same person as the one who left it. Even though Bilbo claims on the return journey that "our back is to legends and we are coming home," Bilbo is different: he is part of a global history and, more importantly, he is aware of it. Henceforth, his interactions with elves or dwarves are not isolated encounters with creatures from a mist-enveloped, legendary past, a region that might as well be a fantastic otherworld, but are woven into a spatiotemporal continuum that includes Bilbo and his kin, along with kings and counselors, gods and monsters. But Bilbo also remains the happy-go-lucky creature who, when reminded by Gandalf he is "quite a little fellow in a wide world," can declare "Thank goodness!" as he passes the tobacco-jar. A fittingly everyday end to a historical novel.[53]

The Cauldron of Story

Tolkien's artistic and narrative trajectory moved from the mythic world of his "history of the gnomes" (elves) in his early "Silmarillion" writings to the historical world of hobbits, men, and the readers themselves once he wrote *The Hobbit* and *The Lord of the Rings*. Tolkien had began with myth, and specifically with a desire to create a distinctively English mythology "dedicated" to England. In his first complete novel whose characters and events find themselves on the margins of that mythology, as well as on the margins of a sort of epic mode, Tolkien created a fairly straightforward romance, an adventure story in which an unlikely and anachronistic hero becomes caught up in the grand historical movements of his time, and thus finds himself both subject to, and an agent of, history itself. For its sequel, the use of similar generic model—that is, a heroic, historical romance—was suitable for establishing a compelling plot, but Tolkien was unable to simply stick with this sort of tale; rather, he allowed his full range of interests in myth, fairy-story, folklore, and "real" history to be indulged. The result is a sort of expansive novelistic monument, a *modern epic* that exceed the bounds of these other genres while also helping to establish many of the conventions of the new genre entirely.

In shifting from a more mythic to a more historical mode, Tolkien's interests in Faërie do not subside. *The Lord of the Rings* is in some respects "an ennobled fairy tale for adults," as Fimi called it,[54] featuring those elements of fantasy that Tolkien had discussed in "On Fairy-Stories." However, with the focus now on mortal men, rather than elves, along with the very human-like and anachronistic (not to mention very English) hobbits, the narrative registers and bears the weight of history. Even in *The Silmarillion*, arguably, the real drama does not fully begin until mortality becomes a factor, starting with the death of the trees and the rape of the Silmarils, which itself was accompanied by the "first" death, that of Finwë, who is killed by Melkor. Feanor's anguish and the flight of the Noldor are thus tied to a death and the quests to avenge it and to recover the stolen jewels. It is perhaps noteworthy that *The Silmarillion* introduces "mortal" humans in a chapter, "Of Men," shortly thereafter. The fact of mortality seems to make for greater drama, and as compelling as the various tales of Valinor and of the Noldor may be before the moment, it is probably not surprising that the three most fully elaborated and tragic tales involve human protagonists: Beren, the children of Húrin (Túrin and Nienor), and Tuor (who survives the fall of Gondolin). The mythic adventures of these mortals, along with the tragedy of their and others' deaths, betokens a shift from the elvish and otherworldly domain of myth to the far more human realm of history, the Realm of Necessity, to use the Marxian idiom.

The Hobbit, as noted above, is marked by anachronism. Its titular hero is a sort of fantastic being, who is not quite human while also being about as anthropomorphic as can be imagined. Hence, hobbits are generally understood as a "race" distinct from men, elves, dwarves, and others, even though Tolkien makes clear that hobbits are actually a form of mankind: "The Hobbits are, of course, really meant to be a branch of the specifically *human* race," Tolkien explained in a letter, adding "They are made *small* (little more than half human stature, but dwindling as the years pass) partly to exhibit the pettiness of man, plain unimaginative parochial man [...] and mostly to show up, in creatures of very small physical power, the amazing and unexpected heroism of ordinary men 'at a pinch.'"[55] Along these lines, Bilbo is also quite clearly an Englishman, and his love of comfort, including his enjoyment of the anachronistic tobacco (a term which was judiciously replaced with *pipe-weed* in the sequel), marks him as a typical bourgeois of his time.[56] Then history and myth, in the guise of Gandalf, Thorin, and the dwarves, literally come knocking at his door, entreating him to venture forth from his present, quasi–Edwardian existence into the depths of time and space beyond. Yet even these apparent "errors" in the overall world-building of Tolkien's universe have their unforeseen advantages. For instance, in *The Historical Novel*, Lukács notes that the realist text includes "necessary anachronisms" that help to enable it to, as it were, step outside of itself and present something like a social totality.[57] Additionally, much as Tolkien may have wished he had not included references to football or golf in *The Hobbit*, and much as he endeavored to avoid linguistic and other anachronisms in *The Lord of the Rings*, the "estrangement effect" of such jarring moments, as Bertolt Brecht might have noted, does recall the reader to the historicity and historical situation of the narrative, which is yet another way of "realizing" history in the seamless web of story.

Tolkien recognizes and emphasizes the distinction between myth and history, as when he points out that the One Ring is "a mythical feature, even though the world of the tales is conceived in more or less historical terms," for example.[58] However, like Lukács and Jameson, Tolkien also understand the degree to which they overlap or rather imbue one another in the form of narrative, that is, in the way the humans make sense of and give form to the world. Tolkien notes in "On Fairy-stories" that "History often resembles 'Myth,' because they are both ultimately of the same stuff."[59] That is, even if the mythical characters or events did not exist in the "real world," some account of the nameless persons they are made to represent is nevertheless thrown into what Tolkien refers to as "the Cauldron of Story." In that Cauldron, "where so many potent things lie simmering agelong on the fire," "the great figures of Myth and History" emerge, and the forms that their narratives take will depend on the mythmaker, the historian, or, more simply, the storyteller. As Tolkien puts it,

> [b]ut if we speak of a Cauldron, we must not wholly forget the Cooks. There are many things in the Cauldron, but the Cooks do not dip in the ladle quite blindly. Their selection is important. The gods are after all gods, and it is a matter of some moment what stories are told of them. So we must freely admit that a tale of love is more likely to be told of a prince in history, indeed is more likely actually to happen in an historical family whose traditions are those of golden Frey and the Vanir, rather than those of Odin the Goth, the Necromancer, glutter of the crows, Lord of the Slain. Small wonder that *spell* means both a story told, and a formula of power over living men.[60]

As in Elrond's Hall of Fire, not to mention the more menacing figure of the Voice of Saruman, the enchantments are to be found less in magic *per se* than in stories: that is, in tales well crafted and well told.

The Lord of the Rings combines myth and history, along with the shape of the heroic romance or adventure story, in order to most fully map out the entire world for its readers. The experiences of the various characters, individually and collectively, trace their courses over the map, which is made richer and more meaningful by the deep and varied historical layers. Many works of fiction, whether categorized as fantasy or not, are able to give the impression of a fully realized "world," but Tolkien's in *The Lord of the Rings* presents an entire geopolitical system in which each hill or dale, mountain or cave, village or city, bears the weight of the centuries of imagined history. Thanks in part to the many genres and forms that make up its soup, and thanks to the ways that Tolkien dips his own ladle into the Cauldron of Story, the effect of the world-building in *The Lord of the Rings* is striking. As with Legolas's surmise concerning Fangorn Forest, the entire world of Tolkien's novel seems "old and full of memory."[61]

Tolkien's world takes on a sort of historical reality not merely through his use of detail and care with linguistic authenticity, but also through the formulae of power that are the multiple genres in which his world is framed and given life. The combinations of forms, including the epic, fairy tale, romance, realism, historical fiction, and even the modernist novel, makes *The Lord of the Rings* especially, but also the entire legendarium in which the Saga of the Jewels and the Rings unfolds, a geopolitical and historical plenum. In this grand system elaborated through Tolkien's multi-layered fantasy masterpiece, with its many textual and linguistic forms, we may descry the outlines of our own history as well, thus enabling us to imagine new ways of thinking it and its potential futures.

Chapter 3

Three Rings for the Elven Kings
Trilogizing Tolkien in Print and Film

J.R.R. Tolkien's *The Lord of the Rings* is almost certainly the most famous trilogy in the fantasy genre, or perhaps even in modern literature at large. But, as some first-time readers are surprised to learn, *The Lord of the Rings* is not so much a trilogy, in the sense of three distinct but related novels, but really a single narrative like *The Hobbit*. Subdivided into six books, plus a Prologue and Appendices, *The Lord of the Rings* is a massive novel, a modern epic that incorporates many forms and styles, but it was not written in the form of a trilogy, and following its publication its author generally disavowed descriptions of the work *as* a trilogy. Extraliterary considerations alone, such as the cost of paper and sales projections, conspired to make Tolkien and his publisher break the single novel into three installments, *The Fellowship of the Ring* (first published in the U.K. on June 29, 1954), *The Two Towers* (published November 11, 1954), and *The Return of the King* (October 20, 1955).[1] However, in what might be called a ruse of literary history, Tolkien thereby effectively became a founding father of the fantasy trilogy, which remains a popular and conventional format within the genre.

The decision by director Peter Jackson to adapt the novel by making *The Lord of the Rings* film trilogy thus seems natural enough, even if he had originally envisioned it as requiring only two films.[2] But Jackson's decision to stretch *The Hobbit*, a much slighter text, across three feature-length movies amounts to a sort of narrative and cinematic overkill. The former, which drew strength from the conceit that it was already an adaptation of a trilogy, involved division, condensation, and carefully considered omissions; the latter, in taking a relatively short children's book and turning it into a more than eight-hour film trilogy, required multiplication, extension, and ultimately some additional "fan fiction" wholly unrelated to the narrative that unfolds in the novel itself in order to fill the hours. In the matter of "trilogizing" Tolkien, both the print text and the film adaptations altered the substance of the narrative and created different effects, not necessarily for the better.

As for the novels, *The Lord of the Rings* was, of course, the sequel to *The Hobbit*, but its length, tone, and subject matter set it apart as a massive fantasy epic-novel in its own right. After the publication of its sequel, *The Hobbit* thus appeared as merely a "prelude" to *The Lord of the Rings* (a term used in marketing the book); apart from Bilbo Baggins's discovery of a magic ring that is later revealed to be the One Ring, most of the events of the earlier work do not bear directly on the plot of *The Lord of the Rings*, although Tolkien made some efforts to connect the plots more in relation to the geopolitical order of Middle-earth, particularly with respect to Gandalf's machinations.[3] At over 450,000 words, *The Lord of the Rings*' inordinate length caused its publisher to divide it into three more or less equally long volumes, on the grounds that the price of a single-volume edition would have been too high to be effectively marketable. It was strictly a business decision. As Tolkien insisted in a letter,

> [t]he book is *not* of course a "trilogy." That and the titles of the volumes was a fudge thought necessary for publication, owing to length and cost. There is no real division into 3, nor is any one part intelligible alone. The story was conceived and written as a whole and the only natural divisions are the "books" I–VI [which originally had titles].[4]

Leaving aside the circumstances that led Allen and Unwin to publish Tolkien's immense tome of a manuscript as *The Fellowship of the Ring*, *The Two Towers*, and *The Return of the King*, which appeared separately over several months in 1954 and 1955, there would be no real reason to view *The Lord of the Rings* as a trilogy. That is to say, there is no diegetic or textual evidence to support this modern epic's triplicity. And yet, one might argue that the historical trilogizing of this otherwise unified narrative has had real effects.

In this chapter, I discuss these effects in relation to the trilogy form, using Tolkien's famous "trilogies" as exemplary cases, while showing how the format affects both his novel, *The Lord of the Rings*, and the film adaptations by Peter Jackson of that novel and of *The Hobbit*. I argue that the use of the trilogy format alters the way in which the stories are understood, and I suggest that the popularity of this form is connected to a generalized desire for clarifying overview and structure in narrative.

"There is no real division into 3": Defining Trilogy

Tolkien's comment about their being "no real division into 3" in this novel invites us to consider the definition of the word, for if the term *trilogy* is misapplied to *The Lord of the Rings*, then a reader might legitimately ask what constitutes a "real" trilogy. Let me propose the following characterization in lieu of a definitive definition: In literature and cinema, a *trilogy*, properly speaking, would require three related books or films that tell a single overarching story, but with the proviso that each book would also have to be "intelligible on its own," to use Tolkien's language.

Hence, for a given work of art or fiction to be a proper trilogy, it would certainly not be enough to take a single work and then divide it into three volumes. In the nineteenth century, for example, it was common enough for a single novel to be divided and sold in three volumes. For instance, Herman Melville's *The Whale* was originally published in a three-volume English edition in 1851, before its single-volume publication (as *Moby-Dick, or, The Whale*) in the United States shortly thereafter, but neither version of that novel would be called a trilogy. Dividing a long film into three segments with intermissions between them would clearly not make it a trilogy either. A play divided into three acts is not a trilogy, after all. Dividing a work into three parts thus is insufficient grounds for viewing the work as a trilogy.

Alternatively, the mere grouping together of three previously unrelated or otherwise independent works cannot be a sound basis for defining a *trilogy* either. For example, China Miéville has set three of his novels in the fictional realm of Bas-Lag, and although those three have been sometimes thus referred to as "the Bas-Lag trilogy," *Perdido Street Station* (2001), *The Scar* (2002), and *The Iron Council* (2004) each stand alone; they can be read in any order, they do not together tell one single, overarching story, and thus they do not form a trilogy. To cite a well-known cinematic variation on this theme, Roman Polanski's "Apartment Trilogy," likewise, which establishes an *a posteriori* connection between the films *Repulsion* (1965), *Rosemary's Baby* (1968), and *The Tenant* (1976), would not be a trilogy under this definition. Understood in this way, of course, neither would the Theban plays of Sophocles that we commonly think of as the Oedipus Cycle, since *Antigone* (c. 441 BCE), *Oedipus the King* (c. 429 BCE), and *Oedipus at Colonus* (c. 401 BCE) not only stand alone as dramatic units, but were not presented as a unified three-play narrative; moreover, the fact that the order of writing and performance does not follow the chronology of the story of Oedipus and his progeny suggests that Sophocles would not have had a three-play "cycle" in mind when composing these discrete works.

Finally, to make what might seem to be a more controversial distinction, I would argue that adding sequels to a formerly singular work would not render the whole a trilogy (or, for that matter, tetralogy, etc.), even if the number of individual installments stopped at three, since this original work was not conceived *as* a trilogy, and the subsequent additions were, in a sense, "tacked on." Hence, *The Godfather* film saga, which eventually became three movies but which was based on a single bestselling novel, would not qualify as a trilogy by this definition. Neither would the "original" *Star Wars* movie trilogy, since the narrative of the film *Star Wars* (1977) was complete unto itself. The original *Star Wars* movie, now repackaged as *Episode IV: A New Hope* in the ever-expanding *Star Wars* franchise, was not originally filmed with the intent of adding two sequels. In fact, *The Empire Strikes Back* (1980) and *Return of the Jedi* (1983) might not have even been made had the original *Star Wars* resulted in a critical and financial failure. However, the subsequent "prequel" movie trilogy, which could scarcely be predicted to fail, was designed to be a single, tripartite story, so one could legitimately say that *The Phantom Menace* (1999), *Attack of the Clones* (2002), and *Revenge of the Sith* (2005) did form a trilogy within the proliferating series of films branded as *Star Wars*. More recently, the franchise released a "sequel" trilogy, comprising episodes VII through IX, *The Force Awakens* (2015), *The Last Jedi* (2017), and *The Rise of Skywalker* (2019), along with affiliated, stand-alone titles. Interestingly, the saga of Skywalker as told across nine separate films is not so much thought of as a "ennealogy" or nine-part story as it is recognized today as a trilogy of trilogies.[5]

Trilogies, properly speaking, are therefore perhaps more rare than we may think. A good recent example would be Suzanne Collins's *Hunger Games* series, in which each novel (*The Hunger Games* [2008], *Catching Fire* [2009], and *Mockingjay* [2010]) maintains a clear level of semi-autonomy while the three together form a single, longer story. Each novel establishes its own atmosphere, introduces new characters and events, and has a distinctive climax. In other words, each has a clear beginning, middle, and end, and the whole includes an overarching, three-volume plot that comprises the smaller plots of these three others. Although authorial intent need not be most definitive consideration, it ought to be noted that Collins did compose the three novels *as* a trilogy; that is, she did not write a single novel that was then divided into three books, nor did she "tack on" two sequels to a single book previously intended to stand entirely alone. The fact that the filmmakers, in adapting this trilogy for the silver screen, chose to tell its story across four films says more about the economics of contemporary mass culture than about the relative artistic merit of trilogies or tetralogies.[6]

If Tolkien's own novels clearly do not represent trilogies under this definition of the term, then Peter Jackson's film adaptations of *The Lord of the Rings* and *The Hobbit* almost certainly are trilogies, since the finished products were three individually intelligible movies telling a larger story over the course of all three.[7] But, again, from Tolkien's own point of view, as print novels, *The Hobbit* and *The Lord of the Rings* are each single, standalone works. Tolkien was quite critical of the decision to divide *The Lord of the Rings* into three volumes, and one can only imagine how he would have felt about the adaptations of these novels for the silver screen. Not that Tolkien would have been opposed to movie versions *per se*. In a 1958 letter in which he complains bitterly about the proposed film "treatment" of *The Lord of the Rings*, Tolkien insisted that "[t]he canons of narrative art in any medium cannot be wholly different; and the failure of poor films is often precisely in exaggeration, and in the intrusion of unwarranted matter owing to not perceiving where the core of the original lies."[8] This sentence provides an inkling of the critique Tolkien might have reserved for Jackson's films.

In Tolkien's estimation, *The Lord of the Rings*, which he had divided into six "books," formed one complete and unified whole; the six parts did not constitute semi-autonomous works, all the less so when grouped two apiece in the published volumes. Furthermore, once so divided, none of the three volumes of *The Lord of the Rings* sustains itself as a complete narrative with a clear beginning, middle, and end. This caused problems for Tolkien, who recognized that the artificial divisions of the narrative would reveal lack of balance and might cause confusion, introducing potential "spoilers" and unsatisfactory breaks.

For Jackson's film adaptations, by contrast, distinctive climaxes were generated in order to provide a sense of an ending for *The Fellowship of the Ring* and *The Two Towers*. In the former, it comes as a showdown between Aragorn and a recognizable, but unnamed orc leader, in a scene based loosely on one from the first chapter of Tolkien's Book III of *The Lord of the Rings* (i.e., in the volume titled *The Two Towers*), and in the latter, the dual battles of Helm's Deep (a memorable scene from the same Book III) and Osgiliath (a reference to an "off-camera" battle in Book V, that is, in *The Return of the King*) form joint climaxes. Viewers had to wait until the third film for Shelob's appearance, which might have been considered the climactic scene of Frodo and Sam's narrative thread in Book IV of the print edition. In making his film trilogy, Jackson wisely adapted the whole of *The Lord of the Rings* as a single, unified story into three movies, rather than trying to film each volume separately. Yet even with these "endings," viewers of Jackson's films who were unfamiliar with the story may well have been caught off guard when the first or second movie ended with so much of the larger story still left unresolved. Jackson had the advantage of planning a trilogy from the start, whereas Tolkien was forced to come to terms with a largely *post hoc* trilogizing of his singular narrative. Tolkien's consternation at the decision to publish *The Lord of the Rings* in three distinct volumes is evident in his letters, and he remained convinced that this marketing choice had had detrimental effects on the aesthetic or literary value of the work. Trilogizing this book, in his view, not only divided an otherwise unitary or coherent narrative, but actually altered its substance, even if no words or sentences were changed.

To the extent that authorial or artistic considerations have bearing on the finished product, an author's decision to write a trilogy, that is, to start out with "thirds" in mind, also has its literary, interpretative, and marketing ramifications. Its three-books-constituting-one-narrative would already be quite different from an undivided story. Non-literary factors may also play a role in this generic convention. As Farah Mendlesohn and Edward James have observed in *A Short History of Fantasy*, the "para-literary" advantages of publishing a series of books include greater visibility of the author's name and series' title, which can be displayed horizontally across volumes, and the literal crowding out of other works on a bookshelf, a sort of colonization of the physical space in a bookstore.[9] Seriality in general is another matter, beyond the scope of the present discussion. But the idea of a trilogy, with its distinctive reification of beginning, middle, and end, is provocative, as it suggests a desire to clarify and make visible the stages of the traditional Aristotelian plot. When it comes to *trilogizing* a work that was not conceived as a trilogy, whether dividing a long work into three, more manageable parts or adding, extending, or multiplying elements of a short work in order to flesh out a trilogy, the effects are noteworthy.

In the case of Tolkien's novels, as well as that of the recent film adaptations, both sorts of the *faux*-trilogy form are on display. The unitary narrative of the novel, *The Lord of the Rings*, was completed before anyone thought of dividing it into thirds. This decision has had real effects on the way the work is approached and interpreted. Even today, when nearly all of Tolkien's readers recognize *The Lord of the Rings* to be a single, complete work, the very existence of *The Fellowship of the Ring*, *The Two Towers*, and *The Return of the King* as individual titles and volumes disrupts the unity of the modern epic. The trilogy form affects, and in some sense *alters*, the work itself.

In the film adaption of *The Lord of the Rings*, these effects are mitigated, in part because the trilogy format *was* intended at the outset of production, which allowed the filmmakers to reimagine Tolkien's novel, *not* as three novels to be adapted one-by-one, but as a re-unified narrative to be re-imagined in new thirds. Hence, as noted above, the films' invention of climaxes, along with flashbacks or jump-cuts, as well as the free use of materials which had appeared earlier or later in the narrative as represented in the texts. With the adaptation of *The Hobbit* as a film trilogy, however, Jackson and his team enacted a different sort of trilogizing upon

Tolkien's source text. Rather than dividing one narrative into three parts, the filmmakers projected a three-part narrative onto the basic history and geography of Middle-earth which had been previously established on film in the earlier movies, which were also "later" with respect to the narrative's chronology. Jackson's *The Hobbit*, while operating as a "prequel" trilogy à la the *Star Wars* Episodes I–III, is no longer able to function as a prelude to *The Lord of the Rings*, but is awkwardly built upon the latter's already well-known history and geography. In both cases, albeit with different effects, the trilogizing of Tolkien's stories in text and film transformed the narratives.

"The rhythm or ordering of the narrative": Trilogizing The Lord of the Rings

With the success of *The Hobbit* in 1937, Stanley Unwin, chairman of Allen and Unwin (Tolkien's publisher), made clear to the author that a sequel would be desirable. Tolkien was initially reluctant, and in his word "perturbed," explaining that "I cannot think of anything more to say about hobbits. [...] But I have only too much to say, and much already written, about the world into which the hobbit intruded."[10] Along those lines, Tolkien provided Unwin with a stack of papers containing largely unrelated, certainly unpolished, tales and poems that he described as his "private and beloved nonsense."[11] Many years later, these papers were heavily edited and partially revised by Christopher Tolkien to form *The Silmarillion*, posthumously published in 1977, and they form the first five of the 12-volume *History of Middle-earth*, which also includes early drafts of *The Lord of the Rings* and other notes about the history, geography, languages, and cultures of this realm. As Tolkien aficionados know well, the "Silmarillion" materials comprise stories of the cosmogony of his imaginary worlds and the genesis of Arda itself, descriptions of the Valar (or "Powers" of the earth), and especially the long Saga of the Jewels, the Silmarils, whose fates were entangled with those of the high elves and heroic men of the First Age, many millennia before hobbits first appear in Middle-earth. But in 1937, quite understandably, Unwin wanted a proper sequel to a surprising bestseller, and he assured Tolkien that "a large public" would be "clamouring next year to hear more from you about Hobbits."[12] Apparently torn between his own writerly interests and the prospect of financial and other rewards, Tolkien immediately relented, assuring Unwin that, "if it is true that *The Hobbit* has come to stay and more will be wanted, I will start the process of thought, and try to get some idea of a theme drawn from this material for treatment in a similar style and for a similar audience—possibly including actual hobbits."[13] Although a draft of "A Long-Expected Party" was composed by mid–December 1937, Tolkien's sequel would not be completed for another 17 years. *The Lord of the Rings* would go on to become one of the bestselling and most well regarded novels of the century, much to the chagrin of some in the literary establishment and much to the delight of uncounted legions of fans worldwide.

The story behind the story of its construction makes for a fascinating history in its own right, and the journey "from fairies to hobbits" (Fimi) along "the road to Middle-earth" (Shippey) is well worth exploring.[14] However, my main interest here is the way that Tolkien's sequel to *The Hobbit* became a multivolume endeavor, to Tolkien's own dismay and to the potential detriment of the narrative itself. The literary work known as *The Lord of the Rings* is one, single and complete text, which then also included a prologue and appendices that Tolkien deemed necessary for helping readers understand the languages, cultures, and overall history of Middle-earth. Tolkien felt that these appended materials were critically important for comprehending the historical situation of Frodo's adventure, Aragorn's restoration, and the War of the Ring. In fact, Tolkien only grudgingly relented in his insistence that *The Silmarillion* be published first, or at least alongside, *The Lord of the Rings*, for he considered "the Saga of the Three Jewels and the Rings of Power" to be one story, and he feared that *The Lord of the Rings* on its own, "as indivisible and unified as I could make it," would not make sense without the long backstory and "deep" history provided in the former epic collection of tales.[15] The Unwins—by this time, the young Rayner Unwin, who as a eleven-year-old boy had famously "reviewed" the manuscript of *The Hobbit* for the publisher, had joined his father in the business—demurred, not surprisingly. With the Unwins and basic economics united against him, Tolkien acceded to letting unpublished "Silmarillion" be: "Watching paper-shortages and costs mounting against me. But I have rather modified my views. Better something than nothing! Although to me all are one, and the 'L of the Rings' would be better by far (and eased) as part of the whole, I would gladly consider publication of any part of this stuff."[16] Readers would have to wait until 1977, four years after Tolkien's death, for *The Silmarillion*, as compiled from various notes, drafts, and semi-completed stories by his son Christopher Tolkien.

The Lord of the Rings remains one immense, unified work, but Tolkien insisted that it was something of an epilogue to an even grander, earlier mythic history, which shines through in various places in the text. Indeed, he allows Sam, of all characters, to make the most striking connection between the epic narratives, as I discussed further in Chapter 1. In comforting Frodo, Sam recalls the tale of Beren and Luthien, before realizing that their own adventures are tied to those of the epic heroes of the past. As Sam puts it,

> Beren now, he never thought he was going to get that Silmaril from the Iron Crown of Thangorodrim, and yet he did, and that was a worse place and a blacker danger than ours. But that's a long tale, of course, and goes on past the happiness and into grief and beyond it—and the Silmaril went on and came to Eärendil. And why, sir, I never thought of that before! We've got—you've got some the light of it in that star-glass that the Lady gave you! Why, to think of it, we're in the same tale still! It's going on. Don't the great tales never end?[17]

Don't the great tales never end? Faced with printing a 450,000-word sequel to a relatively brief (95,000-word), popular children's book—a sequel which, in the author's own view, presented only about half of what it should—Stanley and Rayner Unwin may have wondered the same!

Having conceded defeat on the "Silmarillion" matter, Tolkien was not particularly pleased with the prospect of dividing *The Lord of the Rings* into multiple volumes. First of all, Tolkien had organized his one narrative into six books, and Allen and Unwin's decision to publish *The Lord of the Rings* in three volumes meant that each volume would contain two books apiece. Yet, as Tolkien noted, the parts themselves are not set up to work as pairs: "the 'books,' though they must be grouped in pairs, are not really paired; and the middle pair (III/IV) are not really related." Tolkien preferred giving distinct titles to each of the *six* books—offering "Vol. I *The Ring Sets out* and *The Ring Goes South*; Vol. II *The Treason of Isengard* and *The Ring goes East*; Vol. III *The War of the Ring* and *The end of the Third Age*"—rather than naming the volumes themselves, but if the volumes must be named, his first suggestion was "I *The Shadow Grows*[,] II *The Ring in the Shadow*[, and] III *The War of the Ring*."[18]

Tolkien was generally unhappy with all the volume-title suggestions, since none really captured the substance of the material contained within them, an understandable disjunction considering that the story was never written with a trilogy in mind. As Tolkien put it in an August 8, 1953, letter to Rayner Unwin, "I am not wedded to any of the suggested sub-titles; and wish they could be avoided. For it is really impossible to devise ones that correspond to the contents; since the division into two 'books' per volume is purely a matter of convenience with regard to length, and has no relation to the rhythm or ordering of the narrative."[19] Tolkien ultimately conceded that "The Fellowship of the Ring will do," since it "fits well with the fact that the last chapter of the Volume is The Breaking of the Fellowship."[20] He was less happy with "The Two Towers," which did and continues to cause confusion among readers, given that there are at least four prominent towers—Orthanc, Barad-dûr, Minas Tirith, and Minas Morgul (Tolkien also mentions the Tower of Cirith Ungol)—in the narrative.

In another letter, Tolkien disclosed that *the* two towers are Isengard's Orthanc and the Tower of Cirith Ungol, but later advised that the cover art for *The Two Towers* ought to depict Orthanc and Minas Morgul.[21] Rayner Unwin apparently preferred the "Return of the King" as a title for the third volume, although Tolkien thought that it, unlike his preference ("The War of the Ring"), gave away a key plot point, since at the beginning of Book V it is not at all certain that the king would "return."

All in all, Tolkien expressed frustration with the whole idea of a trilogy, which not only divided his unified narrative into unnatural and potentially confounding segments, with volume titles necessarily turning six individual "books" into two putative pairings and reifying the thirds over and against the whole, but also damaged the "rhythm or ordering" of the literary work of art. In other words, the quite reasonable business decision to publish a very long novel in three volumes had, in Tolkien's view, real and deleterious effects on art of the novel. For one thing, as he complained to Unwin, "there is too much 'hobbitry' in Vol. I." On the whole, by calling *The Lord of the Rings* a "trilogy" when it is clearly not intended to be one, the reader understandably finds a certain "shapelessness," as none of the volumes can really stand completely alone.[22] In *The Two Towers*, especially, this can be misleading, since the reader is naturally invited to see the adventures of Merry and Pippen (Book III) as paralleling those of Frodo and Sam (Book IV), somehow together forming a more-or-less whole story unto itself, whereas Tolkien intended the two narrative threads to remain separate and distinct. Only rarely, as in *The Return of the King*, does the narrator expressly make connections between them; for example, we see Frodo and Sam pondering their next move while "Théoden lay dying on the Pelennor Fields."[23] Tolkien's elaborate narrative, with its multiple storylines and odd contemporaneities, is thus altered by becoming a trilogy.

Above all, Tolkien was dismayed by the way in which the trilogy format by itself dramatically modified the shape, the rhythm, and ordering of the narrative, even if the actual words themselves were unchanged. That is, the trilogizing of *The Lord of the Rings* had real-world and literary consequences beyond simple division, even for readers who were going to read the entire work. (Obviously, those who quit after only reading *The Fellowship of the Ring*, for instance, would have a vastly different and likely unsatisfying experience.) Although Tolkien scholarship and single-volume editions today may be able to approach Tolkien's *magnum opus* as a single, coherent work, the original decision to divide the narrative into thirds has had lasting effects on both the text and its readers, not to mention films and moviegoers. This is a case of "thirding-as-othering," in which the decision to divide the unitary narrative into three parts changes the nature of the narrative.

"Too much hobbitry": The Hobbit *as a Film Trilogy*

If this is so for Tolkien's literary masterpiece, how much more does the trilogy format affect the film adaptations. Jackson's three-film *Lord of the Rings* adaptation (2001, 2002, 2003), which more-or-less tried to replicate the narrative divisions of the three volumes as they appeared in print, but without slavish adherence to the text, *was* conceived as a trilogy. (Actually, doubting he could get funding for three pictures, Jackson had originally pitched it as a two-film project; on the strength of his presentation, plus Tolkien's popularity, the producers approved three films for the "three books.") Any film adaptation will require compromises, as material will be omitted, dramatically altered, or even supplied afresh in order to satisfy the perceived requirements of a blockbuster film. Thus, for example, Tom Bombadil was omitted entirely (a decision, it seems, even Tolkien may have favored, since he admitted that "Bombadil is not an important person" to the narrative),[24] Arwen's role was enhanced (which had a dual purpose of creating an additional female hero and of providing depth to Aragorn's love story, not to mention allowing viewers to admire actress Liv Tyler for a few additional scenes), elves of Lothlórien rather than Aragorn's fellow human rangers join the fight at Helm's Deep (the more elves, the better, it seems!), and so forth. As noted above, the film trilogy needed to be organized in such a way as to make each movie stand, for the most part, on its own. Hence, for example, climaxes were built in where they did not exist, or were quite different, in the book: a showdown between Aragorn and a particularly notable but unnamed orc in *The Fellowship of the Ring*, plus a battle of Osgiliath added to the one at Helm's Deep in *The Two Towers*; arguably, the climactic events of *The Return of the King* functioned as the climax of the entire trilogy as well, with the Last Battle, the destruction of the Ring, and the "return" of the King rounding out both that discrete film and the series as a whole. Each film is one film, of course, but it might be worth mentioning that the Academy voters seemed to prefer imagining the trilogy as one complete work: although each film was nominated for Best Picture, only the third—in my personal view, hardly the best of the three—won the Oscar, from which fact I surmise that the voters wanted to reward the magnificent accomplishment of the trilogy as a whole.

In adapting Tolkien's books to film, Jackson and his team were able to create a balance and rhythm that Tolkien's divided narrative lacked. Where Tolkien complained that Volume I contained "too much 'hobbitry,'" for instance, Jackson could jump-cut to scenes of Gandalf speaking with Saruman, provide flashbacks to Elrond arguing with Isildur, and generally flesh out the geography and history of the world. (That need for "fleshing out" was precisely why Tolkien was eager to publish the "Silmarillion," either before or alongside *The Lord of the Rings*, and it is why he felt the Appendices to be so crucial.) Artistically, Jackson was able to do this because his funding for three movies was basically guaranteed, and he was able to film scenes from all three movies over the course of the trilogy's production. The success of Jackson's *The Lord of the Rings* undoubtedly contributed to the desire for, and funding of, a film adaptation of its "prequel," *The Hobbit*, not to mention the rush to adapt other Tolkien material in the years that followed.

Speaking of too much "hobbitry," one cannot help but find grim irony in the decision by the filmmakers to turn *The Hobbit* into a movie trilogy. Jackson had originally doubted his chances of getting funding to make three *Lord of the Rings* films, and he first pitched it as a two-film project; the producers themselves, as the story goes, approved a three-movie deal that would conform to the "three parts" of Tolkien's novel. *The Hobbit*, by contrast, was supposed to be a two-film project, arguably already too much for such a short book, one that is about half the length of *The Fellowship of the Ring* volume alone. Only after principal filming was complete did Jackson's team and the studio decide to make what had been shot as two films into a trilogy. Cynics—or, indeed, realists—can chalk this up to a straightforward cash grab, as it seems that revising and recutting the filmed materials into three movies is certainly an easy way to earn an extra $300 million (or, actually, about a billion dollars worldwide). But apart from the additional revenue, one can detect in this aspect of *The Hobbit* franchise a desire to conform to the generic convention of the trilogy-form. Somehow, it "makes sense," from the perspective of filmmakers and moviegoers alike, to have this fantasy adventure organized into a three-part whole, as a complement to the prior (or, with respect to the narrative chronology, later) *Lord of the Rings* trilogy.

The production of *The Hobbit* franchise includes an additional determining factor, which is that its narrative *requires* it to be a "prequel" to *The Lord of the Rings*.[25] If Tolkien struggled to make his earlier hobbit adventure fit with the much deeper, broader, and richer geopolitical and historical world of *The Lord of the Rings*, to such an extent that he had to revise *The Hobbit* itself (most notoriously, altering the "Riddles in the Dark" chapter to create a Gollum and Ring more like the ones we encounter in the later work), then the filmmakers had a different challenge.[26] How were they to fit the narrow, relatively simple story of Bilbo Baggins into the already created, vast and beautiful New Zealand landscapes, and mixing in the casts of characters so beloved by viewers of the earlier film trilogy? It becomes clear that, as with George Lucas's "prequel" trilogy in the *Star Wars* saga (1999, 2002, 2005), Jackson has attempted to link these works together in a single hexalogy, a six-film extravaganza just crying out for DVD commentary and special Blu-ray editions. However, hexalogy is not quite accurate, since in these examples the six-part series comprises what are actually two trilogies that have been hastily spliced together after the fact. Surely Lucas or Jackson (or Tolkien, of course) would have plotted and shot things rather differently had they intended to create a unified work in six parts.

In *The Hobbit* films themselves, the interlinking of the *earlier* films that depict persons and events much *later* in time is tricky, and it led to some rather awkward moments. The framing device, also used in *The Lord of the Rings*, enables *The Hobbit* to appear to be told in retrospect, as Bilbo passes his old story down to Frodo, played again by a still sprightly and enthusiastic Elijah Wood, not yet burdened with the psychological trauma of his own, later adventures. The incorporation of characters from the earlier movies who do not appear in Tolkien's *The Hobbit* (e.g., Saruman, Galadriel, and above all Legolas) provides some small sense of continuity between the *dramatis personae* of the two trilogies, although it invites unwanted questions. For instance, if Legolas played an integral role in aiding the dwarves of Erebor, why is he suddenly such a stranger to all things dwarfish in his burgeoning friendship with Gimli in *The Lord of the Rings*? Drawing on materials outside of the published corpus, the films recreate events that must have taken place, but which are not depicted in *The Hobbit*, such as the attack by Gandalf and the White Council on the Necromancer at Dol Guldur, which in turn helps to establish another connection to the plot of *The Lord of the Rings*. A late scene in the last film of *The Hobbit* trilogy even alludes to Aragorn, who would have been about 10 years old at the time, as Thranduil (in the book version, simply referred to as Elvenking) advises his son Legolas to go looking for this young ranger in the wilderness. A nice touch, but it does make one wonder about the more than six-decade gap between these adventures.[27] Indeed, the long period between the events of *The Hobbit* and those of *The Lord of the Rings*—"A Long-Expected Party" takes place 60 years after Bilbo's return from Erebor, and Frodo and Sam do not leave the Shire until another 17 years have passed—introduces a serious problem for the filmmakers, whose two trilogies do not easily mesh into one long, six-part narrative.

Perhaps the most significant, and unfortunate, result of the filmmakers' decision to make *The Hobbit* into a prequel trilogy is the pacing of each movie, which features the slow slog through far too little expository material, but which then gets papered over by ridiculously out of place action sequences. The effect is to make nearly every single moment both less meaningful and more intense, literally turning the films into a series of roller-coaster rides, as in the Great Goblin's city in the Misty Mountains in *An Expected Journey*, the theme-park-inspired barrel rides of *The Desolation of Smaug*, and the well-nigh interminable fighting sequences of *The Battle of the Five Armies*. In some respects, the adaptation project for *The Hobbit* is the opposite of that of *The Lord of the Rings*; where the latter required scrupulous cutting, condensation, and combination, the former indulged in the most ridiculous sorts of extension, addition, and outright invention.[28] In fact, the first movie (*An Unexpected Journey*) was arguably too fastidious with respect to its adherence to the source materials, depicting nearly every scene and drawing them out to wearisome lengths, but by the mid-point of the second film (*The Desolation of Smaug*) it became clear that these movies were less an adaptation of *The Hobbit* than a sort of fan-fiction inspired by that novel.

In Tolkien's original book, *The Hobbit* is rather episodic, with an almost self-contained adventure in each chapter. As such, it may have been best adapted as a television limited-series, rather than as a film. By making it into one film, as in the Rankin/Bass cartoon version (1977), which did first appear on television, the story could remain centered on the title character, Bilbo. In these films, however, Bilbo's own development as a "burglar" is largely limited to the first movie, whereas the blood-feud between Thorin and Azog (a character who in Tolkien's writings is dead before the events of *The Hobbit* book take place), a ridiculously tacked-on love story between Tauriel and Kili, the bizarre antics of a character named Alfred Lickspittle, along with extended action sequences and special effects, tend to dominate the subsequent installments. Three movies require three distinctive climaxes, again, so the already unbalanced story filled with numerous adventures becomes burdened with the need for a fireworks show's grand finale, which is almost made literal in *An Unexpected Journey*, with an escape from orcs and burning trees, and in *The Desolation of Smaug*, with a bizarre smelting project aimed at gilding an already golden dragon.[29] The result is a hugely speculative extravaganza in which the original source materials become less and less relevant. In trilogizing the narrative of a book rather ill-suited for the format, the filmmakers projected a completely different story, at once far too dense in exposition and far too flimsy in content. Like the derivative security whose value is backed up by worthless assets, the film trilogy finds itself ever more distant from the substance that was, presumably, its *raison d'être* in the first place.

An Artificially Ordered World

In taking a unified work of art and turning it into a trilogy, whether by division (as in *The Lord of the Rings* novel) or by multiplication (as in *The Hobbit* films), the creators of the work—which now must be seen to include not only the author or director, but the publisher, producers, and indeed all those who are part of the conditions for the possibility of the finished product—necessarily alter it. However, one might also argue that the trilogy format can serve a valuable role in helping organize our various plots. As I have suggested, the trilogy provides a distinctive beginning, middle, and end that also highlights the incipience, mediality, and finitude of the story. Reading a book or watching a movie, knowing full well that Part 2 (the middle of the story) and Part 3 (featuring the end of the story) are still to come, dramatically changes the experience, creating an anticipatory desire as well as the comforts of closure in the overall apprehension of the work.[30] The delight of the vast epic form merge with the satisfaction of knowing that, most likely, all questions will be answered, all storylines completed, by the third installment's close.

The apparent predominance of the trilogy format in fantasy, both in print and on screen, is perhaps a sign of the degree to which an artificially ordered world, with distinctive boundaries and limits, demarcating a clear beginning, middle, and end, is all the more desirable in an era typified by its fluid borders or indistinct identities. Fantasy is particularly well equipped to project alternative worlds, and its narrative form may embrace figurative orders such a triads, triangles, and trinities. Such triangulations might aid readers and viewers in orientating themselves in an often bewildering world system, whether it is that of Middle-earth or our own. But in aiding readers as they attempt to make sense of the world, such artifices may have value, just as they may create the conditions for the possibility of further error or confusion. Maps can themselves be disorienting at times, after all. As Albert Toscano and Jeff Kinkle have pointed out, "among the first products of a genuine striving for orientation is disorientation, as proximal coordinates come to be troubled by wider, and at times overwhelming vistas."[31] As with Galadriel's mirror, such conventions, though potentially helpful, may not be the best guides for deeds.

In Tolkien, three rings were borne by elven kings, but there was still the One to rule them all. The trilogizing of his novel *The Lord of the Rings* presented narrative, conceptual, and organizational difficulties that troubled him, as he thought that his unified work of art suffered from these artificial divisions. As a film trilogy, Jackson's *Lord of the Rings* mostly worked well, first by maintaining each film's relative autonomy, then by making sure that the overarching plot remained visible throughout. However, one might argue that Jackson's trilogized adaptation of *The Hobbit* went beyond division and differentiation, extravagantly rushing toward rank speculation, gaudy spectacle, and dubious juxtapositions. The trilogy form complicates the storytelling, even as it also provides a sort of generic map for the reader or viewer. Tolkien's great novels, along with their twenty-first-century film adaptations, evoke the perils and the promise of the trilogy format.

CHAPTER 4

The Geopolitical Aesthetic of Middle-earth
Space, Cinema, and the World System in The Lord of the Rings

In a querulous 1958 letter, J.R.R. Tolkien presented his meticulous comments on a draft "story-line" of a proposed film adaptation of *The Lord of the Rings*. Tolkien's irritation is palpable as he details the misrepresentations, misreadings, and outright mistakes in the "treatment." Tolkien concludes that the writer of this unacceptable vision of the popular novel is "hasty, insensitive, and impertinent."[1] Lest one assume that the great Anglo-Saxon philologist and medievalist was merely opposed to the modern medium of cinema or to adaptations of books into movies, it should be noted that Tolkien was initially enthusiastic about the prospect of a film version of *The Lord of the Rings*. Indeed, he did not see any particular reason why a film could not reasonably approximate the same power and effects as would stories delivered in the form of an epic or a novel. As he put it, "[t]he canons of narrative art in any medium cannot be wholly different; and the failure of poor films is often precisely in exaggeration, and in the intrusion of unwarranted matter owing to not perceiving where the core of the original lies."[2] Tolkien himself believed that, in the hands of a filmmaker of sensitivity and skill, the vast world of Middle-earth could very well be made visible and knowable on the big screen.

Fans of Peter Jackson's wildly successful *Lord of the Rings* movie trilogy (2001, 2002, 2003) might agree that the spirit of Tolkien's original does come through on screen, although detractors would smile to hear Tolkien's complaints, since some of the most stringent critiques of these films centered on the filmmakers' decisions to alter Tolkien's story, either by cutting memorable scenes and characters (most notoriously, perhaps, the elimination of Tom Bombadil), inserting or exaggerating the role of others (for instance, with the enhanced presence of Arwen Undómiel), or inventing new storylines entirely (Elves of Lothlórien fighting at Helm's Deep, Faramir taking a captive Frodo and Sam to Osgiliath, and so on). In "Mithril Coats and Tin Ears: 'Anticipation' and 'Flattening' in Peter Jackson's *The Lord of the Rings* Trilogy," eminent Tolkien scholar Janet Brennan Croft analyzes a number of the differences.[3] Yet, apart from the fiercest purists, most moviegoers have been struck by how effectively, if not always faithfully, Jackson's films have re-created the world of Middle-earth in all its diverse majesty. The sometimes breathtaking visual imagery and landscapes, perhaps even more than the compelling characters and epic narrative, render Tolkien's Middle-earth "real" in a way that for many viewers matches the power of the original texts. A large part of the films' success lies in their capacity to make visible the geography of Tolkien's world, broadly conceived, which then lays the foundation for the geopolitical aesthetic of the narrative.

In his foundational study of Tolkien's work, *The Road to Middle-earth*, Tom Shippey has argued that *The Lord of the Rings* developed in relation to a fundamentally "cartographic plot." Unlike *The Hobbit*, with its simpler political geography, *The Lord of the Rings* establishes an entire geopolitical world system in which the narrative elements—Frodo's quest, Saruman's treason, Aragorn's reclamation of his birthright, and so on—unfold. Indeed, I would go so far as to say that the literary cartography of Middle-earth is a principal aim of the narrative, given Tolkien's notorious reputation for meticulous "world-building" in the text. In my view, Tolkien's generic or discursive mode might be labeled "geopolitical fantasy," and the projection of an imagined global system, complete with diverse languages and cultures, deeply historical and unquestionably political, in some respects resembles a sort of cognitive mapping in which the individual subject attempts to represent figuratively a social totality that gives form to both subjective experience and objective reality. In *The Lord of the Rings*, this attempt at mapping involves the sometimes conflicting perspectives of an individual subject on the ground, as it were, and the panoptic or god-like view from above.

Starting from Tolkien's own text, we can see the ways in which Jackson's film trilogy adapts, translates, and in some ways enacts the geopolitical aesthetic of *The Lord of the Rings*.[4] Drawing upon Fredric Jameson's call for a "cognitive mapping on a global scale," and particularly his reading of cinema and space in *The Geopolitical Aesthetic*, I would argue that the overlapping narrative spaces of the novel and the films enable readers or viewers to envision a kind of global totality that might not always be available to them in narratives produced in a more strictly mimetic mode. Elsewhere, in such books as *Spatiality, Utopia in the Age of Globalization*, and *Topophrenia*, I have argued that the fantastic mode is a

4. The Geopolitical Aesthetic of Middle-earth 81

necessary element of literary cartography, a process by which writers and readers project imaginary maps of their world. As Tolkien suggested in "On Fairy-stories," by defining that genre in relation to the place (*Faërie*) it represents, the vocation of fantasy is to produce imaginative cartographies of a world. However, the cinematic rendering of Tolkien's particular otherworld in Jackson's film trilogy effectively undermines the force of Tolkien's literary cartography by reducing its variety and nuance to an artificially simplistic image. The movie version of *The Lord of the Rings* also engages in a form of imaginative cartography, but it produces a very different map, with rather different results.

In this chapter, I begin by looking at this "cartographic plot" in Tolkien's work, which forms the basis of visual text in *The Lord of the Rings* film trilogy. Then, using the bizarre image of Sauron as a disembodied eye as a metaphor for the films' geopolitical aesthetic, I examine Jackson's "scopic drive" in recasting Tolkien's subject-centered itineraries and viscerally perceived landscapes as distant panoramas or bird's-eye-view representations. Following Jameson, I discuss the ways in which this formal or aesthetic feature comes to reproduce a sort of sociopolitical content in the guise of a conspiracy, by which the seemingly random or chaotic elements of a shifting geopolitical balance of power becomes somehow "knowable" through a reduction of elements, not entirely unlike the graphic processes used in cartographic art and science. Finally, I examine the effect of this erasure of nuance on the work of art itself, as the epic and novelistic features of Tolkien's narrative are subjected to a profound levelling effect. In this way Tolkien's thoroughly modernist novel gives way to a postmodern cinematic cartography of the twenty-first-century world system, albeit in an uncertain and tenebrous figuration as a place in which "even the very wise cannot see all ends."[5]

For the purpose of the argument in this chapter, I focus only on Jackson's original *Lord of the Rings* trilogy—*The Fellowship of the Ring* (2001), *The Two Towers* (2002), and *The Return of the King* (2003)—and I do not discuss *The Hobbit* trilogy (2012, 2013, 2014), although some of my arguments may also apply to the latter as well. There may be substantive reasons why *The Hobbit* may be safely placed outside of the discussion. For one thing, the attempt to create a prequel trilogy *à la* the *Star Wars* franchise required an eccentric, spatiotemporal reversal of Tolkien's own narrative and geographical project. That is, whereas the original novel of *The Hobbit* provided a glimpse into the world of Middle-earth, the literary cartographic project of that novel was rather limited in scope. As I discuss below, *The Hobbit* included very few distinctive toponyms, as most of the identifiable places on the map were given merely descriptive names, labels that in some respects concealed the deep historical and philological roots of their referents. What is more, as becomes clear only with the sequel *Lord of the Rings*, published 17 years later, *The Hobbit*'s story takes place only in the northern part of Middle-earth, and almost no attention is paid to the vast southern and eastern territories in which the adventures of Frodo, Sam, Merry, and Pippen take place. By operating as it were in reverse, the filmmakers had already transformed the real and imaginary geography of New Zealand into Tolkien's Middle-earth in *The Lord of the Rings* films, so *The Hobbit* trilogy had to be reconstructed on top of the already existing map. By attempting to retell the smaller tale according to the plan of the larger, the filmmakers have resorted to the sort of narrative trickery that Tolkien bemoaned in the aforementioned letter. Thus, for my purposes, the "world" depicted in the film version of *The Lord of the Rings* is already established before *The Hobbit* was conceived, as strange as that may sound to readers of the novels.[6]

"I wisely started with a map"

The Lord of the Rings can be said to have developed in relation to a fundamentally "cartographic plot," as Shippey puts it.[7] Although an actual map is crucial to *The Hobbit*'s narrative, with Thrór's Map providing the motive force behind the quest of Thorin and Company, that novel included surprisingly few distinctive toponyms. That is, the place-names in *The Hobbit* are largely descriptive: geographical features like mountains, forests, rivers, and lakes are given names like the Misty Mountains, Mirkwood (formerly Greenwood, until it became murky), the River Running, or the Long Lake. Proper names are largely reducible to descriptions as well: Hobbiton is a town populated by Hobbits; Laketown is a town on a lake; Elrond's realm of Rivendell is hidden in a deep valley cloven by a river; the Lonely Mountain stands alone on an otherwise relatively flat plain; and so on. In contrast, the expansive geography and distinctive *topoi* of *The Lord of the Rings* establishes an entire geopolitical world system in which the narrative elements unfold. If anything, in that novel's sprawling discourse, there is a surfeit of geographical and historical knowledge, as places are not merely named, but named in multiple languages, and often in connection to distant historical events and personages. Shippey counts some forty or fifty "rather perfunctory" names in *The Hobbit*, whereas *The Lord of the Rings* boasts over 600 named persons and as many places.[8]

The geographical discourse can be at times overwhelming for readers, as when, for example, characters begin to "talk like a map." Shippey cites the farewell of Celeborn to his erstwhile guests, in which the elf lord describes the course they will take along a river, naming the different places to be encountered along the way, and using no fewer than twelve proper names in a short paragraph. Pointing south, Celeborn maps the fellowship's trajectory along the Anduin:

> As you go down the water, [...] you will find that the trees will fail, and you will come to a barren country. There the River flows in stony vale amid high moors, until at last after many leagues it comes to the tall island of the Tindrock, that we call Tol Brandir. There it casts its arms about the steep shores of the isle, and falls then with a great noise and smoke over the cataracts of Rauros down into the Nindalf, the Wetwang as it is called in your tongue. That is a wide region of sluggish fen where the stream becomes tortuous and much divided. There the Entwash flows in by many mouths from the Forest of Fangorn in the west. About that stream, on this side of the Great River, lies Rohan. On the further side are the bleak hills of the Emyn Muil. The wind blows from the East there, for they look out over the Dead Marshes and the Noman-lands to Cirith Gorgor and the black gates of Mordor.[9]

This guidance is helpful for both the characters in the story and the readers of it. As a result of such detail, the world of *The Lord of the Rings* is much richer and, as it were, "realer" than that of *The Hobbit*. In Shippey's words, "[t]he maps and the names give Middle-earth that air of solidity and extent both in space and time which its successors so conspicuously lack."[10] I would go so far as to say that the literary cartography of Middle-earth is the principal effect of the narrative, whose substance is not so much the adventures of a handful of hobbits as the creation—or, as Tolkien would prefer, the "sub-creation"—of a world system.

In focusing on Tolkien's literary cartography, I do not mean to suggest that maps themselves are the key to the narratives, although there is no question of the importance of actual maps to Tolkien's project, both within the writings as narrative devices and outside of them as tools for the writer and for readers. Maps are, after all, particularly significant in Tolkien's work. Tolkien himself drew maps by hand, partly to accompany and to illustrate his work, but also because mapping was a critical element of his literary method. As he put it in a well-known letter, referring to his approach to the composition of *The Lord of the Rings*, "I wisely started with a map, and made the story fit (generally with meticulous care for distances). The other way about lands one in confusions and impossibilities, and in any case it is weary work to compose a map from a story."[11]

In *The Hobbit*, as noted above, there is a map at the very heart of the plot. Without Thrór's Map, the facsimile of which appears in the book and was drawn by Tolkien, there is no quest to reclaim Erebor from the dragon. Bilbo himself is quite the map-gazer, even if his perspective is at first somewhat parochial and limited to the Shire, and detailed geographical knowledge is valued highly by nearly all of the characters. Thrór's

Map is not only crucial to the narrative itself, perhaps most notably when Elrond discovers and translates its "moon-letter" runes, but it also aids the reader in gaining his or her own bearings in the imaginary geography of Middle-earth. The maps in *The Lord of the Rings* are extremely helpful in this regard, and I would imagine that most readers cannot but smile when Peregrin Took rebukes himself for not having studied the various maps available to him in Rivendell.[12] In my own case, that is one of maybe a hundred moments when I would have paused to look at the map included in the front of the book—the original, drawn up by Christopher Tolkien— as I, like the reader and like Pippen himself, try to figure out just where these orcs were going, tracing itineraries through strange lands, finding their "place" relative to places with which we are already familiar. (In their conversation, the orcs debated exactly *where* they should take their captive hobbits, demonstrating their own knowledge of and concerns about geography.) And I confess that my battered copy of *The Silmarillion* has a deep crease in the spine from nearly constant flipping back to that map of "Beleriand and Its Realms,"[13] which is extremely useful not only for gaining one's bearings in the vast physical geography of the territories but also for understanding the geopolitical balance of power, accords, and discord among the various elven enclaves. Indeed, it is fair to say that a significant part of the difficulty of *The Silmarillion* comes from the reader's inability to adequately project a usable map of the various realms depicted in its pages, something allayed somewhat by the intensely spatial or geographical discourse in *The Lord of the Rings*. For it is not merely that the world east of the Blue Mountains and across the sea is so vast and complex, but the mythic lore of an epic like *The Silmarillion* likely precludes the sort of cartographic detail expected of the modern novel.[14]

Having said all of this, my interest in the spatiality of Tolkien's work lies not so much in literal maps, either those in Tolkien's work or those based on it.[15] Rather, I want to suggest that Tolkien's literary cartography is a productive response to the peculiar spatial problems associated with modernity. To write it as a bigger thesis than I could possibly follow through on here, I would say this: Tolkien's writing, especially in *The Lord of the Rings*, produces a cognizable otherworld in its seeming totality as a means of making sense of the fragmentary, uneven, and largely unrepresentable world system of the early-to-mid-twentieth century. By means of this "geopolitical fantasy," Tolkien gives form to the all-too-real world through the creative, imaginative projection of alternative spaces. In this sense, I see Tolkien's literary cartography as a profoundly modern, if not modernist, artistic program. Jackson's film adaption, on the contrary, alters this project dramatically, at once evacuating the narrative of this world-building content and reshaping its form as pure spectacle. At some level, this is probably a matter of the traditional rivalry between the text and the image, but Jackson's conscious decisions to alter the narrative reinforce and supersede this divide, making the story less about telling and more about seeing. Somehow, in the movie version, *The Lord of the Rings* becomes a story of an eye.

The Eye of Sauron

Jackson and the team behind the film adaptation of *The Lord of the Rings* elected to make a number of changes, some of which are more understandable and work better than others. Some changes were undoubtedly made for strictly artistic reasons—for example, they were based on the ways in which the medium of film requires different considerations than that of print—while others were likely more commercial in nature. Of the many departures from Tolkien's original texts, one of the most significant and also perplexing was the decision to represent Sauron as a flaming eyeball perched atop a tower. In the Jackson films, the "lidless eye" is not just a symbol of vigilance and surveillance, but it is literalized as the physical form of the person himself, which leads to the almost comical treatment of the Sauron-Eye as a rather ineffectual searchlight by the end of the third installment in the series. Although there is certainly something spooky about a villain who maintains an eldritch, incorporeal form, it is difficult to imagine any practical threat from such a person. As a symbol, the eye of Sauron compels obedience and inspires fear, but this is only because the symbol is connected to an actual power, that of one who gives orders and exacts punishments. A fiery eyeball seems like an odd and ultimately bad choice.

To be clear, Tolkien not only envisioned Sauron as having the appearance of a man, but the text itself makes clear that Sauron continues to embody a human form. Indeed, in *The Two Towers*, when Frodo mentions that Isildur had cut off Sauron's finger an age earlier, Gollum—who has seen, and presumably been tortured by, Sauron himself—confirms: "Yes, He has only four on the Black Hand, but they are enough."[16] In letters, Tolkien is clear about Sauron's fundamentally human-like appearance. For example, "[t]he form that he took was that of a more than human stature, but not gigantic. In his earlier incarnation he was able to veil his power (as Gandalf did) and could appear as a commanding figure of great strength of body and supremely royal demeanor and countenance."[17] Ironically, then, the filmmakers may have been closer to Tolkien's intent in their depiction of Sauron in the Prologue—which appears in the opening minutes of the movie, *The Lord of the Rings: The Fellowship of the Ring*—in which an admittedly "gigantic" Sauron, masked and clad in steel armor, does battle with Isildur's father, Elendil. In other words, Jackson and his team were well aware of how Sauron was supposed to look, and therefore we may conclude that their decision to render the enemy as a fiery eyeball is not rooted in ignorance. Jackson undoubtedly had his reasons for overlooking Tolkien's fondness for synecdoche,[18] but I am most interested in the effect of the choice. What does it mean that the enemy of the "free peoples" of Middle-earth appears to be merely a lidless eye, wreathed in flame?

One principal effect of *this* Sauron is to underscore that the Dark Lord's power lies in surveillance. Envisioned as a gigantic organ of sight, perched atop what may well be the tallest tower in all of Middle-earth, the Sauron of the films is the very avatar of surveillance. In this vision, the entire world is potentially a panopticon designed and operated by Sauron. Of course, the narrative of the movies complicates this, which inevitably leads to an almost ludicrous disempowerment of Sauron. For example, when Saruman explains to Gandalf that Sauron cannot yet take physical form (but surely the flaming eyeball is physical!), but that the lord of Mordor can see *all*, viewers must wonder why Sauron is so often completely unaware of what's going on throughout the entire movie trilogy. The fact is that Sauron obviously does not see all; he does not even see very much. But as the figural embodiment of surveillance itself, Sauron represents the supremely terrifying force that instills fear in nearly all of the realm's occupants. A literal "overseer," albeit one who also overlooks a good many things, Sauron occupies the subject-position of a celestial cartographer, whereas everyone else in Middle-earth are located (and locatable) as points on the map.

Consider the distinction made by Michel de Certeau between the itinerary and the map, especially as expressed in his discussion of urban pedestrians. Certeau begins his analysis of "walking in the city" by contrasting the perspective of the street-level pedestrian with that of a "voyeur" who looks down upon the entire city from a lofty vantage. Using exceptionally tall buildings as his exemplary point of view, Certeau argues that, from the observation deck of the World Trade Center in New York City in 1977, a person looking out on a clear day could get an excellent view of nearly the whole of Manhattan, as well as of other boroughs and parts of New Jersey across the Hudson River. This overview represents a form of mastery, but it also necessarily requires a distancing and abstraction from the realities below. As Certeau puts it,

> [t]o be lifted to the summit of the World Trade Center is to be lifted out of the city's grasp. One's body is no longer clasped by the streets that turn and return

4. The Geopolitical Aesthetic of Middle-earth

it according to an anonymous law; nor is it possessed, whether as player or played, by the rumble of so many differences and by the nervousness of New York traffic. When one goes up there, he leaves behind the mass that carries off and mixes up in itself any identity of authors or spectators. An Icarus flying above these waters, he can ignore the devices of Daedalus in mobile and endless labyrinths far below. His elevation transfigures him into a voyeur. It puts him at a distance. It transforms the bewitching world by which one was "possessed" into a text that lies before one's eyes. It allows one to read it, to be a solar Eye, looking down like a god. The exaltation of a scopic and gnostic drive: the fiction of knowledge is related to this lust to be a viewpoint and nothing more.[19]

The "scopic drive" motivates the need for panoramic overview, where seeing all is a way of knowing all, and thus the "celestial" spectator wields power over the subjects down below. For Certeau, the image of the city from this perspective is "the analogue of the facsimile produced, through a projection that is a way of keeping aloof, by the space planner urbanist, city planner or cartographer."[20] Concluding with an image that might even call Sauron to mind, Certeau maintains that "[t]he voyeur-god created by this fiction [...] must disentangle himself from the murky intertwining daily behaviors and make himself alien to them."[21]

In contrast to this "solar Eye," Certeau asserts that the "ordinary practitioners of the city" are down below, on the street: "they are walkers, *Wandersmänner*, whose bodies follow the thicks and thins of an urban 'text' they write without being able to read it." Drawing upon Michel Foucault's elaborate vision of disciplinary societies and the "carceral archipelago" in *Discipline and Punish: The Birth of the Prison*, Certeau maintains that pedestrians attempt to locate "the practices that are foreign to the 'geometrical' or 'geographical' space of the visual, panoptic, or theoretical constructions." In the very act of walking amid the hustle and bustle of a metropolis, Certeau argues, the peripatetic pedestrians "elude discipline." For Certeau, the voyeur-god whose scopic and gnostic drive attempts to order the city into an artificial, geometric plan or map is ultimately vanquished from participating in the space so represented, whereas the urban wanderers are the real authors of a city. "They are not localized; it is rather they that spatialize."[22]

I find this description resonant with the contrasting themes of panoptic surveillance and transgressive movement in *The Lord of the Rings* movies. Sauron remains within Barad-dûr at all times, or, rather, in the absurd figuration of the Enemy as a fiery eyeball, he remains atop the tower, in an unceasing act of looking outward and downward upon the world. The Twin Towers of Certeau's voyeur-god are matched by the many towers from which different geopolitical powers attempt to visualize and alter the map of Middle-earth. In addition to Sauron in his fortress, we see Saruman atop Orthanc in Isengard, Denethor in Minas Tirith, the Witch-King mounted on a winged beast over Minas Morgul. Even lesser places, the various watchtowers such as Weathertop or Amon Hen, are sites of scopic (or telescopic) desire, from whose vantage point the vistas seem supernaturally clear. Moreover, there are the apparently magical or monstrous forms of surveillance, including a beast called the Watcher in the Water in the murky pool outside the western gate of Moria or the Two Watchers outside the tower of Cirith Ungol. Indeed, birds themselves, including the "crebain" of Dunland and eagles of the Misty Mountains, function as aerial monitors of events on the ground. Purportedly on the side of the righteous, Galadriel's mirror and the *palantíri* (also known as the "Seeing-stones of Númenor") represent additional means of surveillance, although they are not necessarily reliable ones. As Galadriel says, in what might also be a caveat to all who would rely on surveillance to secure and maintain their positions, "the Mirror is dangerous as a guide to deeds."[23]

Meanwhile, the movement of individuals and groups on the ground tend to operate as antagonists to these functionaries of oversight. The fellowship of the ring is itself referred to as the Nine Walkers (in contrast to the Nazgûl or Nine Riders), and, apart from a brief river journey by boat, they make their way exclusively on foot. Contrary to the abstract projection of spaces enabled by the God's-eye view from above, the walkers experience the places on the ground viscerally, whether swatting at insects (Sam calls the stinging midges "Neekerbreekers") or enjoying a cool draught from the Entwash. In Certeau's sense, the walkers "write" these spaces through their movements and experiences, whereas the Sauron-like eye in the sky can only "map" them. The southerly and eastward advance of Frodo and Sam gives texture and meaning to the places encountered, while the intersecting adventures of Merry and Pippen in Fangorn Forest and Aragorn, Gimli, Legolas, and later Gandalf in Rohan and Gondor also provide substance to the toponyms. While the great powers strive for control over Middle-earth, so the story goes, the small folk actually "move the wheels of the world."[24]

Yet the film version of *The Lord of the Rings* complicates this schematic view of the narrative. As in the books, halflings accomplish great deeds, heroic warriors do battle with the nameless hordes of enemies, while potentates like Saruman, Denethor, and Sauron (not to mention Elrond and Galadriel) remain within well protected fortresses from which they can observe and make plans.[25] But the films offer an additional perspective, that of the camera—the *Kino-Eye* of Dziga Vertov, perhaps—which frequently functions as a surrogate to the all-seeing Sauron. Much like other visual devices used to descry places, persons, and events from a spatiotemporal distance, the Mirror of Galadriel and the *palantíri* or "seeing stones" being the most memorable, Jackson's own cameras offer the viewer a "bird's-eye view" of Middle-earth. This perspective is itself literalized with the eagle, a reliable *deus ex machina* in Tolkien's fiction, one that even he worried might be overused.[26] The preponderance of helicopter shots and sweeping panoramas gives the movies much of their visual power, but they also detract from the pedestrian mission of the *Wandersmänner*-protagonists. Even the many close-ups and intimate shots only serve to emphasize the "scopic drive" of the medium itself, as the eye of Sauron or of the camera "zooms" in on its unsuspecting prey. The special effects, becoming so meticulous and minute as to include the enhanced blue-ing of Elijah Wood's eyes, only augment the power of the visual to capture and control the subjects. When at the end of *The Lord of the Rings: The Fellowship of the Ring*, as Frodo slips the One Ring on his finger in his effort to escape Boromir, he suddenly feels the presence of "the Eye," and an ominous voice emerging (somehow) from the fiery eyeball declares "I see you," it is fair to wonder whether we the audience have been placed in the position of Sauron all along. That is, we "see" Frodo throughout, but our own scopic, gnostic drive and voyeurism is only made effective by the cameras, which definitively dictate what and who will be seen, and how.

In the language of Certeau, the films "map" the terrain in such a way as to undermine the itineraries of the errant walkers on the ground. Of course, one might expand the argument to suggest that cinema is always also a form of mapping. For example, Tom Conley has suggested that, "[i]f cinema is a tool of power (insofar as power is a mode of the control of perception and an agency that forms subjectivity), it bears resemblance to maps that aim to promote and channel both perception and cognition."[27] And as Foucault's researches into the development and exercise of relations of power in modern societies have made clear, an instrument of power is not in and of itself a means of repression.[28] That is, if the cinematic map figuratively resembles the Solar Eye of Sauron or of another force from above, the map might also serve those interested in resisting such forces, in altering the imposed order, and in reversing the relations of power. These cannot escape power or the relations of power, but operating from within the world system to which such power-relations give form, they may challenge or undermine the dynamics of those relations in such a way as to alter the system itself. This productive counter-mapping, then, might be a way of looking at Frodo's resistance to the power of the ring, broadly conceived.

The Conspiracy of the Ring

The distinction between the narrative overview in which a vast space may be rendered visible at once and the narrative trajectory of active subjects "on the ground" finds special resonance in *The Lord of the Rings*, but much more so in the books than in the films. In the books, such an overview is provided by the maps themselves, but otherwise it must be projected or constructed through the literary operations of storytelling and description. Also, Tolkien's updated usage of the medieval-romantic narrative device of *entrelacement*, in which multiple threads of the story-line are narrated separately but occur at the same time, is suggestive of that "spatial form" in modern literature famously identified by Joseph Frank.[29] In this sense, the spatial form of *The Lord of the Rings* may be discovered, as it were, in retrospect, after the narrative itself has ended and the "world" of Middle-earth has been ultimately surveyed. But the narrative movement is largely a matter of boots on the ground, as the reader must accompany the ranging hobbits from the Shire to Rivendell, then follow the "nine walkers" through Moria and Lothlórien, before splitting their attention between Merry and Pippen's adventures in Fangorn Forest, the three "hunters" and their doings in Rohan, and Frodo and Sam's long slog toward Mount Doom.

However, to call Frodo and Sam *pedestrians* seems at once too grand and too quotidian. They are not Baudelairean *flâneurs*, after all, and their epic adventure mostly involves a slow, plodding march through the wilderness. As pedestrians in a strange land, they cause trouble for Certeau's celebratory appreciation of the street-walker's subversiveness, for they reveal the powerful need for a sense of overview. They are much more like the anxious urbanites of Kevin Lynch's *The Image of the City*, whose efforts at "wayfinding" are hindered by the failure to project a mental map of their environs.[30] As a reader of maps, Frodo is better able to connect his own experiences to a geographic totality, but Sam is almost totally lost: "Maps conveyed nothing to Sam's mind, and all distances in these strange lands seemed so vast that he was quite out of his reckoning."[31] Of course, by the time he arrives in Mordor, Sam has more or less discovered ways of making sense of his milieux, using something not unlike Lynch's model of mapping, with stable and visible landmarks (especially Mount Doom) to guide him. Although the spaces are far from urban, one might agree with Jameson that such subject-centered mapping "involves the practical reconquest of a sense of place and the construction or reconstruction of an articulated ensemble which can be retained in memory and which the individual subject can map and remap along the moments of mobile, alternative trajectories."[32] Perhaps Gollum, even more than Sam, represents this sort of cognitive cartographer, since he has wandered widely in Middle-earth in search of his precious heirloom, which enables him to serve as a guide.

From a storytelling standpoint, the interminable walking could become rather boring, map or no maps. In the films, the long slogs are made less dull by frequent jump-cuts to other parts of Middle-earth. This allows for the same sort of *entrelacement* narrative as could be found in the books, but with much faster action. (Tolkien himself felt that each story needed to be told as it was in his narrative in order to preserve the cohesion of each strand, even while the reader understands that many events are occurring at the same time in different places.) The effect of these rapid movements is to establish that the seemingly disparate adventures of the remaining members of the fellowship are in fact part of a single project. Whereas Frodo and Sam's (and Gollum's) part might seem totally disconnected from the goings-on in Isengard or Rohan, the films offer a slightly different narrative, one based on the conspiracy of the ring.

As Jameson has discussed at length in *The Geopolitical Aesthetic: Cinema and Space in the World System*, the conspiracy film can be viewed as an attempt to map a social totality by seizing upon or inventing connections between diverse, seemingly unrelated forces and events, and then projecting a coherent plan in which everything fits together. It is at once similar to the map created by the Solar Eye, inasmuch as it constructs a total picture, and also the opposite, as its perspective is that of a groundling, a worm's-eye view of the elaborate machinations taking place far above it but undoubtedly affecting it in innumerable, largely unseen ways. Yet the attempt to create the map is already a kind of cognitive mapping, which may be more or less useful to the individual subjects who are trying to make sense of the complex, bewildering spatial ensembles in which they are situated.

Jameson argues that the return of conspiracy is a symptom of the postmodern condition. Jameson had earlier suggested that conspiracy could be thought of as a "poor person's cognitive mapping in the postmodern age," insofar as conspiracy is "a degraded figure of the total logic of late capital, a desperate attempt to represent the latter's system."[33] As he puts it in *The Geopolitical Aesthetic*, "confronted with the ambitious program of fantasizing an economic system on the scale of the globe itself, the older motif of conspiracy knows a fresh lease on life."[34] Conspiracy provides a form of cognitive mapping that allows one to situate oneself and others meaningfully within a system that seems now understandably invisible, perilous, and unimaginably vast. By imagining or discovering a conspiracy, one suddenly gives shape to a larger social structure, inevitably tending toward the world system in its totality. One thus projects a discernible if not wholly representable, supra-individual or collective system that is apparently unknowable in our day to day existence, but which might be outlined somewhat allegorically through a figurative representation, such as a constellation or a map. In this way, as with Lynch's urban pedestrian, the individual subject can coordinate his or her quotidian experiences and practices with a larger spatial and social totality.

Astute readers of Tolkien's novel might balk at the characterization of a conspiracy, since the only real conspiracy in *The Lord of the Rings* is the one formed by the heroes. The fellowship of the ring is itself the result of a conspiracy between various representatives of the "free peoples" of Middle-earth, as the Mouth of Sauron openly declares: "Dwarf-coat, elf-cloak, blade of the downfallen West, and spy from the little rat-land of the Shire [...] here are the marks of a conspiracy."[35] Earlier, in *The Fellowship of the Ring*, the word "conspiracy" was used to name the hobbits' plan to elude notice when they left the Shire. There is not really much of a conspiracy on the part of the "dark powers." Yet, in the film version, a conspiracy is precisely what unites the storylines once the fellowship disbands, since Saruman is transformed into a mere servant of Sauron, which requires the creation of a very different character. In fact, I would suggest that, in addition to the rendering of Sauron as a flaming eyeball, the transformation of Saruman is one of the most radical departures from the textual sources made by Jackson and the filmmakers.[36]

The "Voice of Saruman" scene in *The Two Towers*, which was filmed but cut from the theatrical release of *The Lord of the Rings: The Return of the King*, is the first place in the novels where the reader encounters Saruman in person, even though much mischief and bloodshed caused by his treachery has already occurred. There Gandalf, knowing how powerful and useful Saruman could be in the war against Sauron, attempts to bring Saruman over to his side. It is clear from the books that Saruman was never on Sauron's side, but that he tried to trick Sauron into giving him information that would lead him to the ring. This is a crucial plot point: Saruman betrayed Gandalf, Elrond, Galadriel, and the rest of the White Council, not because he joined forces with Sauron, but because he wanted to become like Sauron. Saruman's investigations into ring lore led him to create his own ring of power, but it was not enough to rival the One Ring, so he attempted to acquire that weapon for himself. In the story Gandalf tells, Saruman planned to feign friendship with the Power rising in the East only until such time as they could subdue it and use it for their own (good) ends, but Gandalf—like Galadriel in her own moment of temptation—knows that would only lead to the same tyranny in a different guise. And in a remarkable insight into the enemy's mind, the orc Grishnákh reveals that Sauron is aware of Saruman's double-dealing as well, averring

4. The Geopolitical Aesthetic of Middle-earth

"Saruman's a fool, and a dirty treacherous fool. But the Great Eye is on him."[37] In any event, Tolkien is nevertheless clear on the matter: Sauron was betrayed by Saruman, who never intended to aid the Dark Lord.

In the movie version, Saruman not only sides with Sauron, but is seen taking orders from him and doing his will. The films feature Saruman far more prominently than do the books, as information recounted by Gandalf at the Council of Elrond or mere inferences from the books (such as his breeding "half-orcs" or "goblin-men"), are depicted on the screen. Jackson seems to go out of his way to oversimplify the character, as if unwilling to believe that a person could be mistaken without also being inherently evil. If, in the political allegory Tolkien abjured, Sauron represents Hitler's Germany during World War II, then Saruman is to have been a Stalin, yet he never truly seals any non-aggression pact with Sauron. A telling scene in *The Two Towers* is the one in which orcs from Mordor argue with orcs from Isengard over what to do with their captives (Merry and Pippen). In the film, the argument is merely over whether or not to eat them, but in the novel it is revealed that different factions have different orders, and the various orcs represent groups well regimented, thoughtful soldiers who have been given different orders from their respective leaders. In making Saruman purely evil and thus entirely unsympathetic, the filmmakers simplify the plot and reduce nuance, effectively transforming the narrative map.[38] They also reduced the geopolitical complexity of Tolkien's Middle-earth to the most simplistic, puerile type of binary moralizing, something that appears almost nowhere in Tolkien's work.

The conception of a conspiracy inevitably simplifies matters, not very much unlike the ways in which a map necessarily reduces the elements it purports to represent, while at the same time maintaining a strict selectivity concerning which elements to portray. The conspiracy theorist attempts to make connections between diverse and complex array of states, motivations, and behaviors, thereby constructing a relatively coherent narrative or cognizable totality in which everything may be reasonably explained according to a simple plan. The swirling, oscillatory, and vicissitudinous social relations that constitute our milieu, the uncertain terrain in which we cannot help but move, becomes temporarily stable, fixed, and above all legible in a master narrative which can be accessed by the reader who is "in the know." The bewildering sense of anxiety or being lost comes from an inability to "read" or make sense of the spaces inhabited. A conspiracy thus functions somewhat in the manner of a map, offering an artificial but utterly credible key or legend (in the cartographic sense), which allows one to make sense of "reality," even if that reality is hidden.

The Saruman–Sauron axis of evil in the films helps to eliminate the complexity and nuance from the narrative. Although Tolkien's detractors have often decried the simplistic morality of the tale, any close reading of the text demonstrates the error of thinking in terms of mere good and evil. Not only are many purportedly evil characters—Gollum, Saruman, even Sauron himself—much more interesting and complicated in Tolkien's vision of them, but the supposedly "good" people like Galadriel, Aragorn, and Gandalf are subject to temptation, error, or doubt. As I will discuss more in Chapter 5, from *The Silmarillion*, the reader learns that Galadriel's own decision to come to Middle-earth was rather similar to Sauron's reason for staying there. Whereas "she yearned to see the wide unguarded lands and to rule there a realm at her own will," Sauron "lingers in Middle-earth [...] beginning with fair motives: the reorganizing and rehabilitation of the ruin of Middle-earth, 'neglected by the gods.'"[39] The moral force of Galadriel's refusal to take the ring when offered by Frodo derives from the knowledge that it is something she truly desires, so viewing her as always and already "good" actually diminishes her heroic overcoming of the temptation.[40] Tolkien observes that "frightful evil can and does arise from an apparently good root, the desire to benefit the world and others."[41] Such philosophy cannot be readily discerned in Jackson's treatment of these characters and themes. As happens throughout the films, the complex relationships of fascinating characters are reduced to cardboard caricatures of the most simplistic morality plays, yet the damage done to the narratives is mitigated (or masked) by the sheer spectacle.

The ring itself provides another illustration. In the films, the One Ring is given a much greater role than in the novel. Indeed, the filmmakers went so far as to give it a voice, albeit a barely discernible whisper, which suggests almost a personality (Sauron's, presumably). The filmmakers also made the ring much more perilous to wear, omitting entirely Sam's wholly productive use of it in rescuing Frodo from the Tower at Cirith Ungol, for example. However, Tolkien himself warned against putting too much stock in the power of the ring. As he explained, the idea of a person investing his or her own power or strength in an object is a not uncommon trope in fairy stories. In a 1958 letter to an inquisitive reader, Tolkien warned:

> You cannot press the One Ring too hard, for it is of course a mythical feature, even though the world of the tales is conceived in more or less historical terms. The Ring of Sauron is only one of the various mythical treatments of the placing of one's life, or power, in some external object, which is thus exposed to capture or destruction with disastrous results to oneself. If I were to "philosophize" this myth, or at least the Ring of Sauron, I should say that it was a mythical way of representing the truth that *potency* (or perhaps rather *potentiality*) if it is to be exercised, and produce results, has to be externalized and so as it were passes, to a greater or less degree, out of one's direct control. A man who wishes to exert "power" must have subjects, who are not himself. But he depends on them.[42]

This illuminating explanation helps to demystify the "magic" of the One Ring, which can now been seen as a metonym or symbol for the conventional machinery of political and military power, such as a standing army or repressive state apparatuses.

The use of a "mythical" device in an otherwise "historical" narrative—these terms are Tolkien's, and refer to the mode of presentation rather than to specific mythic or historical referents—also reinforces an image of Sauron that the filmmakers elected to ignore. That is, Sauron is a powerful leader, a dictator perhaps, who governs a country with immense productive capability and who commands a vast military force. But, as with other dictators, his real power, if it is to be exercised, lies outside of his direct control, in the form of those orcs, men, and other creatures who act on his behalf. Additionally, this explains why Sauron can possess a physical, humanoid form and yet not appear outside of Barad-Dûr. Like Hitler, Stalin, Churchill, and Roosevelt, the executive leaders of states and armies in a time of war rarely step onto the field of battle.

Hence, the real conspiracy of the ring is not that which the films imagine existed between Saruman and Sauron or the fellowship of the ring's conspiracy to destroy the artifact, but the filmmakers' conspiracy to reshape Middle-earth according to a simplified worldview, in which irredeemably evil forces threaten irrepressibly good persons. Although Tolkien's novel complicates such facile delineations, the movies go much farther than seems prudent to simplify the "map" of Middle-earth.

Geopolitical Fantasy

Writing shortly after the films came out, Douglas Kellner argued that *The Lord of the Rings* trilogy has served allegorically fascist ends by offering an "escape" from the complex and dangerous global order in the twenty-first century, but that this apparent escape actively promotes a conservative militaristic and political agenda. As Kellner explains,

> *The Lord of the Rings* films were illustrative of a global fantasy-production machine with a creative team drawn from all over the (especially) English-speaking world. [...] The global popularity of *The Lord of the Rings* films was related to a deep need for fantasy, escapism into alternative worlds, and distractions from the turbulent and distressing conflicts of the contemporary era, as well as to the enticements of a technologically dazzling cinematic epic machine generating a fully articulated fantasy universe. Yet the "escape" led precisely into the tentacles of the conservative ideology that has been a major source of the present world disorder.[43]

I find Kellner's interpretation unconvincing, heavy-handed and, at times, erroneous, but considering the baleful serendipity of the films' release amid the post–September 11, 2001, wars on "terror"—complete with the Bush Administration's reassertion of "evil" as a valid category in which to discuss matters of state, the ill-considered celebration of military force, the demonization of largely unknown enemies as well as of those within the United States and elsewhere not unconditionally supportive of the war effort, not to mention the powerfully evocative racial, cultural, and religious overtones of such bellicose political rhetoric—*The Lord of the Rings* undoubtedly supplied imagery suited to a certain neoconservative discourse.[44]

And yet part of Kellner's argument derives its force from the old dismissal on political grounds of fantasy itself, whether defined as a literary genre or as a discursive mode, which has been found by such influential detractors as Darko Suvin, Carl Freedman, and even Jameson himself as escapist at best, reactionary at worse, and perhaps utterly unworthy of serious criticism at the very worst. In closing this chapter, I would like to take a moment to discuss the value of fantasy, which has served as a means not only for imagining alternative universes but also for criticizing the status quo here in the all-too-real world.

Shippey has asserted that "[t]he dominant literary mode of the twentieth century has been the fantastic."[45] Although most of us probably recognize the degree to which the sort of fantasy exemplified by Tolkien *par excellence* is a modern phenomenon, the genre or mode has tended to be viewed differently, as conservative or reactionary, nostalgic, neo-medieval, and so forth. In my own recent work, I have suggested that the fantastic mode is a necessary element of literary cartography, a process by which writers and readers project imaginary maps of their world. For example, the utopian imagination in the age of globalization is not concerned with discovering a hidden island or future ideal state in the world, but involves rather a figurative projection of the world itself. Utopia provides a map in which the system's *other spaces* may be discerned. In these realms, *hic sunt dracones* ("Here, there be dragons"), and utopian spaces emerge in the form of what Herbert Marcuse called "the scandal of qualitative difference," a radical alterity that establishes a profound break with the *status quo*.

For Tolkien the vocation of fantasy is to produce imaginative cartographies of a world—an otherworld—which may be seen in the form as well as the content of *The Lord of the Rings*. The overlapping narrative spaces of the fantasy novel enable readers to envision a kind of global totality that might not always be available to them in narratives produced in a more strictly mimetic mode. This is not to speak of any allegorical content, but to recognize that the very form of Tolkien's geopolitical fantasy requires an extensive, imaginative mapping of the world. The dream of a perfectly rational organization of social space, like utopia itself, is after all a fantasy, and the political policies, economic processes, or urban planning that attempt to realize these fantasies are, in some ways, themselves fantastic. Imagining an alternative reality in which reason and order prevail, if only provisionally and tactically, is an effort to make sense of our own irrational or disorderly experience of the world. In a way, Tolkien's fantasy world of Arda is, in fact, far more "realistic" by appearing clearer in its figural political cartography, something the so-called "real world" and its constantly shifting permutations can rarely offer. The literary cartography produced by *The Lord of the Rings* thus appears *truer* than many narratives lacking its fantastic features.

However, this is where Jackson's film adaptations, with their emphasis on panoptic surveillance, simplistic remapping, and facile morality in fact undermine the spatial and temporal effectiveness of Tolkien's geopolitical fantasy, substituting as passive illusion for the quite active fantasy generated by and enacted in Tolkien's narratives. Jackson's trilogy establishes an empty space into which preconceived, market-tested, and superficial forms can be easily located and slotted into place. By ignoring the ability of the reader (or viewer) to discern nuances, the filmmakers impose upon the narratives a static map, an artificially stable worldview in which the most outlandish beliefs and contradictory sentiments are somehow supposed to be maintained.[46] This inevitably leads to such critiques as those leveled by Kellner, although it is not the "fantasy" that is the problem in the film trilogy. Rather, it is the inability to recognize the power of Tolkienian fantasy to give shape to and make sense of the world in which we live. Tolkien's literary cartography of Middle-earth is exemplary of this modern or modernist project, and despite their many differences, Tolkien would likely agree with China Miéville that "we need fantasy to think the world, and to change it."[47]

In the fantastic maps produced, perhaps even unwittingly, by Tolkien's writings, we may be able to see the sorts of changes that the cinematic versions created by Jackson persistently occlude. There is little doubt that Tolkien himself would have disapproved of many of the choices made in developing these films, although that is certainly no reason to dislike them. No film adaptation can, or should, simply replicate the novel on which it is based, but the decisions to simplify the geopolitical state of Tolkien's world system have deleterious consequences for the aesthetic itself. Still, the literary cartography of Middle-earth may yield a great many different maps, and travelers who visit the Perilous Realm are well advised to take advantage of any that may help them along their way.

CHAPTER 5

The Politics of Character
The Dark Lord, the Witch-Queen, and the White Wizard

Among the more irksome complaints about J.R.R. Tolkien launched by critics antagonistic to his work is the accusation that Tolkien's narratives involve an overly simplistic moral universe. More specifically, Tolkien has been charged with dividing all characters and motives into strictly binary categories of mere good versus evil. Such was the perspective of one of the early reviewers of *The Lord of the Rings*, Edwin Muir, who in 1955 wrote that the novel lacked "the human discrimination and depth which the subject demanded," adding in particular that "Tolkien describes a tremendous conflict between good and evil on which hangs the future of life on earth. But his good people are consistently good, his evil figures immutably evil; and he has no room in his world for a Satan who is both evil and tragic."[1] In a somewhat more acid review originally published in *The Nation* in 1956 under the sarcastic title, "Oo, Those Awful Orcs!," the American critic Edmund Wilson lamented that the epic quest narrative of *The Lord of the Rings* was ultimately unrewarding, since "[w]hat we get is a simple confrontation—in more or less the traditional terms of British melodrama—of the Forces of Evil with the Forces of Good, the remote and alien villain with the plucky little home-grown hero."[2] Such reviewers and their many adherents fail to recognize or to impart much significance to a character like Gollum, for instance, who seems to undermine any sense of purely evil or purely good. They also tend to forget that Tolkien, for various reasons, sees the ostensible victory of the remaining members of the Fellowship of the Ring as part of what Galadriel calls "the long defeat."[3] That is, even though the heroes may be said to have succeeded in their quests, the ending is not entirely a happy one. After the fall of Sauron, the protracted *dénouement* of the novel is suffused with a tone of melancholy, at least as much as that of celebration. The gloom accompanying the victory is well represented, and even embodied, in the psychologically broken

5. The Politics of Character

figure of Frodo, who never fully heals from his wounds and suffers from what today might be recognized as an acute case of post-traumatic stress disorder. Moreover, and despite the prevalent use of the terms "good" and "evil" by Tolkien and by his fans, any close reading of *The Lord of the Rings*, along with other works in Tolkien's overall *legendarium*, reveals that such a simplistic binary opposition rarely if ever holds. The morality of Middle-earth is far more complex.

In the two chapters that follow I will take up this issue with respect to orcs, the creatures who seem to be invented solely for the purpose of representing "evil" forces in Tolkien's world, but for now I will just say that Tolkien himself struggled over their characterization, observing that as sentient beings, the orcs must have been somehow redeemable, and in *The Hobbit* and *The Lord of the Rings*, Tolkien clearly provides them with rather human motives, needs, and desires. In this chapter, I examine three far more important individual characters: Sauron, the chief *diabolus* of *The Lord of the Rings*, Galadriel, "the greatest of elven women," and Saruman, the wizard whose "treason" and malice causes so much suffering. These characters tend to represent the purely evil, purely good, and perhaps tragically evil (i.e., fallen) moral types, respectively. However, Tolkien's own writings indicate how much more complicated these people, and these ideas, really are. Not surprisingly, the Peter Jackson-directed film versions of *The Lord of the Rings* (and later, *The Hobbit*) tended to oversimplify and to confuse their characters, making them more one-dimensionally good or evil than Tolkien ever imagined. In fact, as Tolkien shows, all three (at least for a time) shared similar desires and goals, and in their choices they might be viewed as various cautionary examples of how the devotion to the principles of "Knowledge, Rule, [and] Order," as Saruman puts it,[4] can lead one into trouble, even—or especially—when one's intentions are noble. Tolkien insists that no one is evil in the beginning, but then he finds that no one is entirely good in the end either.

Sauron, Healer of Middle-earth

In the "Valaquenta" section of *The Silmarillion*, "that spirit whom the Eldar called Sauron, or Gorthaur the Cruel" is listed as the "greatest" servant of Melkor, also known as Morgoth, the great Satan figure in Tolkien's mythology. "In all the deeds of Melkor the Morgoth upon Arda, in his vast works and in the deceits of his cunning, Sauron had a part, and was only less evil than his master in that for a long time he served another and not himself."[5] Once Morgoth is utterly vanquished at the end of the First Age, Sauron becomes the real *diabolus* in Tolkien's world, and Tolkien even suggests that Sauron, through his cleverness more than his innate divinity, actually became more powerful than Morgoth in the Second and Third Ages.[6] If anyone in *The Lord of the Rings* could be said to be innately "evil," surely it is Sauron.

However, even Sauron represents a more complicated ethical figure than most would imagine, and Tolkien gives readers many opportunities to consider the nuances of the character. In the Council of Elrond, Elrond himself explains that he or others acting with good intentions would nevertheless become themselves dangers if they tried to wield the One Ring, pointing out that "nothing is evil in the beginning. Even Sauron was not so."[7] Hence, even in *The Lord of the Rings*, the sense that Sauron is not innately evil, that he too may be viewed as having been corrupted, is stated plainly. In fact, there is evidence that Sauron's downfall is rather tragic, owing primarily to what might be called "good intentions," and thus providing more of a cautionary tale relevant to all who consider themselves "good," rather than an example of "evil."

In *The Silmarillion*, we learn that, like Saruman, Sauron was originally "of the Maiar of Aulë, and he remained mighty in the lore of that people."[8] Aulë is the great craftsman-god, the Vala with "lordship" "over all the substances of which Arda is made," "a smith and the master of all crafts."[9] Hence, Sauron is himself a craftsman, as evidenced in part by his crafting of the rings of power, of course. In a fragment Tolkien wrote in the 1960s concerning languages, we discover that Sauron's "original name was *Mairon*, but this was altered after he was suborned by Melkor. But he continued to call himself *Mairon* the Admirable, or *Tar-Mairon* 'King Excellent' until after the downfall of Númenor."[10] Tolkien also informs readers that "it had been his virtue (and therefore also the cause of his fall, and of his relapse) that he loved order and coordination, and disliked all confusion and wasteful friction," and that this—not any inclination toward "evil," whatever that would be—was what attracted him to Melkor in the first place: "It was the apparent will and power of Melkor to effect his designs quickly and masterfully that had first attracted Sauron to him." That is, Sauron desired the *power* to do good, and as with so many tragic tales, this leads to his "fall." Sauron's despotic desire to rule over others was, in fact, a somewhat paternalistic sense that he was helping others in the process, for as Tolkien puts it, the "real good in, or rational motive for, all this ordering and planning and organization was the good of all inhabitants of Arda."[11]

This is also what chiefly distinguishes Sauron from Morgoth, and which also makes him ultimately more dangerous. Sauron was above all a planner, an architect and craftsman who wished to order all things to his will, which in and of itself was not necessarily evil. Melkor, by contrast, had a far more nihilistic character, and from the start of the Music of the Ainur to his eventual defeat at the end of the First Age, he was bent on destruction and chaos, rather than construction and order. To those ends, "Morgoth had let most of his being pass into the *physical* constituents of the Earth—hence all things that were born on Earth and lived on or by it, beasts or plants or incarnate spirits, were liable to be 'stained.'" Sauron was not more powerful than Morgoth, but he was wiser in his use of power. As Tolkien puts it, "Sauron's, relatively smaller, power was *concentrated*; Morgoth's vast power was *disseminated*. The whole of 'Middle-earth' was Morgoth's Ring."[12] With the defeat of Melkor, Sauron emerges as the great Satan in Middle-earth in the Second Age. However, even then, there is some idea that his aims were praiseworthy, at least at first. Given the post-apocalyptic landscape of Middle-earth at the start of that Age, a powerful "healer" like Sauron would likely be welcomed by most of the population. Arguably, in fact, if one imagines alternative histories told from the perspectives of Easterlings, Haradrim, and the men of Mordor, not to mention orcs perhaps, Sauron may well have been a popular leader.

The Silmarillion describes the sight upon which the former thralls of Angband looked when the War of Wrath had ended: "the northern regions of the western world were rent asunder, and the sea roared through many chasms, and there was confusion and great noise; the rivers perished or found new paths, and the valleys were upheaved and the hills trod down, and the Sirion [River] was no more."[13] Indeed, the Second Age was almost literally a post-apocalyptic world, for following the War of Wrath, the lands of Middle-earth were essentially a wasteland, a "world that was changed," now "neglected by the gods."[14] Although the Valar invited the elves and a handful of noble humans (i.e., those deemed so by elves) to leave Middle-earth, giving them almost paradise-like islands on which to dwell and thrive, the remaining elves—including "proud" ones who refused the summons—as well as the men, dwarves, and (of course) all orcs were left in darkness, "troubled by many evil things."[15]

Strange as it may seem to most readers of *The Lord of the Rings*, Sauron in this time took up the role of "healer," hoping to bring order and well-being to the peoples of this blasted landscape. For Tolkien notes that Sauron, at least at first, had "fair motives: the reorganizing and rehabilitation of the ruin of Middle-earth," with due consideration for the "well-being of other inhabitants of the Earth."[16] Indeed, Sauron's "motives and those of the Elves seemed to go partly together: the healing of the desolate lands," which is what set the stage for the crafting of the rings of power, after all.[17] The First Age ends with an almost Ragnarök-like cataclysm, but for those left in Middle-earth for the Second Age, life goes on, and that age's history is a testament to humane survival in a post-apocalyptic condition.

Sauron, arguably, had a point when he suggested to elves of Eregion that the Valar had abandoned Middle-earth, particularly given what we know about the aftermath of the First Age. Once Melkor was "shut beyond the World in the Void that is without," the Valar in their collective might unquestionably could have rebuilt and healed the lands, but Tolkien shows that they clearly had no interest in doing such a thing. As the "Akallabêth" reveals, "the Valar forsook for a time the Men of Middle-earth," apart from the Númenoreans. "Men dwelt in Darkness and were troubled by many evil things [...] And the lot of Men was unhappy."[18] Rather than rehabilitating the lands of Middle-earth, the Valar at that time largely abandoned them, establishing safe havens for a favored minority completely apart from Middle-earth. As such, they preferred Edenic enclaves to widely habitable lands, and they thus allowed—even *beckoned*—the elves to leave these lands and dwell on Tol Eressëa, an island off the coast of Valinor. For the "good men," the Edain, the Valar created a new island kingdom, Númenor, "neither part of Middle-earth nor of Valinor," in which they could live separate from, if not equal to, both the lofty beings to their west and the *hoi polloi* of the east.[19]

The description of the creation of Númenor itself shows how the Valar could have healed Middle-earth, had they wished to do so. Númenor "was raised by Ossë out of the depths of the Great Water, and it was established by Aulë and enriched by Yavanna, and the Eldar brought thither flowers and fountains out of Tol Eressëa."[20] But no reference is made anywhere to any Vala giving thought to a sort of Marshall Plan for Middle-earth. The people who refused the summons were left on their own, as were those who presumably never received it. The vast majority of others, including nearly *all* humans on the planet, were *never* invited to live in anything other than an utterly destroyed, post-war landscape. If Sauron truly believed that the Valar had forsaken Middle-earth and its inhabitants, one can hardly blame him.

In "Of the Rings of Power in the Third Age," we are told that "the lands for the most part were savage and desolate, save only where the people of Beleriand came."[21] These are the elves who chose to remain, most notably the high king Gil-galad, Cirdan the Shipwright, Galadriel and her husband Celeborn, Elrond Half-Elven, and various other Teleri or Noldorin who formed civilized enclaves in Lindon, the Grey Havens, and Eregion. Some Teleri joined up with existing silvan elf societies, too, and perhaps some of these swelled the ranks of the elves of what would become Mirkwood, such as Thranduil's people or the elves in Lothlórien. But the three elven enclaves—Linden, the Grey Havens, and Eregion—functioned as bastions of light and learning in an otherwise benighted world. (The main exceptions, of course, were the Dwarven kingdoms, notably Khazad-dûm,

5. The Politics of Character

which thrived for much of the Age, but these too were largely self-enclosed spaces.) Tolkien tells us that these Elves who remained had their reasons for refusing the summons:

> There was nothing wrong essentially in their lingering against counsel, still sadly with [words missing?] the mortal lands of their old heroic deeds. But they wanted to have their cake without eating it. They wanted the peace and bliss and perfect memory of 'The West,' and yet to remain on the ordinary earth where their prestige as the highest people, above wild Elves, dwarves, and Men, was greater than at the bottom of the hierarchy of Valinor. They thus became obsessed with 'fading,' the mode in which the changes of time (the law of the world under the sun) was perceived by them. They became sad, and their art (shall we say) antiquarian, and their efforts all really a kind of embalming.[22]

The desire to maintain their prestige and elite status was reasonable, perhaps, but hardly noble or praiseworthy, and Tolkien refers specifically to their "pride," a sin proverbially known to go before a fall. But in their desire to heal the desolate lands make their own world more beautiful, they presumably had Sauron-like motives. The elves' attitude, one of antiquarian elitism, is what allowed Sauron to ensnare Celebrimbor and the elves of Hollin with the crafting of the rings of power, after all.

Famously, Sauron took on a "fair form," presenting himself as Annatar, the Lord of Gifts, and being in reality a Maia of Aulë, Sauron almost certainly was the greatest craftsman left in the world. Moreover, as we have seen, Sauron's motives may not have been wholly bad. Elsewhere Tolkien notes that Sauron truly did repent his "evil deeds" of the First Age, and in another letter Tolkien points out that "while desiring to order all things according to his own wisdom he still at first considered the (economic) well-being of other inhabitants of the Earth."[23] Nevertheless, even if we recognize the "evil" Sauron, posing as Annatar and seducing Celebrimbor's people with malicious intent, one cannot help but wonder at how much his words *rang true* for such elves, especially considering that "they had at first much profit from his friendship":

> Alas, for the weakness of the great! For a mighty king is Gil-galad, and wise in all lore is Master Elrond, and yet they will not aid me in my labours. Can it be that they do not desire to see other lands become as blissful as their own? But wherefore should Middle-earth remain for ever desolate and dark, whereas the Elves could make it as fair as Eressëa, nay even as Valinor? And since you have not returned thither, as you might, I perceive that you love this Middle-earth, as do I. Is it not then our task to labour together for its enrichment, and for the raising of all the Elven-kindreds that wander here untaught to the height of that power and knowledge which those have who are beyond the Sea?[24]

This is seductive, yes, but not an unreasonable thing for an elvish community to desire.

A quick note on the Annatar-Sauron gambit. Although we know Sauron to have been a shape-shifter in the First Age, taking on the form of a vampire bat or a great wolf at need, I tend to think of Sauron of the Second Age here not so much as a shape-shifter as a shrewd politician. True, he hid his identity by presenting himself as Annatar, but the "fair form" is really just a pleasing form, and what would most please Celebrimbor is knowledge and craftsmanship, not a pretty face. This is also more consistent with Tolkien's views of "magic," for example, as in his explanation of "the voice of Saruman"; Tolkien insisted that it was not actual "magic" but merely Saruman's eloquence and rhetorical power. "Saruman's voice was not hypnotic but persuasive. Those who listened to him were not in danger of falling into a trance, but of agreeing with his arguments."[25] Along those lines, when we hear that Sauron in the Third Age can no longer take on a "fair form," that is not a sign of an ugly visage or even a changed physical appearance at all, but more likely the case that the elves and their allies would no longer be fooled by his efforts to seduce them. In other words, Sauron does not become monstrous, and he certainly does not become unable to take on a physical form or appear as a flaming eyeball (as in the films). He just becomes better recognized for who he is and will no longer be able to so easily lure his enemies into supporting him.

As we know from so many dystopian tales, a post-apocalyptic condition is ripe for the emergence of tyrants or otherwise totalitarian regimes, which may be one way of viewing Sauron's role as an evil dictator. That is, he is taking advantage of despair, destruction, and darkness, along with a "natural" power-vacuum, to install himself as ruler of the world. Of course, we know that that such tyranny exists "on both sides," as it were, a point frequently made by Tolkien himself. In fact, one might view the elven aristocracy as another form of total rule, particularly considering that in the Third Age the three principal elf leaders (Elrond, Galadriel, and Cirdan) actively use Sauronian technology—rings of power crafted by Celebrimbor based on the knowledge he had acquired through Sauron—to maintain their realms. None of these elves began the Third Age as a ruler, but Galadriel at least had long desired to rule "a realm at her own will," which at least partly explains her *hauteur* at the beginning of the Second Age, when she "proudly refused forgiveness or permission to return" to Valinor.[26] She is redeemed at last by refusing the thing she had desired so much, the power (symbolized by the One Ring) to rule over all, not just those within her local enclave.

At the beginning of the Second Age, Middle-earth appears as a post-apocalyptic wasteland, and even the gods themselves seem to care little for the fate of those who yet dwell there. Sauron, an impenitent Galadriel, and other "proud" elves are among those who still express the desire to see Middle-earth made not only habitable, but also worth living in. Presumably, the many humans, dwarves, and orcs who live in these lands share such a wish, even if they have different ideas of what that would look like. Eventually, most of these peoples will have to deal with the invading imperialist navies of Númenor, which will definitively shape the "world-politics" of that Age and subsequent epochs, but in the beginning of the Second Age, with the Númenoreans safely ensconced upon their utopian Atlantis, all these persons left in the post-apocalyptic landscape of Middle-earth must fitfully eke out a living. In his attempt to bring order to the chaos left behind by the Valar, Sauron could be viewed as a healer of Middle-earth, one whose intentions, if not his ultimate ends and results, are far from "evil."

Galadriel, Witch-Queen of Lórien

At a memorable moment in the movie *The Lord of the Rings: The Fellowship of the Ring*, Peter Jackson's 2001 film adaptation, the company of heroes rushes into a dense forest, where suddenly everything seems eerily calm and still. The dwarf Gimli warns the hobbits to "stay close," explaining, "[t]hey say that a great sorceress lives in these woods, an Elf-Witch of terrible power." The scene does not appear exactly that way in the book, but the general atmosphere of the eldritch or otherworldly does pervade the description of Lothlórien. Gimli is referring, of course, to Galadriel, who is described in Tolkien's writings as "the greatest of Elven women" and "the mightiest and fairest of all the Elves that remained in Middle-earth."[27] Contrary to the prevailing view, Gimli's initial description of her contains a good deal of truth. Galadriel might well be considered the Witch-queen of Lórien.

Apart from many of the hobbits themselves, whose goodness in Tolkien's world derives mainly from their simplicity rather than their inherent beatitude, Galadriel probably represents the most supremely "good" character in *The Lord of the Rings*. In Tolkien's mythic history, Galadriel was born in Valinor, the "Undying Lands," before even the creation of the sun and moon, and she is the last of this high race of elves in Middle-earth. Hence, in *The Lord of the Rings*, she appears as an almost god-like figure, but one even less corruptible than those who are indeed demigods in Tolkien's mythology (that is, *Maiar* such as Gandalf, Saruman, Radagast, and Sauron). Certainly, after Gimli's initial skepticism—he is won over to such an extent that he later threatens to kill any who disrespect the Lady of the Wood—none of the "good" characters in the novel or the film adaptations questions Galadriel's own inherent goodness.

In fact, Galadriel has a rather ambiguous moral character. She is benevolent, to be sure, but one could argue that her own sense of what is good and evil rests on a dubious foundation, particularly inasmuch as she perceives change itself as undesirable. For those beings who are not entirely satisfied with the status quo, Galadriel's intentions may not be so noble, and her powers may well seem like forms of dark magic. As shocking as it would sound to some Tolkien enthusiasts, Galadriel has quite a lot in common with principal villains of *The Lord of the Rings*, Saruman and even Sauron. Galadriel redeems herself through her modest efforts to aid Frodo and others, but most especially by refusing to take the One Ring. As I discuss below, the traitorous White Wizard was really an inverted Galadriel. When she refuses to take up the One Ring, she "passed the test," whereas Saruman's desire for power—even if it was for the power to do good—led him to become a Sauron-like villain. But to suggest that Galadriel's better choice is based on her own inherent goodness is to deny how powerful the temptation really was and in turn to rob her of the truly heroic aspect of her refusal.

As we learn from her fascinating backstory in *The Silmarillion*,[28] Galadriel came to Middle-earth as an unrepentant imperialist. As a proud member of the Noldor, Galadriel took part in the great rebellion of her people against the will of the Valar, although she was not guilty of the worst sins committed at that time. The main reason that she rebelled was that she "yearned to see the wide unguarded lands and to rule there a realm at her own will."[29] In another version, we learn that "she had dreams of far lands and dominions that might be her own to order as she would without tutelage."[30] In fact, "Knowledge, Rule, Order," the things Saruman claims to value above all, are among the virtues Galadriel cherishes as well. Already a powerful elf who had benefited from the tutelage of the Valar, she eventually settled in Doriath, where she learned many seemingly supernatural arts from the queen of that realm, Melian, a Maia, and where she dwelled until the end of the First Age. After the terrible War of Wrath, Galadriel was given the opportunity to return to Valinor, but as Tolkien phrased it in a late letter, "she proudly refused forgiveness or permission to return," choosing rather to remain in Middle-earth, where she found new lands to rule.[31]

Hence, her own desire for (political) power is, at least in part, what led Galadriel to invade these lands in the first place, and her rule over her kingdom seems no less absolute or more democratic than Sauron's rule over Mordor or Saruman's over Isengard. The Fellowship of the Ring encounters her in the Third Age, the particular kingdom Galadriel and her husband Celeborn govern is Lothlórien (or Lórien). This is a realm of silvan elves (the Nandor), who in the racial hierarchy of Tolkien's mythology are considered lesser elves, and there is no other explanation as to why

Galadriel should rule over the people who already lived there other than that she is a superior being to begin with, although we could add that her powers were great enough that those who admire such power would support her rule. As far as the racial or ethnic hierarchy goes, Galadriel is of the Noldor, and her mother was of the highest race, the Vanyar; Celeborn was a Sindaran elf from Doriath, so between the two, the rulers of Lórien have most impressive bloodlines. Galadriel's daughter married Elrond, which makes Arwen is Galadriel's granddaughter and Aragorn, Arwen's husband, is also a distant relative. Hence, Galadriel's kinfolk will continue to reign even after she leaves Middle-earth. Presumably their elevated heritage and status make them fit to rule over the wood elves,[32] but even among the elven peoples, Galadriel seems to be a colonizing potentate, albeit a benevolent one. Furthermore, arguably like Sauron, she maintains her regnant order, at least in part, through magic.

Galadriel is nowhere referred to as a "witch," even though her seemingly magical powers are cited in a number of places. In fact, the word *witch* appears in *The Lord of the Rings* only in the Prologue and the Appendices, and every reference is to the Witch-king (or Witch-lord) of Angmar, an ancient enemy who lives on as Lord of the Nazgûl or Ringwraiths.[33] The Witch-king of Angmar was a sorcerer of terrible power, it seems, and his black magic was undoubtedly linked to the ring of power he wielded. Yet Galadriel also bears a ring of power, as she confesses to Frodo, and she uses it to maintain a rather unnatural dominion over the laws of time and space. Although Galadriel is not depicted as a warrior in Tolkien's writings, she does use some form of seemingly magical power to throw down the walls of Dol Guldur and lay bare its pits, as mentioned in Appendix B of *The Lord of the Rings*.[34] Although Tolkien consistently presents her in a flattering light, any reasonable person would be justified in thinking of Galadriel as a Witch-queen.

Galadriel wears one of the "Three Rings for the Elven-kings," whose power she uses to maintain her own kingdom in a state or perpetual, preternatural changelessness. The weakness of the elves, as immortal beings, is that they "become unwilling to face change," as Tolkien writes in another letter. "Hence they fell in a measure to Sauron's deceits: they desired some 'power' over things as they are," thus wanting "to arrest change, and keep things always fresh and fair."[35] The rings of power are, after all, a technology introduced by Sauron, and even though "the three" were unsullied, their power is connected to his. Galadriel tells Frodo that her only desire is that "what should be shall be," which sounds rather ominous, depending on how you view things.[36] She wields powerful magic as a way of achieving her desire, although she will "pass the test" by declining the opportunity to possess the One Ring.

Tolkien fans might object that Galadriel's magic is not the same as "the deceits of the Enemy," a distinction made clear by Tolkien and voiced by Galadriel herself in *The Lord of the Rings*.[37] Tolkien distinguishes between *art* and *power*, and he associates magic with the latter. In a letter later reprinted as a preface to *The Silmarillion*, Tolkien identifies "Magic" with "the Machine," as both are catalysts "for making the will more quickly effective." They are two names for the same thing: "all use of external plans or devices (apparatus) instead of the development of the inherent inner powers or talents—or even the use of these talents with the corrupted motive of dominating: bulldozing the real world, or coercing other wills. The Machine is our more obvious modern form though more closely related to Magic than is usually recognized."[38] It is an interesting if fine distinction. Tolkien would argue that Galadriel's "magic" is really an art, although I have my doubts.

Take, for example, the "Mirror of Galadriel" episode from *The Lord of the Rings*. The scene begins with Sam and Frodo remarking upon the omnipresence of "Elf-magic" in Lothlórien. "You can see and feel it everywhere," says Frodo, but Sam notes that, unlike Gandalf with his showy fireworks displays, "you can't see nobody working it. [...] I'd dearly love to see some Elf-magic, Mr. Frodo!" Galadriel uses just this term to entice Sam to look in the mirror, although she mildly rebukes the hobbits for confusing "Elf-magic" with "the deceits of the Enemy." Yet Galadriel had already indicated the moral ambiguity of this particular magic, explaining that she is able to "command the Mirror" to reveal many things, often showing "to some [...] what they desire to see." But, she goes on, it is more "profitable" to allow the Mirror to show what it will, even though—whether it displays visions of the past, present, or future—"even the wisest cannot always tell."[39]

If this seems perilous, that is because it clearly is perilous. As Galadriel specifically counsels when Sam becomes agitated and alarmed at the Mirror's vision, "the Mirror shows many things, and not all have yet come to pass. Some never come to be, unless those that behold the visions turn aside from their path to prevent them. The Mirror is dangerous as a guide to deeds."[40] Thus Galadriel's own "art" involves the potential for deceit, as the ambiguities of the Mirror suggest.

Earlier, when the fellowship first arrives in Lórien, Galadriel telepathically "tests" the members, causing them to see visions, unbidden and unwanted. Whether this is "deceitful" or not is another question, but Galadriel is aware that it is violation enough to merit an apology (to Frodo, if not to the others) later. These are painful to bear, especially to Boromir and to Frodo, and Galadriel later observes that Frodo's courtesy toward her is a gentle revenge for "my testing of your heart."[41] Undoubtedly, she

5. The Politics of Character

has her reasons, and the reader is compelled to trust that they are well intended, but her power to probe, to read, and, indeed, to interfere with the minds of others ought to give pause. If Galadriel does not wish to *dominate*, as do Sauron and Saruman, she is certainly willing to exercise power over others, at least for a while and without asking permission.

There is, perhaps, an extradiegetic explanation for Galadriel's character and behavior. One might argue that the elves, particularly the High Elves such as Galadriel, Celeborn, and even Elrond Half-elven, represent the aristocracy, even the *ancien régime*, of Middle-earth. After the War of the Ring, these figures acknowledge that the age of the elves has passed, and for the most part they make their graceful exit from the stage, ceding Middle-earth to "men" as their own power diminishes, and voluntarily departing from both human society and the world itself. At the risk of undue allegorizing, one could envision the graceful evanescence of the elves as symbolic of the fading British aristocracy, whose members in the aftermath of World War II were increasingly challenged by commercial and political transformation of the stable, hierarchical society that they had presided over for centuries and by the rise of a dominant bourgeoisie. A more demotic society—it is the "Age of Men," after all—would not be suited to such "highborn" figures, as the bourgeois civilizations to come would be characterized by a more seemingly democratic and less overtly hierarchical social formations. Rather than continuing to fight what Galadriel calls "the long defeat,"[42] these elites graciously allow the world to change and to continue without them. It is a much more chivalric version of Ayn Rand's *ressentiment*-fueled, self-imposed hermitage of the rich and powerful in *Atlas Shrugged*, but it does offer a similar version of the culturally conservative response to modern social and political formations.

Tolkien himself was rather ambivalent about modern democracy, after all. He certainly opposed fascism and communism, and he supported the Allied war effort against Germany, Italy, and Japan, but in a wartime letter to his son Christopher, Tolkien lamented that the ultimate consequence of victory would be to spread "American sanitation, morale-pep, feminism, and mass production" throughout the world. As he continues,

> But seriously: I do find this Americo-cosmopolitanism very terrifying. Quâ mind and spirit, and neglecting the piddling fears of timid flesh which does not want to be shot or chopped by brutal and licentious soldiery (German or other), I am not really sure that its victory is going to be so much better for the world as a whole and in the long run than the victory of ——.[43]

The final dash or blank space is in the original, which suggests that *any* side's victory might be no worse than if the USA-led forces were to prevail. In the context of Galadriel's "long defeat," Tolkien's wartime fears of the modern world as a spiritual wasteland dominated by commercial, popular culture are all too vivid. Galadriel's true enemy, as her own behavior makes clear, is change itself, whether that change is natural, cultural, or political. In gracefully accepting defeat, she models for a dying aristocracy the sort of elegiac stance with which to confront inevitable social transformations of her revolutionary era.

In my discussion of orcs, which I take up in the next chapter, I argue that the basic humanity of these "inhuman" creatures proved them to be more worthy of our sympathy than the elves, whose near-perfection marks them with a profound otherness. As immortals, elves are always playing a long game in which we finite beings cannot ever hope to be much more than pawns, albeit, occasionally useful ones. The characters who seem most aware of this fact in *The Lord of the Rings* are, in fact, the orcs, as is tellingly revealed in the dialogue between Gorbag and Shagrat. They lament having to work for "Big Bosses," remember the "bad old times" when elves besieged them, and make hopeful plans for a postwar future in which there are "no big bosses."[44] In their fear and loathing of aristocrats and high powers, these orcs express thoroughly modern, even vaguely democratic sentiments. The Witch-queen of Lórien, much like the dark Lord of Mordor, champions a different social order entirely. I am not entirely sure that Galadriel's vision for how the world system should be organized is necessarily the better one. For those of us who are in favor of changing the world, Galadriel and her coterie of hereditary aristocrats represent the enemy, a power to be overcome, and her "long defeat" cannot come soon enough.

Song of Saruman

In an official trailer for *The Hobbit: The Battle of the Five Armies* in 2014, viewers received a tantalizing glimpse of Saruman, no more than two seconds long, intoning in Christopher Lee's inimitable voice, "Leave Sauron to me!" For fans of Tolkien and of the genre he helped to develop and popularize, the prospect of a showdown between the two most powerful persons in all of Middle-earth is delicious. Even Gandalf had deferred to Saruman as the head of his order, acknowledging that "he is both wise and powerful," and thus a potential battle between Sauron and the White Wizard would be something to see. But, of course, we know that the showdown never takes place; nor would it have occurred, since the now six-film saga of *The Hobbit* and *The Lord of the Rings* has made sure to emphasize Saruman's inherently evil status. Although *The Battle of the Five Armies* does include that scene in which Saruman fights alongside Gandalf, Radagast,

Elrond, and Galadriel against the servants of Sauron, the implication in the end is that wizard is really helping Sauron to escape. The oversimplification of Saruman is, in my view, one of the more egregious mistakes made by Jackson and his team. They have taken one of the most interesting characters in Tolkien's story—one who is conflicted and flawed, but not unlike a tragic hero—and turned him into boringly one-dimensional movie villain. Even in *The Hobbit* films, whose story takes place years before any characters had an inkling of Saruman's later treason (first revealed during the "Council of Elrond" scene of *The Fellowship of the Ring*), Saruman is depicted as snide, untrustworthy, and even sinister.

As noted above, one of the knocks on Tolkien, a favorite of his detractors, has been that his world is too neatly divided into good and evil, with the saintly elves, heroic men, doughty dwarves, and innocent hobbits standing their righteous ground against hordes of demonic orcs, trolls, evil or fallen men (who are sometimes coded as racial outsiders as well), along with some great Satan. This simplistic moral universe has even been taken as a hallmark of the fantasy genre itself by such imminent critics of the genre as Darko Suvin, Fredric Jameson, and Carl Freedman, who favor what they take to be the political complexity of science fiction. The "great divide" has been bridged by such fantasists as Ursula Le Guin, Samuel R. Delaney, and China Miéville, among others, but there remains a sense that Tolkien's own writings are almost comically reductive with respect to morality. The Jackson films have only exacerbated this perception by reducing the nuances even further, but a careful reading of Tolkien's writings reveals a far more subtle and complicated view of the motives and goals of various characters in *The Lord of the Rings* and other texts. Perhaps even against his own wishes, in what might be considered a sort of political unconscious, Tolkien's work draws attention to the troubled and troubling political and moral quandaries facing the peoples of Middle-earth. Saruman is an exemplary figure in this regard.

The filmmakers' caricaturishly evil vision of Saruman is unfortunate, as it deprives a fascinating narrative of its complexity, while also being untrue to Tolkien's own vision. Jackson and his team seem incapable of imagining that a person can be in the wrong on a given matter without also being irredeemably evil. Thus, for example, the Master of Lake-town in the novel *The Hobbit* was greedy, but he was an elected official, who was generally well-regarded by the community (at least until he absconds with the municipal funds, a fact revealed only on the last page of the book); in the film, *The Desolation of Smaug*, he is a murderous tyrant, who opposes even the idea of elections. An even worse example is the case of Denethor, Steward of Gondor, who in the books has been driven mad by grief and despair, utterly bereft because of the death of his beloved son Boromir, and tormented by the cruel machinations of Sauron himself, who has projected visions of a bleak, hopeless future using the *palantir*. In the film (*The Lord of the Rings: The Return of the King*), he is made to appear so loathsome and so irredeemably evil that Gandalf actually attacks him, causing his death, while we the viewers are expected to cheer. Where in the novel Gandalf desperately tries to save Denethor, in the film he enthusiastically murders him. If this is what Jackson does to weak and pitiable characters, what must he do to Saruman, who is much more of a legitimate "bad guy" in *The Lord of the Rings*?

In addition to limiting his screen-time, the answer seems to be: to make him both more evil and less interesting. In the original movie trilogy, Saruman is depicted strictly as a willing servant of Sauron, even going so far as to take orders from him. Saruman's own servants appear to acknowledge the pecking order, as one asks "What orders from Mordor?" and "What does the Eye command?" while Saruman ponders how best to serve his "master." In his brief appearances in *The Hobbit: An Unexpected Journey* and *The Battle of the Five Armies*, he comes off as a querulous, dismissive boss, who is already shown to be subverting the council he heads. For this reason, the "Leave Sauron to me!," uttered in response to Elrond's insistence that they pursue the temporarily banished Sauron into Mordor, appears as a dilatory tactic that would benefit Sauron, thus revealing to the viewers (if not yet to Gandalf, Galadriel, and Elrond) that Saruman is already a servant of the Dark Lord.

In the novel, Tolkien makes clear that Saruman was never really in league with Sauron. Saruman only feigns allegiance for a time, in order to trick Sauron into revealing secrets about the ruling ring or to stall him while Saruman himself seeks the ring. True, Saruman betrays Gandalf and the rest of the White Council, but not in order to side with the enemy. Rather, as Gandalf himself might put it, Saruman would *become* Sauron. As Gandalf does put it in the movie *The Lord of the Rings: The Fellowship of the Ring*, "there is only one Lord of the Ring [...] and he does not share power." In the book, the line is a bit different, as Gandalf notes that "only one hand at a time can wield the One,"[45] and indeed, at various points in both the film and print versions of the story, Gandalf, Galadriel, and Aragorn each reveal how powerfully tempted they are to take the ring, only to "pass the test" by declining the opportunity. Saruman is no more evil than these other characters to start with, and thus he serves as the cautionary example of what happens to the wise and good who succumb to the temptation. (Denethor, who also covets the ring but only out of his desire to defeat Sauron and save Gondor, is another example, as is Boromir.) By missing this crucial point, the films misrepresent Tolkien's most fascinating villain. Like Gollum, Saruman is deeply conflicted, and he is deserving

5. The Politics of Character

of the pity he receives from Gandalf, Frodo, and others. Saruman's downfall is, however, more tragic than Gollum's, since the former had so much farther to fall.

Saruman's back-story is illuminating in this regard. He was the first of the *Istari* or wizards to arrive in Middle-earth, and even Gandalf acknowledges him as the wisest, most powerful of that order. Some would dispute the characterization; in an unpublished fragment, Tolkien reveals that Galadriel had wished to name Gandalf as head of the White Council, which caused Saruman to mistrust her and to envy Gandalf thereafter.[46] Following Gandalf's own fall in his battle with the Balrog, he is resurrected in *The Two Towers* as "Gandalf the White," declaring "I *am* Saruman, one might almost say."[47] Gandalf's deference to Saruman early on, as well as his continuing respect for him later, should be indication enough that Saruman is not an innately evil person. Saruman's downfall, somewhat like Sauron's own, is based in part on his good intentions, a desire to make the world an orderly, peaceful, and rational place.

In Tolkien's mythology, both Sauron and Saruman are Maiar originally in the service of Aulë. (Of course, there's ultimately only one god, Eru or Ilúvatar, but the Valar are the "Powers of Arda" itself.) It is significant that the two "evil" characters in *The Lord of the Rings* have this association, for the connection between creativity or craftsmanship and power is, for Tolkien, a perilous one.[48] In a famous letter describing his "private and beloved nonsense," the materials that make up his "Silmarillion," Tolkien explains that the "creative desire" can lead to the "Fall," as the maker can become possessive, wishing to become "Lord and God of his private creation." This leads to a desire for what Tolkien views, almost interchangeably, as "Magic or the Machine," the power of "making the will more quickly effective." With these elements, it is only a short step toward tyranny and domination, as the "sub-creator" imposes his will on others, dominating and "bulldozing" them, and hence becoming a force of "evil." However, Tolkien explains that "this frightful evil can and does arise from an apparently good root; the desire to benefit the world and others—speedily and according to the benefactor's own plans—is a recurrent motive."[49] This is, after all, why the ring is so dangerous. Contrary to the film's portrayal of the device, the ring is not inherently "evil," such that any user of it will become evil. Rather, one might say, what we think of as "evil" is the power to control the wills of others, which is ultimately the power of rule itself. In other words, what had been cast as a moral or ethical problem comes down to a fundamentally political one.

Stepping away from Tolkien's own philosophy for a moment, one can easily imagine a revisionist reading in which Saruman's good intentions are vindicated, as he attempts to thwart the designs of an authoritarian, aristocratic, and preternaturally conservative regime—that of Elrond, Galadriel, and Aragorn, who are all also related to one another by blood and marriage—in favor of a more progressive, modern society. In *The Last Ringbearer*, Kirill Yeskov's unauthorized alternative vision of the War of the Rings, Saruman is depicted as defending the rights of an increasingly industrial civilization in Mordor against a warmongering Gandalf, who is intent on nipping the revolution in the bud. There are no orcs in this version, presumably because what Tolkien names *orcs* are really just humans who have been demonized by their enemies. In fact, Tolkien himself gives credence to that view, as he once described the physical appearance of the orcs as resembling "the least lovely Mongol-types," which is suggestive of a cultural or racial conflict masquerading as an ethical one.[50] Seen from this perspective, the geopolitical and moral landscape of Middle-earth looks quite different. This view of history from below informs such revisionary fantasy as we find in Delaney's *Return to Nevèrÿon* series, for example, and it lends color to other more complicated and interesting works of fantasy literature in recent years. However, many elements of such perspectives, if not the authorial intent, can still be found in Tolkien's own writings.

Returning to Tolkien's mythology, then, we can see how Saruman's background as a skilled and wise craftsman-demigod helps us to understand his motives, as well as his corruption, and it also explains why Gandalf, Treebeard, and the hobbits pity him and hope to save him. The movie version of Saruman ignores his good intentions, and it also ignores his efforts to combat Sauron. In the book, for instance, the resurrected Gandalf the White states that "[t]he Enemy [Sauron] has failed—so far. Thanks to Saruman"; that is, Saruman's desire to possess the ring, which led to his double-dealing with Sauron, had prevented Sauron from capturing the hobbits. Were it not for Saruman's treachery, Gandalf asserts, all would have been lost.[51] However, by making Saruman a mere lackey of Sauron, the filmmakers vastly simplify the narrative, effectively insulting the audience by assuming its members cannot handle the idea of multiple enemies at once or that they cannot imagine conflicting values irreducible to simple "good versus evil." (Even Harry Potter fans know that one can be bad without being evil, after all, and not because they have studied Nietzsche, presumably.) Like Gandalf, Elrond, and Galadriel, Saruman was never in league with Sauron, and, like them, he was always trying to undermine and ultimately defeat Sauron. Unlike those others, however, Saruman gives in to the temptation to rule, to seek a power over others to arrange things in what he takes to be their best interest. As one of the most knowledgeable beings in Middle-earth, Saruman understandably feels that he is most capable of ordering it for the good, and thus desires to rule. In his study of the Enemy's "arts," Tolkien suggests, Saruman became ensnared by this

Machiavellian desire, but this is precisely why Gandalf is so eager to forgive, and even to rejoin forces with Saruman in the aftermath of the Battle of Helm's Deep. This wise, powerful, and ultimately well-intentioned Saruman would be a most useful and worthy ally in the War of the Ring.

Saruman's story is therefore tragic. In his desire to do good, to protect the people of Middle-earth and to organize (and rule) the world according to rational, benevolent principles, Saruman succumbed to the ultimate evil, which is the desire for power, in Tolkien's view. The ring itself is a symbol of this peril. In the films, the One Ring is given a rather different role than it had in the novels. The filmmakers even went so far as to give it a voice, albeit a barely discernible whisper, which suggests almost a personality (Sauron's, in fact). The filmmakers also made the ring much more dangerous to wear, omitting Sam's effective use of it in Cirith Ungol, for example. However, Tolkien himself warned against putting too much stock in the power of the ring. As he explained in a 1958 letter to an inquisitive reader, the One Ring is a device:

> a mythical way of representing the truth that *potency* (or perhaps rather *potentiality*) if it is to be exercised, and produce results, has to be externalized and so as it were passes, to a greater or less degree, out of one's direct control. A man who wishes to exert "power" must have subjects, who are not himself. But he depends on them.[52]

This explanation helps to demystify both the purported "magic" and "evil" of the One Ring, which can now be seen as a symbol for the sort of conventional machinery of political and military power, such as a standing army, police forces, or bureaucratic apparatuses.

Saruman's investigations into ring lore led him to create his own ring of power, but it was not enough to rival the One Ring, so he attempted to acquire that weapon for himself. As I suggested above, in the political landscape of Middle-earth during the War of the Rings, Saruman is really the inverted Galadriel; he "fails the test" that she passes near the end of *The Fellowship of the Rings* (both the book and the film). In *The Silmarillion*, Galadriel's own desire for rule and order is what led her to forsake the Undying Lands and travel to Middle-earth in the first place. Her motives were almost identical to Saruman's, and even to Sauron's originally, but she eventually—after many millennia of apparently absolute rule over her own kingdoms, by the way—abjures her own desire for power, allowing herself to "diminish, and go into the West, and remain Galadriel."[53] Seen in this light, Saruman's inability to "remain" Saruman is the stuff of high tragedy.

Saruman was diminished, becoming in his resentment and malice a mere Sharkey for a time, whereas Gandalf the White became "Saruman as he should have been."[54] This is not to say that Saruman in *The Lord of the Rings* is not a bad guy, only that Tolkien allows for far more nuance than his detractors imagine. Things are not nearly as black and white as many critics think, and it is a shame that the films have, by and large, gone even further in oversimplifying things. Although Gollum comes across as extremely sympathetic, a victim of the ring, some other "villains" are presented as almost cardboard cut-outs, with no depth of character at all. The filmmakers' bizarre decision to render Sauron as a disembodied, flaming eyeball, despite the clear description of Sauron's humanoid form in the books, is an extreme example of their unwillingness to view "bad" characters as having even a modicum of humanity. Saruman appears at his most villainous in two scenes from the books that were either cut from the movies ("The Voice of Saruman," which appears in the extended-edition DVD of *The Return of the King*) or never filmed ("The Scouring of the Shire"), but even in those moments, Tolkien presents him as an object of pity, a once-great and noble, now "fallen" figure. It is a shame that moviegoers are not given enough credit to understand this, and that Tolkien's greatest villain loses his tragic graces in a farcically fiendish depiction on film.

"Satan fell": Ethics as False Consciousness

Apart from the insights that a revisionist reading can provide, the reevaluation of such characters as Sauron, Galadriel, and Saruman, particularly considering their overly simplistic characterization in the popular film adaptations of *The Hobbit* and *The Lord of the Rings*, underscores the degree to which Tolkien's universe is far more complex and interesting than even his most ardent supporters normally find. Undoubtedly, my interpretation might go beyond what Tolkien himself would find tolerable, but the fact that his writings are so amenable to such a reasonable, revisionary perspective is itself a sign of the richness and depth of the narrative universe in which these figures and events exist.

Moreover, Tolkien explicitly denied the existence of "Absolute Evil," which he did not believe in, and added "I do not think at any rate any 'rational being' is wholly evil. Satan fell. Morgoth fell before the creation of the physical world," and Sauron himself fell victim in part to his own good intentions—rehabilitating Middle-earth and bringing order to a state of desolation and disorder—but above all to his sense of pride.[55] Saruman's fall, like Sauron's (and Galadriel's), is related to this desire for knowledge, rule, and order, which is enough to say—along Nietzschean or Foucauldian lines, perhaps—that such obviously desirable things carry their own terrible perils. When at the end of the Mirror scene Sam expresses his wish that Galadriel *would* take the Ring, stating "You'd put things to rights. [...] You'd make some folk pay for their dirty work," Galadriel's offers simple, chilling response, a line as ominous as any in the novel: "I would [...]. That is how it would begin."[56]

The moral or ethical question of whether someone is "good" or "evil" is shown to be false, and worse, to be used as ideological cover to obscure the fact that the issues were political all along. That is not to say that ethics or morality has no role to play in politics, only that such categories as "good" or "evil" are not helpful, and are in fact quite unhelpful, in understanding the processes, problems, and ideas involved. As Tolkien observed, "tyrants are seldom utterly corrupted into pure manifestations of evil will," and even if we could imagine some to be so corrupted, "they must rule subjects only part of whom are equally corrupt, while many still need to have 'good motives,' real or feigned, presented to them."[57] This is a matter of politics, not just in the narrow sense of representing a given polity, but in the capacious sense of the fundamental problems of the *zoon politikon* that is man, a social animal in Aristotle's terminology, who must inhibit the world and abide within it. To imagine Sauron as "evil" or Galadriel as "good" is to fail to appreciate the complexity of Tolkien's world system and of his art.

Given the manifest perils of knowledge, rule, and order, it is a wonder that more sympathy is not accorded to beings associated with ignorance, misrule, and disorder. In addition to the supernatural "enemies," such as Sauron, Saruman, or Smaug (in *The Hobbit*), and the various human ones, such as the Easterlings, Southrons (Haradrim), or Wild Men, fighting alongside the men of Mordor and confronted by the apparent "good guys" in *The Lord of the Rings*, the orcs represent the most salient and difficult to deal with conceptually. As the embodiment of "demons," they represent a force that the noble races can oppose, and kill, without any moral compunction whatsoever, and yet Tolkien himself struggled over their status. As "rational beings," after all, they could not be "wholly evil," but they are certainly treated as such by the various heroes in the novel, perhaps best exemplified by the lurid and cruel "counting game" played by Legolas and Gimli, who vie over who can kill the most orcs. In the following two chapters I examine the problems posed by the orcs, first in Tolkien's own legendarium, writings, and in the film adaptations, then in connection with the wartime demonization of the enemy more broadly. Not unlike the cases of the Dark Lord, the Witch-queen, and the White Wizard, the stories of the orcs are far more nuanced than most readers acknowledge. They are also far more political, as the world system itself depends on the vast underclass figured forth in the form of these demonized populations.

CHAPTER 6

Let Us Now Praise Famous Orcs
Simple Humanity in Middle-earth's Inhuman Creatures

In J.R.R. Tolkien's sprawling legendarium, the mythic world of Middle-earth and its suburbs, orcs provide a seemingly endless supply of enemies to challenge the mettle of the noble elves, men, dwarves, and hobbits. As every reader of the books knows, along with every viewer of the blockbuster films, orcs are the immutably terrible foot soldiers of "evil," employed by both the traitorous wizard Saruman and the great *diabolus* Sauron in *The Lord of the Rings*, forming the infantry of Morgoth's vast armies in *The Silmarillion*, and being the one race against which all others unite in *The Hobbit*'s Battle of Five Armies. As I discussed in Chapters 5 and I will discuss further in Chapter 8, for instance, the tendency to view Tolkien's moral universe as strictly demarcated between good and evil is both widespread and oversimplified, as Tolkien regularly introduces far more ethical nuances in both his characters and in their actions. However, orcs are presented with surprising uniformity as loathsome, ugly, cruel, feared, hated, and especially terminable. In Tolkien's narratives, the only good orc is a dead orc.

Yet, as dedicated readers discern, Tolkien could not resist the urge to flesh out and "humanize" these inhuman creatures from time to time. In such examples as those I discuss below, Tolkien presents orcs who have rather human, even *humane*, qualities, notwithstanding their generally negative characteristics.[1] This fact makes it a bit disturbing, then, that Tolkien's heroes, without the least pang of conscience, dispatch orcs by the thousands. Indeed, letters and unpublished manuscripts reveal that Tolkien himself struggled with the metaphysical and moral problems he had set up by inventing, characterizing, and using orcs as he does. Orcs were, and are, problematic.

"Whence they came or what they were"

This uneasiness is understandable when considering the origins of orcs (i.e., in Tolkien's world, not the philological or folkloric origins in ours),[2] a subject of some disagreement as even Tolkien changed his mind over time. The canonical view presented in *The Silmarillion* is that the Elves "by slow arts of cruelty were corrupted and enslaved; thus did Melkor breed the hideous race of the Orcs in envy and mockery of the Elves."[3] In *The Two Towers*, Treebeard explains to Merry and Pippen that "Trolls are only counterfeits, made by the Enemy in the Great Darkness, in mockery of Ents, as Orcs were of Elves."[4] Elsewhere in *The Silmarillion*, the surmise that Orcs were former Elves—specifically the Avari or "the unwilling," who did not make the long journey to Valinor as did the "light elves"—is given further credence: "Whence they [the orcs] came, or what they were, the Elves knew not then, thinking them perhaps to be Avari who had become evil and savage in the wild; in which they guessed all too near, it is said."[5] This explanation would make the most sense in Tolkien's legendarium, if only because orcs appear after elves but before men in the mythic history of Arda. However, as Dimitra Fimi points out, "the thought that the hideous and malicious Orcs were once Elves—the 'highest' beings of Middle-earth—became increasingly unbearable to Tolkien."[6] Indeed, in unpublished manuscripts written during the 1950s and 1960s Tolkien toyed with several different ideas to explain the orcs' existence, ranging from corrupted men (rather than corrupted elves) to low-level Maia (and hence, fallen "angels" like Sauron himself) and even to automata without reason or sentience who were essentially puppets controlled by Morgoth or Sauron (an admittedly unlikely scenario).[7] There is even the vague suggestion that Orcs *were* a kind of man, distant cousins of the Drúedain or related to the Púkel Men who appear in *The Lord of the Rings*: "some thought, nonetheless, that there had been a remote kinship, which accounted for their special enmity. Orcs and Drûgs each regarded the other as renegades."[8] Ultimately, as Christopher Tolkien concludes, "[t]his would appear to be my father's final view on the matter: Orcs were bred from Men."[9]

The crucial philosophical point in the various arguments concerning orc origins is that their very existence shows they have value and are worthy of being. An article of faith in Tolkien's world holds that only God (that is, Eru or Ilúvatar) can *create*, and the evil ones—whether Melkor (a.k.a. Morgoth, Tolkien's original Satan figure), or Sauron (Melkor's acolyte and successor), or Saruman (who apparently breeds his own orcs or "half–Orcs")—can only *pervert* that creation. To put it another way, no new "souls" or "spirits" can be created. Frodo explains as much to Sam when he avers that "[t]he Shadow that bred them [the orcs] can only mock, it cannot make: not real new things of its own. I do not think it gave life to the Orcs, it only ruined them and twisted them."[10] Indeed, this principle is dramatized and made perfectly clear in *The Silmarillion* in a myth that explains the origins and existence of the dwarves. In this story, Aulë, a Vala who longs to share his great knowledge with pupils and becomes impatient waiting for the elves to awaken, actually creates dwarves, but they are merely as clay figurines or puppets with no independent being. Eru Ilúvatar chastises Aulë for attempting a thing "beyond thy power and thy authority," but even so grants his wish by giving his dwarves life.[11] What this episode underscores is that not even the most powerful beings in Arda, the Valar, can create new sentient beings or imbue creatures with life. What this also means, of course, is that anything that in fact *has life*, has it with the tacit if not explicit approval of Ilúvatar. As Tolkien concedes in a letter, drafted but unsent, "by accepting or tolerating their making—necessary to their actual existence—even Orcs would become part of the World, which is God's and ultimately good."[12] Hence, like men and elves, orcs are in a way also the "Children of Ilúvatar."

In a nutshell, as Tom Shippey puts it, "though he became increasingly concerned over the implications of the Orcs in his story, and tried out several explanations for them, their analogousness to humanity always remained clear."[13] Orcs partake of a humanity that renders them familiar and akin, albeit loathsome, to the race of men, at least as far as can be discerned from the texts of Tolkien's Saga of the Jewels and the Rings. For example, although readers never encounter any female orcs, *The Silmarillion* establishes that orcs "had life and multiplied after the manner" of elves and men, that is, sexually.[14] Indeed, it seems that orcs, like elves, can interbreed with humans, as Saruman is said to have bred "half–Orcs" or "goblin-men."[15] What is more, Tolkien alludes to particular orc families and communities, including whole cities (such as the "capital" city, Gundabad) and diverse cultures. Although "Orcs entered Middle-earth originally just because the story needed a continual supply of enemies over whom one need feel no compunction,"[16] Tolkien obviously provides more ethnographic and cultural background for orcs than such a plot-device would require. The orcs of Middle-earth are shown to have their own languages, customs, communities, and even families. In *The Hobbit*, for instance, Gandalf declares, "[t]he Goblins are upon you! Bolg of the North is coming, O Dain! whose father you slew in Moria"; the actual battle in which Bolg's father, Azog, is killed by Dáin Ironfoot is described in Appendix A to *The Lord of the Rings*.[17] Hence, vengeance and familial honor motivate the assault, more so than some inherent "evil." Vengeance is undoubtedly one of the human, all-too-human impulses driving the orc attack, especially after Gandalf had killed the governor, the Great Goblin, of an orc village in the Misty Mountains, not to mention dozens if not hundreds of members of that community. Far from being mindless drones, robots, or clones (which was one of George Lucas's solutions to the ethical problem in the *Star Wars* universe), orcs are "rational, incarnate beings," who have deeply human feelings, conventions, and cultures.[18] Indeed, perhaps even more than the elves, whose near-perfection marks them with a profound otherness, orcs are shown to be human.

One may well wish to view "the orcish question" through the lens of race or racism. It is true that one can only read about the "swart" and "slant-eyed" orcs so many times without becoming offended. In a letter in which he describes the physical appearance of orcs, Tolkien himself invites a racial characterization of orcs: "[t]he Orcs are definitely stated to be corruptions of the 'human' form seen in Elves and Men. They are (or were) squat, broad, flat-nosed, sallow-skinned, with wide mouths and slant eyes: in fact degraded and repulsive versions of the (to Europeans) least lovely Mongol-type."[19] Race, in the modern sense—therefore also in a somewhat anachronistic sense within Tolkien's quasi-medieval universe—is a pressing concern in Tolkien's world, as Tolkien establishes elaborate hierarchies based upon bloodlines and heritage not just between but also *within* the races of elves, men, dwarves, and hobbits, not to mention in distinguishing them from the "evil" races of orcs, plus perhaps trolls, dragons, and so on. Fimi has discussed the problem of race in Tolkien at length, concluding that Tolkien's sometimes objectionable racial characterizations are consistent with the discourse of his time and, in any event, consistent with the "hierarchical world" in which his mythic history unfolds.[20] In a somewhat less forgiving interpretation, Peter E. Firchow has concluded that the underlying ideology of *The Hobbit* and other writings supports an essentially fascist worldview.[21] Robert Stuart, in what is perhaps the most thorough treatment of the subject to date, *Tolkien, Race, and Racism in Middle-earth*, has endeavored to split the difference, in a sense, by thoroughly documenting the racism in Tolkien's work, in his time, and in his own ideas, while also rejecting the view that Tolkien's writings or ideas should be considered in any way sympathetic toward fascism.[22] Racism and racial ideologies are worth exploring in greater detail elsewhere, but it is also clear that the generic conventions of fantasy-adventure narratives seem to necessitate this sort of hostile alterity. That is, the overall system of fantasy adventure requires a broadly understood enemy class, which may or may not be identifiably a race or a species, such that the heroes have an endless source of enemies to fight. For example, in the Tolkien-influenced world of *Dungeons & Dragons*, along with the numberless video-game derivatives, a veritable "Orc Holocaust" is not only the result but the aim of the adventures, and the language of race makes this practice seem all the more abominable.[23]

However, even if one were to accuse Tolkien of racism (which I am not doing here), racism alone would not explain Tolkien's treatment of the orcs. The apparently racialized image of orcs is still wholly different from Tolkien's treatment of different "races" of men, and orcs are not treated in the same way that humans putatively "of color" are, whether enemies like the Southrons, the Easterlings, and the Wild Men near Rohan, or allies like Ghân-buri-Ghân and the Drúedain. For example, it is enough to consider Sam's sympathy for the "swarthy" Southron, cut down while fleeing, his "brown hand" still clutching a broken sword, to see that Tolkien envisioned a place for sympathy among different races and toward one's enemies.

> It was Sam's first view of a battle of Men against Men, and he did not like it much. He was glad he could not see the dead man's face. He wondered what the man's name was and where he came from; and if he was really evil at heart, or what lies or threats had led him on his long march from his home; and if he would not really have rather stayed home in peace.[24]

Needless to say, perhaps, but Sam—who frequently longs for home and peace while on his own long march into foreign lands—does not for a moment consider what potential "lies and threats" may have brought his own company to wage war on diverse peoples and races of the South and East. More to the point, neither Sam nor anyone else shows a bit of sympathy for slain orcs. Humans seen to be in the service of "evil" may not be "evil at heart," but the assumption among even the good-natured hobbits remains that orcs must be inherently and irrevocably evil.

Later, when the ring is finally destroyed and Sauron vanquished, many of the humans in Mordor's service flee, surrender, or continue fighting, but Tolkien depicts orcs as mindless ants that "wander witless and purposeless and then feebly die,"[25] a characterization that does not easily square with what readers had learned of orcs in earlier scenes, as I discuss below. It is noteworthy that, in the distinction between enemy men and enemy orcs, Tolkien is willing to accord some rights and respectability even to these fallen or lowborn races of men who had sided with Sauron, as when Aragorn—now King Elessar of Gondor—releases the Easterlings who had surrendered on the battlefield, makes peace with the swarthy men of the South, and frees the thralls of Mordor, granting them lands in that region.[26] No such accommodations are made for the orcs, who are accorded no human rights in Tolkien's world, notwithstanding their being understood to be "corrupted" elves or men themselves. If, indeed, orcs are "corrupted" elves or men, twisted and tortured by Morgoth, then one would imagine that they could be seen as victims, and that the enemies of "the dark powers" would sympathize with them.[27] Hence, traditional notions of race or racial prejudice is not really the issue when it comes to orcs. Even with Tolkien's race-based hierarchies, even with racial description of orcs (as Mongol-types), and even with the surmise that orcs are in fact a twisted or corrupted form of men, orcs in Tolkien's universe are not treated so much as an inferior race as an inferior and despised order of being entirely. Given how many "noble" animals appear in *The Lord of the Rings*, from the well-nigh god-like Shadowfax of the Mearas or Gwahir the Windlord to the sturdy, faithful pony Bill, one might add that even being *inhuman* is far from an insult, but orcs are treated worse, and as being worse, than nearly all creatures that inhabit Middle-earth.

No More Big Bosses!

Yet Tolkien occasionally reveals a not entirely unsympathetic view of orcs, in which what might be called their simple humanity becomes visible. I am thinking especially of two scenes from *The Lord of the Rings*—that is, the conversation between Shagrat and Gorbag at Cirith Ungol and the interactions of Uglúk, Grishnákh, and other unnamed orcs amid the fields of Rohan—which disclose more than one would expect about the orcs' personal and social character, not to mention the role of orcs in the geopolitical system of Middle-earth in the Third Age.

The conversation between Shagrat and Gorbag takes place after Frodo and Sam have sneaked past the great citadel of Minas Morgul and ventured through a tunnel leading into Mordor that is guarded by the giant spider Shelob and patrolled by orcs. After Frodo is paralyzed by Shelob and Sam defeats her, Sam overhears a discussion between Shagrat, the commander of the Tower of Cirith Ungol, and Gorbag, a captain of a group of orcs from Minas Morgul. Shagrat mentions that the captured "spy" (Frodo) is "something that Lugbúrz wants," employing a familiar metonymic form: *Lugbúrz* is the orcs' name for Barad-dûr, the tower that stands as Sauron's seat of power in Mordor (thus, this is like saying "the White House wants it" or "the Kremlin wants it"). When Shagrat cannot explain why such a trifle is actually so significant, Gorbag scoffs, "Oho! So they haven't told you what to expect? They don't tell us all they know, do they? Not by half. But they can make mistakes, even the Top Ones can." The scene is revealing. These two commanders are hardly mindless drones, slaves to their masters' bidding, carrying out orders without question. Indeed, Shagrat is circumspect enough to note warily that Gorbag's statement is dangerous—in a whisper he says, "They may, but they've got eyes and ears everywhere"—and he urges them to slip into a recess to continue the discussion more freely. The gist of this conversation is that Shagrat and Gorbag have each noticed that "something has slipped," that the war may not be going as well as they had been led to believe, and that "big bosses"—namely, the fearsome Nazgûl or Ringwraiths and Sauron himself—are troubled by new developments. As Gorbag puts it, "ay, even the Biggest, can make mistakes. Something nearly slipped, you say. I say, something *has* slipped. And we've got to look out. Always the poor Uruks to put slips right, and small thanks."[28] Shagrat and Gorbag, both captains in the armies of Mordor, here appear as worried employees, not sure if their superiors are as competent as claimed, but absolutely certain that the decisions made by their bosses will directly affect them, likely for the worse. These are reasonable, and altogether human, concerns.

More human still, Shagrat and Gorbag grant themselves the limited space to imagine a life without "big bosses." As unseemly as their dream may be, it clearly expresses a desire for freedom, opportunity, and friendship that most readers—in another context, perhaps—would find laudable. After sparring over which was worse, serving under a Nazgûl or having to keep Shelob company, Gorbag concludes:

> "I'd like to try somewhere where there's none of 'em. But the war's on now, and when that's over things may be easier."
> "It's going well, they say."
> "They would," grunted Gorbag. "We'll see. But anyway, if it does go well, there should be a lot more room. What d'you say?—if we get a chance, you and me'll slip off and set up somewhere on our own with a few trusty lads, somewhere where there's good loot nice and handy, and no big bosses."
> "Ah!" said Shagrat. "Like old times."[29]

This might as well be the American Dream![30] Gorbag's hope for a future *if* the war goes well is underscored by Shagrat's nostalgia for the good old days. The message is clear: These orcs are not having any more fun than the men of Gondor, the elves of Rivendell, or the dwarves of the Iron Hills. War is Hell, for all parties involved.

An earlier scene offers further perspective on orcish cultures. After Merry and Pippen have been abducted by orcs and the Fellowship of the Ring disbanded, two prominent orc leaders debate the best course of action. Tolkien employs a kind of free indirect style to present Pippen's own limited perspective, which is how we learn that the orcs speak different languages or dialects, but they can also speak the *lingua franca* of all races in *The Lord of the Rings*. "One of the Orcs sitting near laughed and said something to a companion in their abominable tongue. 'Rest while you can, little fool!' he said then to Pippen, in the Common Speech, which he made almost as hideous as his own language." A bit later, Pippen hears many orcs speaking heatedly; to his surprise, "many of the Orcs were using the ordinary language. Apparently the members of two or three quite different tribes were present, and they could not understand one another's Orc-speech." As it turns out, there are at least three distinct groups, and each has its own priorities with respect to the mission.[31]

Uglúk, a commander of the Uruk-hai loyal to Saruman, insists that the prisoners be returned as quickly as possible to Isengard, Saruman's redoubt. Grishnákh, an orc from Barad-dûr (or Lugbúrz) who seems to be looking out for Sauron's interests, opposes him. A third group of unnamed, northern orcs, presumably of the same ilk as those who fought under Bolg's leadership the Battle of Five Armies or perhaps of the large community of "goblins" from the Misty Mountains in *The Hobbit*, aim to kill the prisoners and want nothing to do with the contest between the various powers in this world war. "We have come all the way from the Mines to kill, and avenge our folk. I wish to kill, and then go back north."[32] The three groups bandy about insults, calling the others *apes*, *swine*, *maggots*, and *fools*, employing the sort of language that might well have been used by disparate groups of humans in conflict. Uglúk and his elite forces win out, but clearly the "evil" so often mentioned in Tolkien is not nearly as monolithic as it is usually thought. Orcs, like men, may debate strategy, question authority, and dream of a better future. And orcs, like men, have different cultures, languages, and philosophies.

This applies to orcish morality and politics as well. Uglúk reminds the company that "these lands are dangerous: full of foul rebels and brigands."[33] Of course, he is referring to noble warriors like Éomer of the Rohirrim. As readers, we understand the reversal in meaning; when Uglúk says "rebel," we know that we should be on that rebel's side, as he is likely referring to the Rohirrim, whom the readers are positioned to admire. Similarly, when Gorbag makes reference to a "regular elvish trick,"[34] we see how an adjective used throughout *The Lord of the Rings* in a most positive sense would be employed in the pejorative by one whose people had been at war with the elves since ... well, forever. Significantly, this is not a reversal of values à la Milton's Satan ("Evil, be thou my good"), but rather a moral valuation consistent with that of elves, men, dwarves, and hobbits; all agree with orcs that a given characteristic—here, disloyalty—is immoral, and that trickery is not to be valued. These orcs do not call a thing "good" that an elf or man would call "bad" or "evil." Rather, orcs actually maintain the same values, and quite understandably they recognize their own enemies to be "bad" most of the time. As Shippey puts it, "Orcs here, and on other occasions, have a clear idea of what is admirable and what is contemptible behavior, which is exactly the same as ours."[35]

Human, All-Too-Human

Orcs reveal themselves in these scenes to have quite human qualities. Or rather, and perhaps against his own better judgment, Tolkien depicts orcs as having such qualities. Orcs seek wise leaders and freedom from tyranny. They want loyal companions ("trusty lads") as do Sam, Frodo, and the rest of our heroes. They want peace and a life without anxiety. Their open fear of "Whiteskins" and elf warriors falls directly in the same category as Gondor's fear of orcs, trolls, and other invaders. Remarkably, we find many instances in which orcs take captives alive and relatively unharmed (as with Merry and Pippin here, and Frodo later, as well as the dwarves in *The Hobbit*), but at no point do the heroic elves, dwarves, or men ever take a single orc hostage; rather, they are killed on sight and pursued unto death when they try to flee. Indeed, Uglúk's fear of the Whiteskins proves all too valid when the Éomer and his troops destroy them all, while "the keen-eyed Riders hunted down the few Orcs that had escaped."[36] As much as many readers wish to view orcs as mere monsters, evil ones at that, Tolkien himself depicts them as reasonably fearful, cautious, and canny with respect to those who are out to destroy them.

One might even go so far as to suggest that the Orcs are, at times, *more* humane than the heroic men, dwarves, hobbits, and elves appearing in *The Lord of the Rings*, at least when it comes to certain matters. For example, Frodo tells Sam that, while he was Shagrat's prisoner in the Tower of Cirith Ungol, he was given food by the orcs.[37] During their forced march toward Isengard, Uglúk gives Pippen a liquor or draught that, though unpleasant to taste (like many medicines), invigorates him; perhaps this elixir is the orcish equivalent of the elves' *miruvor*. Uglúk then rubs a salve into Merry's wound, essentially healing it: "[t]he gash in his forehead gave him no more trouble."[38] Of course, one might object that this "humane" treatment of the hostages is founded upon practical reasons having nothing to do with kindness: Shagrat needs to deliver his prisoner unspoiled to Sauron, and Uglúk needs to keep his captives alive but also requires that they to be able to run under their own power. Nevertheless, it is worth noting that in the many long wars and fearsome battles in the three Ages of Middle-earth, nowhere does Tolkien depict any kindly treatment towards orc prisoners-of-war on the part of elves, dwarves, men, or hobbits. Indeed, only a single orc is ever taken prisoner at all, even for the reasonable purposes of learning of enemy plans, but that one was brutally executed immediately after being "forced" to speak.[39] That one orc (goblin), and all others by the hundreds and thousands, are killed unceremoniously or with no remorse whatsoever.

This is not to say that orcs are "good" people. They are often horrid, and the violence and cruelty among them, towards others as well as among themselves, is well documented in those scenes in which they appear. Yet these baleful attributes are to be found in men as well, including among many of the "good" men in Tolkien's legendarium, not to mention among the more vexed characters to be found in those pages. Along similar lines, orcs can be extremely greedy, and in their desire for treasure (or loot) they can exhibit great rapaciousness. But if greed is a vice they have, in that too they are not unlike nearly all who inhabit Middle-earth, where the greed of dwarves and men is matched if not exceeded by the avaricious compulsion of the elves to keep things in a state of pure changelessness. In his repudiation of the idea of "Absolute Evil," discussed in the previous chapter, Tolkien also observes that there is not really an absolute "good"; although he would not countenance moral relativism, Tolkien's idea of "being good" derives from a political sense of being on the "right side," and he explains that "I have not made any of the peoples of the 'right' side, Hobbits, Rohirrim, Men of Dale or of Gondor, any better than men have been or are, or can be."[40] It stands to reason that, in turn, Tolkien has not made the orcs or the others on the "wrong" side particularly worse than people have been, are, or can be. In this, too, orcs are exhibited to be fundamentally human.

Owing to his religious beliefs, perhaps, Tolkien was reluctant to pronounce orcs "irredeemably bad,"[41] although he could not really envision any real salvation for them, unlike Gollum, who at least comes close to redemption, which makes Gollum one of *The Lord of the Rings*' most interesting characters. Tolkien affirms that, for him, "the most tragic moment in the Tale comes [...] when Sam fails to note the complete change in Gollum's tone and aspect," such that Gollum's "repentance is blighted and all Frodo's pity (in a sense) wasted."[42] It is another example of a character who only aims to do "good," in fact, perpetrating a terrible "evil." Moreover, Gollum is the one who, albeit inadvertently, destroys the ring and thus saves the world, something that so many of the "good" characters in the novel—including Bilbo, Gandalf, Tom Bombadil, Elrond, Galadriel, Aragorn, and Frodo himself—could not bring themselves to do. Hence, even the most "evil" creatures, in theory, ought to be redeemable. There is no transcendental or absolute principle that would preclude Uglúk or any other orcs from being redeemable as well. In various letters, Tolkien explicitly connects what we might call the spiritual condition of orcs to that of "real" humans, as when he states that the orcs "are fundamentally a race of 'rational incarnate' creatures, though horribly corrupted, if no more so than many Men to be met today." Also, he avers, that God would "tolerate" their corruption and remodeling by the Dark Lord "seems no worse theology than the toleration of the calculated dehumanizing of

Men by tyrants that goes on today."[43] Tolkien expressly locates orcs within the moral landscape of mankind more generally, and thus highlights the problem of treating them as a completely inferior and innately evil race of beings.

Furthermore, as a survivor of the Great War and the father of a Second World War veteran, Tolkien also exhibits a knowing ambivalence towards the horrors of battle. It is not coincidental that almost all orcs encountered are by training, in fact, or in effect *soldiers* of one sort or another. Even amid the tremendous bloodshed of his tales, there should be at least grudging respect for the orc soldiers and their fearsome battles with the heroes of the West, not to mention the struggles they face with their own leaders and colleagues. Writing during World War II, Tolkien famously stated, "I think the orcs as real a creation as anything in 'realistic' fiction […] only in real life they are on both sides, of course." He was writing to his son Christopher, then serving in the Royal Air Force and stationed in South Africa, who had complained bitterly about his fellow British soldiers, prompting his father to say, "Well, there you are: a hobbit amongst the Urukhai." Note that here, the "Urukhai" refers exclusively to the troops on Tolkien's own "side," not to the Germans or Japanese with whom they were at war. In another missive written three months later in 1944, Tolkien tells Christopher that, while "there are no genuine Uruks" that are completely irredeemable, there are some "human creatures" that seem to come close, for "I have met them, or thought so, in England's green and pleasant land."[44] Although Tolkien is not necessarily sympathizing with those he compares to orcs, he is certainly acknowledging the humanity of orcs. In fact, if anything, such persons are "all too human," to borrow Nietzsche's well known formulation.

Orcs' Untold Stories

Tolkien never seems to invite the reader to sympathize with the orcs directly, for he has no admirable characters who do so, but neither could he make them entirely inhuman or completely lacking in those characteristics which would allow for their possible redemption. At the same time, however, he could not go so far as to endorse their humanity, perhaps for reasons having to do more with narrative integrity than overall morality. It is true, as Shippey has pointed out, that a definitive recasting of the origins of the orcs and of their behaviors in the books "would have involved, to be consistent, a complete revision of all his earlier work."[45] However, imagining orcs in terms of their cultures, ethnicities, and basic humanity, as with the Easterlings and Southrons, the Dunlendings and the Drúedain, would go a long way toward alleviating some of the metaphysical problems posed by their treatment in the published writings, even if some of the more disturbing issues of race and racism would persist.

One might protest that in making my argument in this chapter I have been awfully selective in my emphases, that the orcs—regardless of whatever human qualities on display in these few passages—are horrible creatures, with utterly appalling characteristics and behavior. Yet that position is already well established, as it is the prevailing view of Tolkien's readers and of all of the heroes in Tolkien's work, not to mention the perspective afforded by the filmmakers in the adaptations of *The Lord of the Rings* and *The Hobbit*. In those two main scenes I have described, and in a number of other places here and there across Tolkien's legendarium, orcs can be viewed in a somewhat more nuanced way. Moreover, as we have seen from his own comments in letters and elsewhere, Tolkien remained uncomfortable with the spiritual status of the orcs in his writings. My purpose here is not to show how orcs are in fact good and not evil, but to trouble the facile assumption that they are inherently evil. Orcs, along with Gollum, Saruman, or even Sauron, are much more complex, and a proper consideration of the overall ethics and politics of Middle-earth will require moving beyond good and evil, to borrow another one of Nietzsche's evocative phrases.

Without giving this matter undue gravity,[46] I would mention that every appearance of orcs in Tolkien's legendarium is necessarily situated in a context that must present them in a bad light, owing to the elvish ideological position from which they are given. That is, the tales are told from the point of view of hobbits, elves, and the "noble" men of the West, and in Tolkien's marvelous conceit of the Red Book of Westmarch, they are even imagined as tales transmitted by the Eldar and the Númenoreans, translated by Bilbo Baggins in Rivendell, and supplemented by Bilbo, Frodo, and other hobbits later. From these perspectives, naturally, orcs would be demonized. (By contrast, the exchanges among orcs cited above demonstrate that the orcs depict their enemies in a similarly negative light, as when Gorbag refers to the Great Siege, during which Sauron was defeated and Isildur took the Ring as "the bad old times.") The perspective and orientation of the reader, who is definitively positioned as already anti-orc before the stories even begin, influences this discussion. One simply views orcs differently if they are established from the beginning as inherently evil.[47] Readers more attuned to possible injustices in the West—for example, readers not pleased by the imperialism of the Númenoreans in conquering the southlands and establishing Gondor to begin with, or by the lack of opportunity or social mobility for those not immortally established at the top of the hierarchy in Lothlórien or Rivendell (where Celeborn and

Galadriel and Elrond have ruled for thousands of years)—might be more open to the worldview and potential reforms in societies benefiting from a victorious Saruman or Sauron, if not a world in which, as Gorbag dreams of, there are no "Big Bosses" at all. Who knows? From the *orcs*' point of view, the War of the Ring may very well be seen as a war of Gondorian aggression against their own ways of life.[48] In these texts, Tolkien's orcs are given just enough humanity to make one wonder.

As Tolkien has explained, "it is the untold stories that are the most moving," and in the handful of scenes in Tolkien's legendarium that offer a glimmer of the orcs' perspectives on the world we get that "sudden sense of endless *untold* stories" that so fire the imagination and enchant the reader,[49] so long as that reader is willing to give orcs a chance. Hence, when you reread *The Hobbit* and *The Lord of the Rings* (or when you watch the films), by all means cheer on your doughty, good-natured hobbit heroes, respect the industrious and faithful dwarves, admire your wise and beautiful elf leaders, and celebrate the courage and skill of the noble human warriors. But also, in some small part of your imagination, raise a glass to Shagrat and Gorbag, to Uglúk and Grishnákh, to Bolg and Azog, and to some billion unnamed but "rational, incarnate creatures" who struggle to make a life worth living in this perilous realm. Perhaps, in some divine plan only hinted at in their own metaphysics, it is the orcs who will inherit Middle-earth.

CHAPTER 7

Demonizing the Enemy

Monstrosity, Ethics, and the Sense of the World Wars

In his magisterial study of the First World War, Paul Fussell elaborated upon the logic that seemed to underwrite a soldier's ability or willingness to kill his fellow man. Fussell pointed to what he called "gross dichotomizing," which he identified as "a persisting imaginative habit of modern times, traceable, it would seem, to the actualities of the Great War." As he explained,

> "We" are all here on this side; "the enemy" is over there. "We" are individuals with names and personal identities; "he" is a mere collective identity. We are visible; he is invisible. We are normal; he is grotesque. Our appurtenances are natural; his, bizarre. He is not as good as we are. Indeed, he may be like "the Turk" on the Gallipoli Peninsula, characterized by a staff officer before the British landings there as "an enemy who has never shown himself as good a fighter as the white man." Nevertheless, he threatens us and must be destroyed, or, if not destroyed, contained and disarmed.[1]

The racial distinction, of course, is part of the demonization of the enemy as well—Fussell's quotation of the British officer comes from Robert Rhodes James's *Gallipoli* (1965)[2]—but racial difference explains little about the gross dichotomizing Fussell identifies, particularly as the "sides" in question were equally "white," that is, British and German. (It is worth recalling that the British Royal Family itself *was* German, and during the war, in June 1917 specifically, King Georg V cannily opted to change the family's ancestral moniker from the rather Teutonic-sounding House of Saxe-Coburg and Gotha [i.e., *Haus Sachsen-Coburg und Gotha*] to a more English-like House of Windsor, owing to quite understandable anti–German sentiment in the United Kingdom at the time.) Fussell goes on to quote British soldiers apparently in awe of the enemy's "monstrous and grotesque" attributes. "Sometimes the shadowy enemy resembled the vilest animals," with enemy soldiers being compared to water-rats scrambling into their holes or earwigs scattering under a rotten tree stump. Fussell notes that descriptions of the German dead frequently mentioned the bodies' porcine qualities.³ All of this contributes to the general idea that one's wartime enemy is not entirely human.

At the very moment when these impressions were being felt and expressed by many of his fellow enlisted men, a young soldier in the Lancashire Fusiliers was working on what he referred to as "my nonsense fairy language."⁴ J.R.R. Tolkien was developing this language in connection with an elaborate series of connected myths, a legendarium in which fair but tragic elves and bold but equally tragic men took up arms against an insuperably powerful evil Enemy, one whose "vilest deed," it could be said, was to create the demonic race of orcs.⁵ As Tolkien later confessed to his son, while the latter was serving in the Royal Air Force during the *next* world war, part of the urgency with which he wrote these tales emerged from a longing to make sense of the terrible world in which he was living, to express his "*feeling* about good, evil, fair, foul in some way: to rationalize it, and prevent it just festering."⁶ Tolkien encouraged his son to write, as a way of dealing with these pains that come with serving as a common soldier in a great war. As he continued,

> [i]n my case it generated Morgoth and the History of the Gnomes [i.e., the earliest versions of the "Silmarillion"]. Lots of the early parts of which (and the languages)—discarded or absorbed—were done in grimy canteens, at lectures in cold fogs, in huts full of blasphemy and smut, or by candle light in the bell-tents, even some down in dugouts under shell fire. It did not make for efficiency and present-mindedness, of course, and I was not a good officer.⁷

Tolkien may have neglected some of his duties as an officer, but his urgent *mythopoeia* and desire for narrative helped him to make sense of his own horrid condition and of the world more broadly. Most wars involves some aspect of senselessness, few more so than "the war to end all wars" in which Tolkien found himself, but storytelling is an inherently sense-making practice, and Tolkien's "Silmarillion" helped him give form to the chaos surrounding him, if only provisionally and through his art.

Tolkien does not here, or really anywhere else in his letters, demonize Britain's or the Allies' wartime enemies. He has too much respect for Germanic cultures—though not for Nazis, whom he blamed for perverting and abusing the majestic Nordic mythologies and folklore to serve their own foul ideological ends—to imagine the German soldiers as subhuman.⁸ John Garth has suggested otherwise, noting that Tolkien during World War I may have connected his idea of goblins (also known as orcs) and trolls to Germans, particularly in his earliest version of "The Fall of Gondolin," but Garth concedes that "Tolkien later insisted there was no parallel between the Goblins he had invented and the Germans he had fought, declaring 'I've never had those sorts of feelings about the Germans. I'm very anti that kind of thing.'"[9] Moreover, as a combat veteran of "the Great War," Tolkien arguably had too much respect for the common soldier on either side of the lines of battle to envision them as inhuman, animal-like, or unworthy of life. Even during and after World War II, Tolkien expressed anger at those in England who called for destroying the Germans, stating that "[t]he Germans have just as much a right to declare the Poles and Jews exterminable vermin, subhuman, as we have to select the Germans: in other words, no right, whatever they have done."[10]

Nevertheless, as I discussed in the last chapter, Tolkien's legendarium quite literally demonizes the enemy in the form of orcs, a race treated as monstrous, inferior, savage, and in need of annihilation by the more "heroic" characters in *The Hobbit*, *The Lord of the Rings*, and *The Silmarillion*. If Tolkien's fantasy narratives required the presence of orcs in order to have a distinctively demonized enemy for the heroes to battle, it was certainly not a matter of substituting orcs for Germans or any other real-world enemy of England's during the world wars. Indeed, in one of the few instances among his wartime letters in which he refers to orcs metaphorically, Tolkien does so only to note that "in real life they are on both sides, of course."[11] Janet Brennan Croft has analyzed the manner by which Tolkien's use and characterization of the orcs parallels the demonization of the enemy in wartime, and she specifically connects Fussell's observations with Tolkien's own.[12] However, Croft also examines Tolkien's misgivings about the demonization of the enemy, whom he could not find utterly irredeemable, which led him to revise his ideas about the orcs over the years, often in the attempt to make them less worthy of sympathy by denying their free will and humanity. But still, the stories required enemies to be clearly demarcated as such, and the orcs served that purpose. Tolkien's desire for narrative, as it might be called, is not informed by a need to demonize the enemy, but by a need to make *sense* of the war and the world in which it is waged.

In this chapter I want to discuss these two elements of the wartime narrative impulse in terms of modern fantasy's effectiveness as a means for imagining the world system as whole, but especially in the context of World Wars I and II. The demonization of the enemy is, I believe, a critical element of *Realpolitik*; if it is so useful in wartime, that is in part because of its intensely practical political value, war after all being merely the continuation of politics by other means, as Carl von Clausewitz famously put it. As such, the practice is subject to political critique. But the demonization of the enemy is also a crucial element in formulating incidents, persons, and events into a cognizable narrative, and this narrative impulse in turn shapes the way in which the world and everything in it is understood. Narrative is, in this manner, a sense-making system, and the more readily elements within a narrative can be assimilated into identifiable tropes, themes, categories, and patterns, the more easily the purportedly underlying reality can be given shape and made meaningful.

Manufacturing Monsters

Demonizing the enemy makes for a pragmatic short-cut for overcoming the genuine apprehension of confusion and complexity by offering a simplistic, straightforward identity, which in turn serves as its own justification for action and reaction. The development, deployment, and legacy of Tolkien's orcs, which function in both *The Hobbit* (where they are referred to as *goblins*) and *The Lord of the Rings* as enemies to be dispatched without the slightest hint of moral compunction, offer a case study in the literal demonization of the enemy, but Tolkien's orcs also suggest ways in which this facile demonization can inspire meaningful critique of the very system they were meant to help make visible. The basic humanity of Tolkien's inhuman creatures invites readers to question the racial and moral hierarchies presented in the narratives themselves, and also in the world we live in.

Again, I do not mean to suggest that Tolkien used orcs or other enemies as allegorical counterparts to any "real-world" enemies fighting in the world wars. As I discuss in the next section, Tolkien was extremely wary of such demonization of the enemy, particularly when connected to race, even though his own racialized rhetoric and descriptions in *The Lord of the Rings* can be problematic at times. The orcs of *The Lord of the Rings* most certainly do not represent German, Italian, Russian, or Japanese soldiers, and Tolkien makes clear in his wartime letters to his son Christopher that the "real" orcs, viewed metaphorically as violent, boorish, uncivilized persons, would be well represented in every country in the world. Yet, in the fantasy writings for which he is most famous, the orc stands out among the various enemies—a category that includes "evil" men, as well as such traditional monsters as dragons, trolls, fell beasts (wolves, for instance), and god-like villains, Morgoth or Sauron—as a special case of demonization.

Contrary to much popular belief, Tolkien did not create the race of orcs, although his writings did more to shape the characteristic images of these creatures in fantasy novels, films, and video games than perhaps any other twentieth-century writer. As Tolkien himself noted, the word *orc* appears in Old English, where it had the apparent meaning of "demon."[13]

Indeed, the word *orcnéas* appears in *Beowulf*, where Tolkien translated it "haunting shapes of hell." In Tolkien's overall legendarium, orcs emerge as the mortal enemies of the primordial elves, later men (although some men fight alongside the orcs), and sometimes dwarves (but in *The Hobbit*, it is suggested that some "wicked" dwarves had made alliances with orcs or goblins). Their primary narrative function seems limited to the role of cannon fodder for the enemy's war machine, and orc regiments form the rank-and-file of Morgoth's armies in *The Silmarillion*, while also representing a core of both Sauron's and Saruman's armies in *The Lord of the Rings*. Interestingly enough, whether affiliated with "Bolg of the North" or the goblins of the Misty Mountains, the orcs in *The Hobbit* appear to fight for *themselves*, not for any "Big Bosses," as two memorable orcs in *The Lord of the Rings* will later refer to them. As enemy soldiers within the narratives, the orcs are certainly demonized, but Tolkien's writings concerning the origins and character of the orcs make it clear that he does not view them as literal demons.

Tolkien's published and posthumously released writings give different accounts of the origins of orcs within Middle-earth, but for the most part he did not imagine them to be *demons* in the traditional sense of the word. In order to understand to role of orcs in his writings, one first needs to get a basic understanding of the broader mythological system upon which Tolkien's narratives rest. In Tolkien's mythology, which is ascribed to the beliefs and histories of the elves, there is one god, Eru or Ilúvatar, but from him emanates an infinite number of god-like, or perhaps angelic, beings known as the Ainur. At the beginning of the world, some of these Ainur descended to Arda (i.e., the planet Earth), and the mightiest of them formed the pantheon of Tolkien's myths, the Valar or "powers" of the Earth. Lesser Ainur, but still very powerful god-like beings, also came to Arda, and many of these served the Valar in one capacity or another. These were the Maiar, whose numbers includes such famous characters as Gandalf, Saruman, and Sauron. The most mighty of all the Ainur was Melkor, whom the elves later named Morgoth, a great Satan-figure for these mythic narratives. Melkor seduced many of the lesser Ainur into his own service, Sauron most significantly; some of these evil demigods took the form of monsters, with the balrogs (also known as "demons of might") and possibly even dragons are among the most striking examples.[14] It is well worth noting that, here in the early characterizations of these creatures, Tolkien might have chosen to list orcs among the lesser Ainur as well, effectively making them minor demons or devils, fighting alongside the balrogs, for example, but he does not. Far from considering the balrog a kindred spirit or even ally, for instance, the orcs of Moria in *The Lord of the Rings* seem to fear it and flee from it.[15] However, Tolkien's characterization of orcs and his speculations as to their origins show that he was not comfortable assigning them the role of the actual demon, even if his narratives seemed to require that these creatures be thoroughly demonized later.

Regarding the origins of orcs, perhaps it is telling that even Tolkien changed his mind over time, as he seemed uneasy about the ways in which they fit into the mythic histories of Middle-earth. The standard view is that orcs were once elves, who through various means had somehow become ugly, violent, uncouth, and altogether monstrous. As *The Silmarillion* relates the matter, the elves "by slow arts of cruelty were corrupted and enslaved; thus did Melkor breed the hideous race of the Orcs in envy and mockery of the Elves."[16] In *The Lord of the Rings*, the authority of Treebeard is asserted, as he explains to his hobbit guests, Merry and Pippin, that "Trolls are only counterfeits, made by the Enemy in the Great Darkness, in mockery of Ents, as Orcs were of Elves."[17] Elsewhere in *The Silmarillion*, there is also the surmise that orcs actually *were* elves, specifically the Avari or Dark Elves, which is to say, the ones who did not migrate to the holy realm of Valinor, which is what distinguished the Light Elves from the Dark. As Tolkien writes, "[w]hence they [the orcs] came, or what they were, the Elves knew not then, thinking them perhaps to be Avari who had become evil and savage in the wild; in which they guessed all too near, it is said."[18] If orcs were merely another race of elves, however, it would be much more difficult for their demonization to be secured and their annihilation to be met with such universal approval. At least, one would hope so.

The hypothesis that orcs are simply different races or types of elves probably does make the most sense in accordance with Tolkien's overall legendarium, if only because orcs appear in these tales after elves but before men, and the special hatred that the elves bear toward orcs suggests some kind of ancestral if not personal grudge at the heart of the conflict. However, as Dimitra Fimi has elaborated, "the thought that the hideous and malicious Orcs were once Elves—the 'highest' beings of Middle-earth—became increasingly unbearable to Tolkien."[19] In fact, Tolkien entertained a number different ideas regarding the origins and characters of his orcs. Of the more bizarre explanations, Tolkien briefly considered the possibility that orcs were automatons, robots or puppets controlled by Morgoth or Sauron, without free will, languages, or thoughts of their own. This was an admittedly unlikely scenario, especially after readers had already been exposed to various goblins and orcs in *The Hobbit* and *The Lord of the Rings* who clearly had their own views, spoke independently of their "masters," or had no masters at all. Whatever else orcs may be, they are most assuredly sentient; moreover, the orcs we meet in Tolkien's writings are imbued with fears, desires, values, families, languages, and even cultures.

Tolkien did toy with the idea that orcs might be lesser Maia, which was certainly possible given that balrogs were already so understood, but he abandoned that notion as well. It seems that the orcs were far too *human* to be categorized definitively as either angels or demons.

If one had to make a case for which of the various origins stories were most likely to be believed by Tolkien himself, the best bet seems to be that orcs are some form of human being. Rather than being tortured, twisted, or corrupted versions of elves, they were more likely corruptions of men. There is one crucial philosophical or religious point in the various arguments concerning the origin of orcs that clearly troubled even Tolkien himself. To wit, their very existence shows they have value and are worthy of being. To put it another, less formal way, one could say that by their very nature, it seems, orcs must have souls, and being so endowed means that they must be, in theory at least, redeemable. By their very existence, then, orcs cannot be viewed as literal demons, yet in the stories, they are demonized throughout and dispatched thoroughly without pause or pity.

The extent to which the orcs are demonized, by the other characters if not by the author himself, can be measured by the vastly different treatment of orcs when compared to other characters. Notoriously, in the midst of terrible bloodshed in the Battle of Helm's Deep and in the Battle of Pelennor Fields, Legolas and Gimli maintain a friendly competition to see who can kill the most orcs. This grisly entertainment would seem almost inhuman were it not for the demonization of the enemy in this case. Contrast the positive glee these heroes express when killing orcs to the famous scene in which Sam for the first time witnesses a battle between armies of men. Looking upon the corpse of a "swarthy" Southron soldier, who had been cut down while fleeing, his "brown hand" still clutching a broken sword, Sam "wondered what the man's name was and where he came from; and if he was really evil at heart, or what lies or threats had led him on his long march from his home; and if he would not really have rather stayed home in peace."[20] In *The Lord of the Rings*, Sam witnesses orcs both living and dead, but never does he wonder about their motivations and preferences, and needless to say, despite frequently longing for home and peace himself, Sam never considers what potential "lies and threats" have brought his own friends to wage war on diverse peoples and races of the South and East. Later, after the war had ended, Aragorn (now King Elessar) releases the Easterlings who had surrendered on the battlefield, makes peace with the swarthy men of the South, and frees the thralls of Mordor, granting them lands in that region,[21] but no reference is made to any such accommodations or humane treatment of orcs. Likewise, after the Battle of Helm's Deep, "[n]o Orcs remained alive; their bodies were uncounted," but the "wild men" of Dunland who had fought alongside those Orcs were pardoned.²² Tolkien thus emphasizes the difference between the treatment of orcs and that of men, even where the men in question are enemies.

No pardons, forgiveness, or even sympathy is offered to any orc in these texts. Moreover, living orcs are not taken hostage or held as prisoners of war by the heroes, not even for the legitimate purposes of gathering information. Instead, the heroes happily slaughter the enemy even as they recognize the baleful effects of war on men and elves. Within these pages, Tolkien's characters may view even humans in the service of "evil" as being potentially good, as with Frodo's sympathy and kind treatment of the treacherous renegade Wormtongue, for example. Gollum is an "evil" enemy to be pitied and rehabilitated, and Gandalf reprimands Frodo for even suggesting that Gollum "deserves" death. Even Saruman is forgiven by Gandalf, who attempts to enlist him in their service, and when Saruman dies, Frodo pities him and mourns his death.

All orcs who can be killed are killed, and it is somehow assumed that the orcs in the armies of Mordor simply die off after the ring was destroyed; as noted above, that seems rather unlikely given what the reader would have gleaned about orcs and their character from earlier scenes. If anything, orcs may well have celebrated their liberation from Sauron's big bossiness, and those who were never in Sauron's service would have probably rejoiced to see an end to the war. Tolkien somehow manages to give the reader enough information about orcs and their desires to make these surmises at least possible, if not wholly plausible, but then he bizarrely pulls the rug out from under us, stating that, after the destruction of the One Ring, orcs "ran hither and thither mindless; and some slew themselves, or cast themselves into pits, or fled wailing back to hide in holes and dark lightless places far from hope."²³ That certainly does not sound like the sort of thing that would be done by the orcs readers had met earlier in the novels, most of whom expressed a longing for being left alone by not only elves and dwarves, but by "bosses" of all stripes. Nevertheless, and despite ample opportunities throughout his novels to show sympathy toward the orcs, the reigning assumption of the "good" characters in *The Hobbit* and *The Lord of the Rings* that orcs must be inherently evil, demons to the end.

Sympathy for the Devils

If Tolkien's orcs appear to be merely one-dimensionally evil beings, or even worse, simplistic and racist caricatures, it is worth noting that Tolkien himself had his concerns about the matter. For example, Shippey has pointed out that, "though he became increasingly concerned over the implications of the orcs in his story, and tried out several explanations for them, their analogousness to humanity always remained clear."[24] Elsewhere Shippey had conceded that "Orcs entered Middle-earth originally just because the story needed a continual supply of enemies over whom one need feel no compunction,"[25] but Tolkien could apparently not resist "fleshing out" these default enemies with almost the same sort of cultural and historical detail with which he had made his elves and men so compelling.

For one thing, as noted above, Tolkien gives different groups of orcs distinctive cultures, languages, and even families. Orcs can bear grudges and be motivated by vengeance just as humans can. Shippey even points out that the basic sense of morality (e.g., their views of good and evil) aligns with that of the heroes, even if, in practice, the orcs engage in what appear to be immoral activities. As Shippey puts it, the orcs "have a clear idea of what is admirable and what is contemptible behavior, which is exactly the same as ours."[26] Far from being mindless drones, orcs are "rational, incarnate beings," with what we might recognize as deeply *human* feelings. As I discussed in the last chapter, later in *The Two Towers*, Tolkien depicts a scene in which two orc captains are discussing the war that they find themselves waging, and each expresses his concerns over its potential failure, doubting the word of their own leaders as to its inevitable success and complaining about the circumstances of their own service. Moreover, these two express the sincere desire to live free, without "Big Bosses" to rule them, which is a far cry from the notion that all orcs are mindless slaves or minions. True, the freedom they seek is to become itinerant raiders and pillagers, but their desire for autonomy and independence clearly indicates that they are all too human, and not merely creatures controlled by the "dark" powers. In fact, by complaining about their jobs and their supervisors, these orc soldiers seem more realistically human than most of the heroic men fighting against the armies of Isengard or Mordor.

Of course, the question of race is part of the problem when examining the role of orcs in Tolkien's world. In this fantasy universe, the "races" usually involve types of beings, such that elves, men, and dwarves each constitute a separate race, yet within these racial categories, there exist other racialized hierarchies: Calaquendi (light elves) *versus* Moriquendi (dark elves), for instance, or even the various elven kinship groups, such as the Vanyar, the Noldor, the Teleri, and so on. Orcs may well be merely corrupted men or perhaps another race of men, of course, but even limiting the discussion to those beings called "men" in Middle-earth, Tolkien clearly distinguishes a number of different racially identifiable cultures and creates hierarchies among them. In *The Lord of the Rings*, Faramir offers a "Gondorian theory of anthropology" (as Virginia Luling has called it): "For so we reckon Men in our lore, calling them the High, or Men of the West, which were Númenoreans; and the Middle Peoples, Men of the Twilight, such as are the Rohirrim and their kin that dwell still far in the North; and the Wild, the Men of Darkness."[27] However, regardless of the specific culture or kinship group they belong to, orcs are almost invariably described as "swart" and "slant-eyed," to the extent that one cannot help finding the characterization offensive at times, all the more so if one is familiar with Tolkien's description of orcs as being Mongol-like in appearance. In a 1958 letter, Tolkien averred that the "Orcs are definitely stated to be corruptions of the 'human' form seen in Elves and Men. They are (or were) squat, broad, flat-nosed, sallow-skinned, with wide mouths and slant eyes: in fact degraded and repulsive versions of the (to Europeans) least lovely Mongol-type."[28] By granting that orcs bore the appearance of Mongols or east Asians, Tolkien emphasizes their basic humanity even as he underscored their profound Otherness when compared to the Northern European physical types comprising his various heroes. Although the racial stereotyping is problematic, this nevertheless allows readers to see orcs as discernibly human, if also demonized by their enemies.[29]

Admittedly, Tolkien's own texts are somewhat inconsistent on this matter. For example, even though *The Hobbit* and *The Lord of the Rings* contain scenes in which orcs are shown to operate in well-organized societies, ones that can be completely independent of such "bosses" as Saruman and Sauron, for example, the story manages to kill off or otherwise render nonexistent the entire race of orcs after the War of the Ring has ended. Indeed, the aforementioned bizarre scene where orcs mindlessly run off or slay themselves, there is no further mention of orcs at all, not even among Saruman's ruffians in "The Scouring of the Shire."[30] Orcs simply disappear as soon as the Ring is destroyed. Needless to say, such a fate makes little sense given the conversations already depicted among the orcs, but this does serve the narrative function of allowing the war to end at the very moment that Sauron's power is overthrown. Such a fantasy makes for a neat, simple narrative of victory or defeat, and allows the characters to avoid the long, messy aftermath of battle, and the far more complicated process of rebuilding and reorganizing the geopolitical frameworks of a postwar world. And yet, to Tolkien's credit, he does include elements of the postwar aftermath, from Aragorn's reestablishment of his kingdom in Gondor to the need to purge the Shire of Saruman's treachery. Nevertheless, for reasons that do not truly fit with the otherwise "realistic" aspects of Tolkien's fantasy world, there seems to be no way of imagining a postwar Middle-earth that include orcs in it.

Tolkien was reluctant to pronounce orcs "irredeemably bad," although he could not really envision any real salvation for them, but even the most evil creatures, in theory, ought to have redeeming qualities. Undoubtedly, the vast majority of Tolkien's readers do not necessarily sympathize with the orcs directly, but they can hardly have missed scenes such as those I have discussed, in which the basic humanity of orcs, in both the good and bad senses of the word "human," is on display. However, the narrative structure and plot requires an endless supply of enemies to be defeated, in which case the literal demonization of the enemy—orcs *as* demons— serves a valuable purpose. As Shippey has pointed out, recasting the origins of the orcs and of their behaviors in the books "would have involved, to be consistent, a complete revision of all his earlier work."[31] Honestly, I am not so convinced, for I see little reason beyond a profoundly racist dehumanization of these otherwise "humane" beings (a term used by Tolkien himself in reference to all "speaking creatures")[32] why orcs could not be treated as the Dunlendings, Easterlings, or Haradrim are, as enemies to be defeated, not as a race to be annihilated. The bloodlust of the heroes who express their eagerness to kill and delight in killing orcs is likely the biggest problem that arises in imagining orcs as human beings, but then such demonization of the enemy is common enough in wartime. The unlikely end of the orcs at the conclusion of the War of the Ring allows for the sort of narrative closure that most real-world wars cannot. Here demonization becomes a "strategy of containment," as Fredric Jameson famously called it in *The Political Unconscious*, which ideologically delimits the narrative field in order to make the story more easily comprehended.[33]

After the Wars

Tolkien's two great completed works of fantasy feature warfare, but in each case, the depiction of the fighting is mostly ambiguous. In *The Hobbit*, for example, the Battle of Five Armies would appear to be the climactic event of the novel, except that most of it takes place, as it were, off camera, since the protagonist and eponymous hero, Bilbo Baggins, is knocked unconscious early on in the great skirmish. When he awakens, the war is over, and the leader of the "good" forces, the dwarf King Thorin Oakenshield, lies wounded and dying, hanging on only long enough to express his admiration for the hobbit's humility, peacefulness, and love of simple things like food and the comforts of home. Not that Tolkien himself is a pacifist exactly; he seems to recognize that some wars may be necessary, and in any case, like Kurt Vonnegut, he knows that wars are inevitable so long as humans are imbued with their all-too-human nature. But Tolkien certainly does not celebrate warfare, nor does he delight in it. Faramir likely voices his opinion best, when he says "I do not love the bright sword for its sharpness, nor the arrow for its swiftness, nor the warrior for his glory. I love only that which they defend."³⁴ Good warriors and leaders, such as Aragorn, do their fighting out of a sense of duty and at need, but do not seek renown on the battlefield. In *The Lord of the Rings*, both Éowyn and Théoden come to realize that their desire for glory in battle was wrongheaded, and, while many characters are regarded as great warriors, they generally fight only when necessary, taking little pleasure in the fighting. (Here, again, Legolas's and Gimli's cruel orc-killing game stands out in sharp relief to the more sober, even grim sense of duty seen in Aragorn, Faramir, or Gandalf.) As noted above, King Elessar actually forgives the people (i.e., the men, but not orcs) of Mordor, allowing them to live and to thrive in their homelands. Only the demons, the demonized enemies, are dispensed with at the conclusion of Tolkien's two novels. Their defeat, presumably, must be total and, indeed, genocidal.

It is not so simple in the real world, after all. The rank artificiality of these forms of demonization becomes all the more apparent when a given conflict ends and the ideological commitments of a postwar political order are established. Almost immediately after World War II, within days or weeks (at most) of the end of the hostilities in Europe and the Pacific, the American people were expected not only to stop demonizing the Germans and the Japanese, but to offer sympathy and aid to them. At the same moment, many people in the United States, France, and Great Britain found that they were now supposed to shift their allegiances sharply away from former Allies, such as the Russians, which in some cases required "demonizing" their erstwhile friends.

Studs Terkel's monumental oral history of World War II, *The Good War*, details some of these paradoxes. As Dellie Hahne, a retired music teacher and one of Terkel's interlocutors, recalled,

> The OWI, Office of War Information, did a thorough job of convincing us our cause was unquestionably right. We were stopping Hitler, and you look back at it and you had to stop him. We were saving the world. We were allied with Russia, which was great at that time. Germany had started World War One and now it had started World War Two, and Germans would be wiped off the face of the map. A few years later, when we started to arm Germany, I was so shocked. I'd been sold a bill of goods—I couldn't believe it. [...] As soon as the war was over we dropped Russia. During the war, I never heard any anti-Russia talk.³⁵

It is remarkable how quickly, in the minds of the public, an ally can become an enemy and *vice versa*, but Hahne goes on say that her "disillusionment was so great, that was the beginning of distrusting my own government."³⁶

To offer another example from the same moment, consider a statement from a well-known journalist, the *Chicago Tribune*'s Mike Royko.

Royko was too young to fight in World War II, but he fought in the Korean War, where he saw clearly just how absurdly insubstantial the earlier demonization of the enemy had been. "I didn't know anyone who was in Korea who understood what the hell we were doing there," he told Terkel, adding,

> We were over there fighting the Chinese, you know? Christ, I'd been raised to think the Chinese were among the world's most heroic people and our great friends. [...] I was still mad at the Japs. The Japanese are now our friends, our pals. I'm going from Japan to Korea, where I'm supposed to fight the Chinese, who are now our enemies. A few years earlier, I was mad at the Japanese and I was supposed to love the Chinese. Now I gotta love the Japanese and hate the Chinese. [Laughs.] That's when I decided something's wrong.[37]

One of the most telling things about these observations is that both Hahne and Royko, in their moment of revelation, discovered that "something's wrong," which in turn caused them to distrust their own government, as well as other sources of information, when they saw the eerie reversibility of the demonization of the enemy.

The propaganda of the war machine finds outlets throughout mass culture, not merely through the news media or official government reports. In Terkel's *The Good War*, legendary film critic Pauline Kael complained about the egregious representation of the enemy in films from that period. Films, like novels and other forms of narrative, helped to shape the way both allies and enemies would be viewed, which in turn shaped how the entire narrative of the war would be understood. As Kael put it,

> Oh, I hated the war movies, because they robbed the enemy of any humanity or individuality. In all these films you were supposed to learn a lesson: even the German or the Japanese who happened to be your friend, even the one who was sympathetic, had to be killed because he was just as dirty as the others. Even those who were trapped trying to save American lives were weaklings and untrustworthy. We had stereotypes of a shocking nature. They could never be people, who were just caught in the army the same way Americans were and told what to do. They always had to be decadent, immoral people, sneaks.[38]

The demonization of the enemy, while quite effective for ideological purposes (which is also to say, for *narrative* purposes), rings hollow to those who can read beyond the surfaces. But in oversimplifying matters, this trope also made the war all the more cognizable or *sensible* to the soldiers and, moreover, to the average citizen.

Tolkien's depiction of the orcs at the end of *The Lord of the Rings* is, in my view, clearly an error, given what the reader would have gleaned about orcs and their cultures in those revealing moments of the novel in which orcs are observed talking amongst themselves. Moreover, Tolkien's presentation of the orcs' origins in *The Silmarillion* and other posthumously published writings indicates that he was well aware of their "humanity," if we may call it such. Yet in creating the orcs as a race to be demonized in wartime, Tolkien demonstrates the perverse effectiveness of this form. He also proved himself able to see beyond the mere demonization of the enemy, by showing that whatever demonic or orcish behavior there was to be found in the world, it was not limited to the ranks of the enemies. As he famously put it in a wartime letter to his son Christopher, "I think the orcs as real a creation as anything in 'realistic' fiction," before adding, "only in real life they are on both sides, of course."[39]

Tolkien's perhaps unconscious sympathy for the orcs, as a demonized enemy, clearly affected his view of the moral or immoral attitudes of his own countrymen. He feared that, in their delight in humiliating their enemies, they too were becoming "orc-like," which at that point indicates less of a racial characteristic *per se* and more of a strictly behavioral and intellectual one. Tolkien emphasizes their contempt for the beautiful and the orderly, along with their cruelty and hard-heartedness. Tolkien was angered by the "gloating" of the English in their impending victory over the Germans, comparing their attitude to those who not only want to execute a criminal, but also "to gloat, or to hang his wife and child by him while the orc-crowd hooted."[40] As we see, many of Tolkien's fictional heroes gloat over the deaths of orcs, but none feel any shame for so doing, which may show the degree to which they are themselves more orc-like than they imagine.

The acknowledgment that "there are orcs on both sides" cannot stand long without calling into question the entire ideological program associated with demonizing the enemy, which at least suggests a crack in the armor, a scarcely visible yet undoubtedly real utopian element in the martial narratives of both Tolkien's fantasy novels and the stories of the world wars. From this fissure, one can imagine, might emerge a more powerful sense of sympathy with one's fellow man, during times of war and times of peace, in which the demonic characteristics for the moment evanesce, and the face of our shared humanity shines forth. In this moment, our fellow "orcishness" may also be acknowledged, along with the profound desire for freedom from "Big Bosses" and other repressive authorities. That Tolkien allows this image of freedom to be voiced by disgruntled orc soldiers, Shagrat and Gorbag, indicates his own, perhaps unconscious sense that "both sides" deserve respect and sympathy.

Chapter 8

"Places where the stars are strange"
Fantasy, Utopia, and Critique

In the opening lines of *J.R.R. Tolkien: Author of the Century*, Tom Shippey observes that "the dominant literary mode of the twentieth century has been the fantastic," and—after listing such writers as H.G. Wells, George Orwell, William Golding, Kurt Vonnegut, Ursula Le Guin, and Thomas Pynchon—Shippey notes that, "[b]y the end of the century, even authors deeply committed to the realist novel have often found themselves unable to resist the gravitational pull of the fantastic as a literary mode."[1] The rise of fantasy as a genre, almost certainly among the most popular genres of literature and popular culture today, is itself one of the significant features of twentieth-century literary history, on par with (and, perhaps, not unrelated to) the development of modernism in the late-nineteenth and early-twentieth century. Beyond the question of genre or subgenre, however, the fantastic as a discourse or mode permeates "high" literature as well as "low." The modernism of William Butler Yeats or James Joyce finds itself infused with Celtic, Greek, or medieval mythologies, just as the advent of magical realism in Gabriel García Márquez or Julio Cortázar has uncovered the interrelations of the fantastic and the realistic in everyday life, and the postmodern extravagancies of a John Barth or Georges Perec disclose that the lines between imaginary and real are at best oscillatory, provisional, and uncertain. All of these, and many more, partake of the fantastic, sometimes in more or less obvious ways. As Kathryn Hume has made clear in her magnificent *Fantasy and Mimesis: Responses to Reality in Western Literature*, the fantastic and the imitative or realistic modes "seem more usefully viewed as the twin impulses behind the creation of literature."[2] In any event, the overlapping territories of fantasy and *mimesis* are significant features of the literary and critical landscape of our time.

The somewhat defensive tone of Shippey's arguments, as well as the implied defensiveness in Hume's, appears a bit justified when confronting critics who would insist upon more clearly mimetic or realistic literature.

However, some the harshest critics of fantasy are not so much the proponents of a sober realism, as they are readers whose own preferred forms of creating imaginary worlds are set in opposition to Tolkien's mythmaking and mapping of Middle-earth, not to mention the many and varied successors to Tolkienian fantasy. In particular, I am thinking of the distinction frequently made between fantasy and science fiction, in particular the politically oriented science fiction associated with utopia. Champions of the latter, as a discourse or a genre, often resist and even condemn fantasy as a retrograde, reactionary, immature, or unworthy approach to the otherworldly. Utopia, which had appeared to be a quintessentially modern genre and discourse, has reasserted itself in recent decades. I myself have argued for the persistence of utopia in postmodernity, and the utopian impulse may have found its moment in the era of globalization, ironic perhaps given the widespread dystopianism in our time.[3] The idea that fantasy and utopia are incompatible or opposed strikes me as false, although this notion permeates the discussions of these ostensibly related discourses. In this chapter, I examine the utopian critique of fantasy, specifically with regard to Tolkien's imaginary world or "Other-world,"[4] and I want to take up the challenge of our era's greatest utopian critic, Fredric Jameson, who has provided one of the most authoritative critical voices in distinguishing utopia from fantasy. The fantastic world of Middle-earth is not so neatly defined as some anti-fantasy critics would have it, and I argue that Jameson's critique, which appears in the context of his analysis of science fiction as the genre most suited to the utopian impulse, mistakes its opponent and thereby overlooks the utopian function and potential of fantasy.

Surveying the Great Schism

In their imaginative visions of alternative social, cultural, or historical formations, fantasy and utopia share generic aims and effects, but they are frequently set in opposition, often on political grounds. For example, in his landmark treatise on utopian discourse, *Archaeologies of the Future: The Desire Called Utopia and Other Science Fictions* (2005), Jameson speaks of a "great schism" between fantasy and science fiction.[5] Here Jameson follows Darko Suvin in seeing utopia as a "sociopolitical subgenre of science fiction."[6] Fantasy is thought to be anti-utopian in the sense that it is escapist or that it withdraws from the "real world," rather than projecting meaningful alternatives to our present "real world" problems as utopia, or even dystopia in some cases, is supposed to do. Jameson is not alone in treating fantasy as an escapist, indeed reactionary, genre: a genre that presents a lost world of magic, a realm of clear-cut morality, an inhabitable space that is preferable to our own, but also unavailable to us except as "fantasy."

Indeed, Jameson's discussion of this great schism is largely meant to define utopia in such a way that it can no longer be tainted by fantasy; he even introduces his discussion by observing the popular conflation of such different genres and saying, "[w]e must now lay this misunderstanding to rest."[7] In Jameson's analysis, science fiction (or utopia) offers the possibility of imagining a radical alternative to the present order by allowing us to think its limits, rather than presenting a distant otherworldly realm which has no bearing on the actually existing conditions of our lives, or worse, which tacitly supports the status quo. For Jameson, severing utopian discourse from the follies of fantasy is a crucial step in establishing the necessity of utopianism for the project of comprehending our present, world-historical condition. Of course, one might declare that this difference in view is largely unremarkable, as Tolkien's many supporters are in no way threatened by the critique of one or more literary theorists. Nevertheless, Jameson is perhaps the most significant utopian theorist and cultural critic of our time, and I believe his objections to fantasy as a genre or a discursive practice ought to be addressed. As I will discuss further below, I question whether Tolkienian fantasy really is antithetical to the utopian project, and I find that the fantastic mode offers productive areas for literary and political criticism of the world as we experience it in the here and now. By exploring Tolkien's Middle-earth, perhaps the archetypal and paradigmatic fantasy world, I intend to show that even Tolkien's fantasy operates with a utopian and critical force to energize the reader's engagement with this world and with its possible alternatives.

Jameson's analysis of the great schism in *Archaeologies of the Future* focuses on three elements that are thought to distinguish the genres—or, perhaps better, the discursive practices or modes—of fantasy or utopia. The first and most general element is the *fantasy world* itself. In fantasy, so the anti-fantasy argument goes, this fictional world in which the narrative takes place is definitively an "otherworld," unrelated to and incommensurable with our own "real world." Presumably, in science fiction, even the entirely invented worlds are themselves connected, allegorically if not more directly, to our present condition and circumstances. One might also characterize this fault line here as that between *escape* and *extrapolation*, insofar as fantasy is viewed as a mode of escaping from the all-too-real world in which we currently live, whereas utopia or science fiction attempts to extend various aspects of our real world to their logical conclusions. In fairness, Tolkien himself comes to the defense of the "escapist" impulse, while disavowing the usually apolitical or anti-political valences associated with the term.[8]

The second element is the prevalence of *magic* in fantasy, especially as distinguished from *technology* in science. Fantasy is thus understood as invoking an irrational, metaphysical, or non-cognitive substitute for science that "magically" avoids the material or logistical problems that would normally take place within the fantasy world. From this perspective, the technological or mechanical details of utopian or science-fictional schemes is preferable, since these aspects more closely relate to our own, again, "real world" experience. However, in theory and in practice, it is not always clear how well this distinction can be maintained, since magic is often functionally similar to technology, and *vice versa*, in the narratives and, in some respects, in the real world as well.

The third element is the perceived predominance of *ethics* or an ethical system, especially understood as a stable *good-versus-evil* binarism, in fantasy. This is contrasted with the more nebulous morality (or amorality) of the typical science-fictional world. Or, to put it more pointedly, this distinction is ultimately revealed to be that between ethics and politics, where the former insists upon a once-and-for-all judgment of what is or is not "good," and the latter acknowledges the contested terrain upon which humans struggle to make a life worth living. In Jameson's view, for instance, Fantasy with a capital *F* ultimately suppresses or turns its back on the political sphere in its recourse to often crudely moralistic worldviews. It is a valid critique, particularly as I have been arguing for a more nuanced understanding of heroes and villains throughout this book. Clearly, I believe that the political remains not only possible, but necessary and active, in the practice of fantasy, and that the utopia-versus-fantasy arguments are misplaced.[9] Indeed, these three elements turn out to be red herrings: the utopian fantastic in Tolkien's Middle-earth combines, but also troubles, these notions.

"The world as it appears under the sun"

For many critics skeptical of fantasy, utopia in science fiction offers the possibility of imagining a radical alternative to the present order, rather than a distant otherworldly realm that cannot affect the actually existing conditions of our lives. For example, Jameson draws on the rather anti-fantastic arguments in Suvin's trailblazing study, the *Metamorphoses of Science Fiction*, in which science fiction or utopia is understood to be a genre of "cognitive estrangement."[10] For Suvin, fantasy is not "cognitive" but "metaphysical," employing myth, religion, or magic in the place of rational thought. At a superficial level, Tolkien's "mythophilia" and his own religious beliefs lend support to Suvin's argument, at least with respect to Tolkien's own fantasy writings, but the reality of Tolkienian fantasy is more complex than the anti-fantastic utopian critics would have us believe.

In truth, Tolkien's Middle-earth would seem an archetypical example of a fantastic realm, with its elves, orcs, trolls, wizards, and dragons. Furthermore, Tolkien's distinction between fairy-stories and traveler's narratives might be viewed as confirmation of his distaste for traditional utopian literature. We recall that utopia often appears in the form of the travel narrative, and even Thomas More's *Utopia* takes on the form of a second-hand reporting of a traveler's tale; Raphael Hythlodaeus—his very name suggests that he is a "dispenser of nonsense"—encountered the island nation while taking part in one of Amerigo Vespucci's voyages. But Tolkien's commitment to the creation, or "sub-creation," of a world apart does not necessarily mean that Tolkien turns away from an engagement with the "real" world. The imaginary projection of an alternate reality combines the fantastic and the utopian in Middle-earth, where the integrated or closed *Lebenstotalität* ("totality of life"), as Georg Lukács refers to the world of the epic,[11] figures forth a kind of truth not seen in more crudely allegorical narratives. As Tolkien insists, "creative Fantasy is founded upon the hard recognition that things are so in the world as it appears under the sun; on a recognition of fact, but not a slavery to it."[12]

The view of the fantasy world as wholly unrelated to our own underlies a key objection to the genre, especially on the part of more politically minded critics. That is, so the story goes, where science fiction offers images of an alternative reality through cognitive estrangement, its world is still an extrapolation of our own real world. To cite the most familiar version of this, the science-fictional world is a look into our future, where certain contemporary problems, like poverty, nuclear weapons, overpopulation, and so forth, are extended to what seems their logical consequences. So, for instance, in a world of growing and rampant overpopulation and consequent food shortages or famines, of course we would find that "Soylent Green is made out of people!" (as immortalized by Charlton Heston's *cri-de-coeur* in that film's final scene). In contrast to this science-fictional world, according to the argument of fantasy's detractors, fantasy either creates a wholly unreal, Never-Never-Land completely unconnected to the world in which we live, or it creates a simplistic and romantic vision of our past that is somehow preferable to our present condition. In both cases, the political message is deemed inappropriate to effecting real social change in the here-and-now, or even worse, it operates in support of a reactionary, right-wing political program of nostalgia, an evasion of the world we live in and its urgent concerns. That is, the unreal world is merely an escape into utter "fantasy," a realm of the impossible.

For example, this is a large part of Michael Moorcock's critique of Tolkien (and, more so, of Tolkien's epigones):

> Since the beginnings of the Industrial Revolution, at least, people have been yearning for an ideal rural world they believe to have vanished—yearning for a mythical state of innocence [...]. This refusal to face or derive any pleasure from the realities of urban industrial life, this longing to possess, again, the infant's eye view of the countryside, is a fundamental theme in popular English literature.[13]

In a sense, and perhaps somewhat ironically, this comports with Karl Marx and Friedrich Engels's critique of "utopian socialist" in *The Communist Manifesto*, where the revolutionary critics saw the desire to return to a pre-capitalist social formation as both philosophically wrongheaded and politically reactionary.

In Tolkien's Middle-earth, there certainly seem to be elements of both escapism and nostalgia. Tolkien concedes that escapism may be a goal of fantasy, but he disputes the assumption that escape is a bad thing, as when he argues that the "misusers" of the word have confused "the Escape of the Prisoner with the Flight of the Deserter": "Why should a man be scorned if, finding himself in prison, he tries to get out and go home? Or if, when he cannot do so, he thinks and talks about other topics than jailers and prison-walls? The world outside has not become less real because the prisoner cannot see it."[14] Middle-earth is not exactly our world, nor is it even our past world, even though Tolkien suggests as much. Yet the otherworldly domain, while independent of our real world, is not altogether incommensurable with our own. As Tolkien notes in "On Fairy-stories," fairy tales are not so much stories about "fairies or elves" but about the Perilous Realm itself: "*Faërie* contains many things besides elves and fays, and besides dwarfs, witches, trolls, giants, or dragons: it holds the seas, the sun, the moon, the sky; and the earth, and all things that are in it: tree and bird, water and stone, wine and bread, and ourselves, mortal men, when we are enchanted."[15] That is, although this otherworld is clearly not the same as our world, it is not altogether an escape from our world either. The place where we exist (when enchanted) is also a vision of our world that, like the classical utopias and even more like the speculative fiction of modern utopian literature, encourages us to imagine alternatives to our own condition, while actively exploring what might be called "real-world" problems through this imaginative activity of fantasy.

The title of this chapter obliquely refers to the overall point about fantasy worlds, as Tolkien's view of Middle-earth as a world very much like, but not crudely homologous to, our own is figured forth in the idea of "places where the stars are strange." As fans and scholars of *The Lord of the Rings* will recognize, the phrase comes from Aragorn's speech during the Council of Elrond, in which he mildly rebukes Boromir, who had just complained of his long journey from Gondor to Rivendell, by asserting just how far and widely he himself had traveled over the years. Indeed, if one regards the map while reading this passage, one discovers that Aragorn had sojourned to and possibly beyond its outer limits. As Aragorn puts it, "the leagues that lie between here and Gondor are a small part in the count of my journeys. I have crossed many mountains and many rivers, and trodden many plains, even into the far countries of Rhûn and Harad where the stars are strange."[16] As beautiful or poetic as this image of lands "where the stars are strange" is, Aragorn's comment might be reasonably viewed as stating a mere matter of fact: to wit, we can discern that he had travelled to regions which lie south of the equator, where he could perhaps view Cetus, the Southern Cross, and other constellations not always visible in the Northern Hemisphere. Although we ought never simply graft Tolkien's Middle-earth onto a map of "our" world,[17] Tolkien is nevertheless still speaking of our world, albeit figuratively and in such a way as to maintain the internal coherence and "totality" of his own imaginary geography. Aragorn's journeys take place in a fantasy world, but as readers of this fantasy, we still "know" it to be akin to our own, at least as much so as the worlds of utopian or science-fictional literature.

This is not at all to say that the fantasy world of Middle-earth *is* our real world. Tolkien plainly states that the fantasy world is an "Otherworld," and that "Fantasy" itself is "the making or glimpsing of Otherworlds."[18] And, although Suvin quotes this as a sign of Tolkien's escapism, Tolkien's view that "Fairy-stories were plainly not primarily concerned with possibility, but with desirability" is actually closer to Jameson's idea of "the desire called Utopia" than we typically imagine.[19] Tolkien's youthful desire to know a world of magic, dragons, and whatnot seems to me quite similar to the desire for a world of spaceships and time-travel. Indeed, Jameson has suggested that the dragon is fantasy's equivalent or analogue of science fiction's spaceship.[20] It really seems that the *enchantment* of such worlds, rather than the otherworldliness of them, is what really disturbs certain utopian critics. But, as Tolkien indicates in several places, the very idea of "magic," so intimately tied to the "sword-and-sorcery" form of fantasy that he helped to launch, is much closer to machinery, technology, and science than is generally supposed.

Reflections on Magic

In his well-known letter to Milton Waldman, Tolkien essentially identifies what is called "Magic" with what he calls "the Machine." In Tolkien's view, both have the same function, both are means to the same end, and both are catalysts "for making the will more quickly effective."[21] Or, to put it more accurately, "magic" and "the machine" are really two names for the same thing. As Tolkien states, in using the term "the Machine (or Magic),"

> I intend all use of external plans or devices (apparatus) instead of the development of the inherent inner powers or talents—or even the use of these talents with the corrupted motive of dominating: bulldozing the real world, or coercing other wills. The Machine is our more obvious modern form though more closely related to Magic than is usually recognized.[22]

Tolkien tries to distinguish "art" from "magic" along these lines, by suggesting that for his elves so-called "magic" is more of a creative power in which the product and the vision are "in unflawed correspondence."[23] However, such a poetic *art* is very much like a creative *power*, and it may not always be clear that one is inherently less perilous, ethically or politically, than the other.

Interestingly enough, for a corpus that so influenced the sword-and-sorcery fantasy sub-genre, Tolkien's writings include very few instances of actual magic being wielded or performed. Magic would seem to be the particular province of wizards, but even the named wizards in Tolkien's world but rarely perform magical acts. In *The Hobbit*, Gandalf—who is, of course, known to hobbits for his impressive fireworks displays—uses a sort of weaponized fireworks on goblins and wolves, as the pine-cones ignited with magical fire and tossed from the treetops suggest an early use of hand-grenades and incendiary bombs, but he is far more likely to draw his sword for battle. In *The Lord of the Rings*, Gandalf utters spells, famously in contesting with the balrog in Moria; the balrog apparently utters some curses of its own, and Gandalf continues to wield fire. But in both *The Hobbit* and *The Lord of the Rings*, Gandalf is perhaps handier with the sword than with the wand or spell. Contrasted with his many epigones, such as the celebrated Albus Dumbledore, Gandalf scarcely does magic at all, but for another kind of "magic," to which I will return shortly.

By way of illustration, let us look at one particular example of magic in *The Lord of the Rings*: the Mirror of Galadriel. It is a memorable scene, and, by virtue of its framing, it may operate as a meditation on the nature of magic itself. We recall that the scene begins with Sam and Frodo remarking upon the omnipresence of "Elf-magic" in Lothlórien. "You can see and feel it everywhere," says Frodo, but Sam notes that, unlike Gandalf with his showy fireworks displays, "you can't see nobody working it. [...] I'd dearly love to see some Elf-magic, Mr. Frodo!"[24] Galadriel uses just this term to entice Sam to look in the mirror, although she mildly rebukes the hobbits for confusing "Elf-magic" with "the deceits of the Enemy": "this is what your folk would call magic, I believe; though I do not understand clearly what they mean; they seem to use the same word of the deceits of the Enemy. But this, if you will, is the magic of Galadriel. Did you not say that you wished to see Elf-magic?" Yet Galadriel has already indicated the ambiguousness of this particular magic, noting that she is able to "command the Mirror" to reveal many things, often showing "to some [...] what they desire to see," but that it is more "profitable" to allow the Mirror to show what it will, even though—whether it displays visions of the past, present, or future—"even the wisest cannot always tell."[25]

This is clearly a dangerous bit of magic, as Galadriel specifically counsels when Sam becomes agitated and alarmed at the Mirror's vision. "Remember that the Mirror shows many things, and not all have yet come to pass. Some never come to be, unless those that behold the visions turn aside from their path to prevent them. The Mirror is dangerous as a guide to deeds."[26] Most famously, after Frodo has seen his own perplexing visions in the Mirror, he offers the One Ring to Galadriel, who—like Gandalf earlier in the Shire, but even more vehemently—admits that she is sorely tempted, but then she "passes the test" by declining the offer. The wielder of this Elf-magic has survived the "deceits of the Enemy." Hence, the hobbits were not entirely wrong to characterize Elf-magic and the magic of Sauron with the same word. Many of Galadriel's own magical actions involve forms of potential deceit, as the ambiguities of the Mirror suggest. Before she passes her own test, she quite pointedly tests the members of the Fellowship, causing them to see "visions"; whether these visions are "deceitful" or not is another question, but they certainly can cause pain, as they definitely do to Boromir and to Frodo. In fact, the mirror itself, not Galadriel's magic mirror but our own quotidian one, is perhaps an apt figure for the ambiguities of magic in Tolkien's Middle-earth. A mirror presents a false image, that is, a reflection of the "real world," that may or may not be useful to those who employ it. The reflected image might be an accurate representation of the look of things, but it is also a distortion of reality. Certainly the mirrors can be used to trick the eye just as easily as to satisfy it. The scene in which the hobbits encounter "Elf-magic" in the Mirror of Galadriel reveals a deep ambiguity about magic in Tolkien's world, and this ambiguous stance is not really much different from the concerns over technology in the worlds of science fiction.

Although Tolkien wishes to distinguish the so-called "magic" of the elves from the magic or machinery of others, this distinction does not really hold. As we have just seen, the Mirror of Galadriel is a not wholly reliable or salutary form of magic, but this is not atypical. Other examples in *The Lord of the Rings* include the *palantíri*, whose manifest usefulness is revealed to cause far greater dangers to those, like Saruman or Denethor, who employ them, and of course the *rings* themselves, which ultimately are shown to cause harm, even the "Three Rings for the Elven-kings," as Galadriel notes sadly. While Tom Bombadil and the elves use a type of homeopathic or nature-based "magic"—allowing them to speak to trees, for example, or to command the river to flood—the agents of evil, as they are imagined, use a more artificial or technological form, as with the One Ring or even bombs, such as the explosives that Saruman contrives for blowing a hole in Helm's Deep. The art, magic, and machinery on display in Middle-earth functions very much like technology throughout.

But again, for all of the magical power of the White Wizard and the "Necromancer" Sauron, very little actual magic is wielded. Indeed, for the most part, as Tolkien's letter to Waldman had indicated, the real force of this "black" magic lies in its influence or domination over other wills; that is, the function of magic or machinery for its user is primarily to impose one's will upon orcs, trolls, and corruptible men. However, in a more positive sense, this is also the power wielded by a Gandalf or a Galadriel, although we would prefer to think of theirs as the power of inspiration—for instance, in kindling men's hearts—rather than domination, the results, however, are similar. Once it is known that Gandalf himself is wearing "the Third Ring, Narya the Great," it becomes apparent that his real magical power is the ability to "rekindle hearts in a world that grows chill."[27] Like Galadriel, who does not claim to offer counsel, but who clearly offers some anyway, Gandalf's greatest magic is in motivating and guiding others, a more beneficent, but not dissimilar, form of "making the will more quickly effective."

The difference, for Tolkien, comes down to the intent of the magic user and the effect of the magic used, it seems. The fundamental issue is Art itself, which Tolkien characterizes as "sub-creation," since what Tolkien calls the "real primary world" of creation has only one Creator, and its relation to the "primary world." In a reflection on the natural desire for art, for sub-creation, Tolkien considers the origins of "the Machine (or Magic)," as he explains in the letter to Waldman.

> This desire [to create Art] is at once wedded to a passionate love of the real primary world, and hence filled with the sense of mortality, and yet unsatisfied by it. It has various opportunities of "Fall." It may become possessive, clinging to the things made as "its own," the sub-creator wishes to be Lord and God of his private creation. He will rebel against the laws of the Creator—especially against mortality. Both of these (alone and together) will lead to a desire for Power, for making the will more quickly effective,—and so to the Machine [or Magic].[28]

Hence, art itself, when combined with the usual sin of pride, quickly leads to power and the use of "un-natural" devices. However, in attempting to distinguish the "good" magic of the elves from this baleful form, Tolkien avers that "its object is Art not Power, sub-creation not domination and tyrannous re-forming of Creation." But, as the entire tragic history of *The Silmarillion* recounts, the problem is "that this frightful evil can and does arise from an apparently good root, the desire to benefit the world and others—speedily and according to the benefactor's own plans—is a recurrent motive."[29]

Thus magic, which is supposed to infuse the fantasy world, is really related to the broader questions of ethics and politics. In other words, the distinction between magic and technology dissolves in Tolkien's world—and, more generally, in fantasy at large—as they become names for the same thing: means of enhancing the aesthetic ability of the artist or sub-creator. Perhaps this is why so many would-be Saurons or Gandalfs appear as hybrids of the magician and the scientist, like Faust, Frankenstein, Ahab, and so on. What counts, then, is not the mythological versus the cognitive estrangements in the world, but the ethical approach to being in the world. This is the seemingly inevitable problem of good versus evil.

Beyond Good and Evil

The anti-fantasy arguments of those favoring science fiction or utopia frequently cite the simplistic ethical system that undergirds the fantastic realm. That is, to use Jameson's words here, one of the "structural characteristics of fantasy which contrast sharply with SF and which can serve as *differentiae specificae* for this genre" is "the organization of fantasy around the ethical binary of good and evil," in addition to "the fundamental role it assigns to magic."[30] Some of Tolkien's detractors cite this seemingly simplistic, good-versus-evil ethical code as a primary objection to the fantasy world of Middle-earth. It is not just that Tolkien seems to have adopted a strictly Manichean worldview, at least in their view of it, but that his world also establishes once and forever just who is good (elves, for instance, or noble men, "good" dwarves, and well-bred hobbits) and who is evil (Sauron above all, but then the various monsters, such as the orcs, trolls, dragons, and so on). From this ethics, a reactionary politics must inevitably emerge. For instance, in what I take to be a serious misreading or oversimplification, Moorcock objects that

> *The Lord of the Rings* is a pernicious confirmation of the values of a morally bankrupt middle-class. [...] If the Shire is a suburban garden, Sauron and his henchmen are that old bourgeois bugaboo, the Mob—mindless football supporters throwing their beer-bottles over the fence—the worst aspects of modern urban society represented as the whole by a fearful, backward-yearning

class for whom "good taste" is synonymous with "restraint" (pastel colours, murmured protest) and "civilized" behaviour means "conventional behaviour in all circumstances."[31]

There is some truth to Moorcock's critique, but by drawing up the sides along class lines, he also shows how the ideological framework of the "real world" shapes this fantasy world system of Middle-earth. That is, Tolkien's only apparently moral dichotomy between the good and the evil turn out to involve far more nuanced political power, strategy, and organization.

This view of Tolkien's as a strictly binary, good-versus-evil worldview cannot long withstand scrutiny, and a careful consideration of Tolkien's texts reveals a far more nuanced ethical framework, whatever Tolkien's own personal religious or moral tenets. Shippey has quite rightly undercut Edwin Muir's notion that *The Lord of the Rings* contains a formulaic happy ending in which "[t]he good boys, having fought a deadly battle, emerge at the end of it well, triumphant and happy, as boys would naturally expect to do." As any serious reader would recognize, the ending not nearly so simple: Frodo is literally and figuratively scarred for life (Shippey calls him a "burnt-out case"),[32] Théoden's prophetic words—"much that was fair and wonderful shall pass for ever out of Middle-earth"—come true,[33] Elrond's and Galadriel's powers wane, the "high" elves depart from the land, and so forth. Far from presenting a neat victory for good over evil, Tolkien introduces us to Galadriel's poignant concept of the "long defeat." Moreover, as the magic of Galadriel's Mirror or of Denethor's *palantír* suggests, the basic morality of things is not so clear cut in Tolkien's world. Whatever Tolkien's own view on the matter, the ethical framework of his Middle-earth cannot be reduced to a good-*versus*-evil caricature.

As I have pointed out in the prior chapters, orcs—the representatives of so-called "evil" in Tolkien's world—are themselves far more complex and ambiguous than generally supposed. The problem of any inherent orcish evil troubled Tolkien, and he felt that their mere existence meant that they could not be beyond redemption. But then, this must be the case with all "evil" beings in this world, right? So many of the "evil ones," such as Sauron, Saruman, and even the great original Satan-figure, Melkor or Morgoth, are really the Fallen, figures of pity rather than pure hatred. Gollum, of course, is the very avatar of this concept of pitiable "evil." Similarly, with the Ringwraiths and Denethor and Fëanor and so on, each of whom commits horrific acts but who are also the victims of some greater "evil," like pride or hopelessness. Furthermore, as Tolkien had indicated in his letter to Waldman, in almost every case, this so-called evil emerges out of a desire to do good. (Morgoth would seem to be the exception, as noted by Tolkien, but I think a case could be made for even his greater moral ambiguity. Like

Milton's Satan, Melkor *fell*, in large part because he aspired to be a supreme god. One could argue that his motives are not that different from Galadriel's initially, only on a much larger scale and far more vexed.) This is of course why both Gandalf and Galadriel decline Frodo's offer of the Ring. As Gandalf puts it, the Ring would corrupt him precisely because of his "pity for weakness and the desire for strength to do good."[34] But, as Tolkien makes clear in his identification of Magic with the Machine, all the ring really does is enhance the inherent power of the user, and the very desire to do good is at the root of all evil. In fact, in a later letter, Tolkien explicitly writes that "Gandalf as Ring-Lord would have been far worse that Sauron. He would have remained 'righteous,' but self-righteous. [...] Gandalf would have made good detestable and seem evil."[35] This is enough to show that Tolkien, notwithstanding his use of the conventional terminology, does not strictly imagine his moral universe in terms of "good" *versus* "evil."

Tolkien is no moral relativist, but his work does invite the possibility of a kind of Nietzschean perspectivism which would undermine the simplistic, binary ethical model attributed to him. When Sam wonders if the fallen enemy soldier "was really evil of heart," he is close to seeing the difference, but his perspective is not labile enough to imagine that an Easterling or orc might wonder the same of him, even though he is at that very moment attempting to invade a foreign country in service of those who would overthrow its government.[36] Not long after that scene, Sam overhears the conversation between the orc captains Shagrat and Gorbag, who clearly indicate that they see elves and others on Sam's "side" as the enemies, treacherous and deadly.

Shippey has made much of how evil in Tolkien is characterized by the ambiguous figure of "the Shadow."[37] A shadow is, of course, simultaneously a presence and an absence, existing and nonexistent at the same time, much like the reflections in Galadriel's mirror. This evocative figure is well suited to the depiction of evil in Tolkien's world, since it both is and is not present, and when visible, it is largely seen in its effects; moreover, those effects may not be recognizable or able to be evaluated until much later. The "ruse of history" does not spare Middle-earth, and Jameson's view of the dialectical reversal might also bear on the events in this imaginary place. The dialectical reversal, "that paradoxical turning around of a phenomenon into its opposite," as Jameson puts it,

> [c]an be described as a kind of leap-frogging affair in time, in which the drawbacks of a given historical situation turn out in reality to be its secret advantages, in which what looked like built-in superiorities suddenly prove to set the most iconclad limits on its future development. It is a matter, indeed, of the reversal of limits, of the transformation of the negative to positive and from positive to negative.[38]

Tolkien's narratives are filled with such dialectical reversals, perhaps most notoriously visible in the fact that Gollum, whom Bilbo considered killing and who Frodo initially thought had deserved to be killed on the spot, is the one who actually "achieves" the quest, destroying the One Ring, and thus effecting the eucatastrophe that enables something like a happy ending for the heroes who survive the ordeal. Of course, one might argue that the very drama of the One Ring is itself part of a dialectic reversal of Sauron's own intentions in crafting it to begin with, for had he not tried to "concentrate" his powers in an object that he could then be deprived of and that could potentially be used against him, he would have undoubtedly survived and likely won the War of the Ring, thus achieving his own goals. As Gandalf had put it while mildly rebuking Frodo for wishing Gollum dead, "even the very wise cannot see all ends."[39]

Jameson's critique of the ethical oversimplifications of the fantasy genre are tied to his critique of moralizing more generally, since the lessons of the dialectic and the dialectical reversal (*peripeteia*) show that what may seem "good" at a given moment might prove deleterious, even "evil," in the fullness of time. Tolkien's contention that "evil" arises largely out of a desire to do good—that the human, all-too-human desire for sub-creation, for Art itself, is what makes possible, if not *inevitable*, the Fall—seems applicable to this worldview, even if he is not coming out the Marxist tradition.

In the end, the ethical framework of Tolkien's Middle-earth is much more complex, even muddied, than either his detractors or his champions frequently believe. Tolkien's apparently idealized elves turn out to have much to find fault with, and even in their most noble images, they do not always stand for what is good, as seen most clearly in long series of tragic decisions and terrible actions of nearly all the major characters in *The Silmarillion*. If elves are the "highest" beings, hobbits and dwarves are somewhat more nuanced, which also makes them more interesting, and men are far more complex in their tendencies toward good or evil or that which lies beyond good and evil. The fact is, as the angelic (*Maia*) Gandalf indicates at the very outset of the adventure, the ethical argument should not require either some adherence to an abstract and unchanging ideal or the repulsion of an ever-nefarious evil, but rather it must involve the basic ways we comport ourselves in our world. That is to say, it involves something far more like politics, broadly understood. The scene is memorable, and the lines have become so salient as to have been made into memes and widely circulated in our own dark times. Echoing a sentiment felt by everyone at some point, or rather at many points, in his or her life, Frodo wishes this "evil" had not arisen in his own lifetime, and Gandalf replies, "So do I [...] and so do all who live to see such times. But that is not for them to decide. All we have to decide is what to do with the time that is given us."[40]

The wisdom here lies partly in a recognition of the degree to which all we are ever doing is muddling through. We are undoubtedly doing our best with the materials at hand in the time available, but nothing can prove to us in this time and place that we are doing some transcendent "good." Indeed, even the good we feel pretty sure we are doing will have consequences that are to our minds baleful, as when Galadriel notes that the destruction of the One Ring will inevitably lead to the disintegration of Lothlórien and of elven culture more generally. The end of Sauron, which is followed a bit later by the end of Saruman, is not at all the Hollywood happy ending some would suppose. The catastrophic transformation of Middle-earth resembles, dare I say, the more *realistic* vision of a world altered by the forces of history. As with real history, in Gandalf's words, "even the very wise cannot see all ends." Hence, the apparent "good-versus-evil" worldview gives way to a more nuanced and more realistic ethics, one which shares a great deal with the aims, if not always the methods, of politics, insofar as the political realm is always understood to be a site of contest, compromise, second-looks, and reevaluation. This too helps in transforming the image of the real world by establishing an imaginary space in which to envision our own world in a new light.

Gandalf later acknowledges this again in language that seems to echo Marx's famous line about not making recipes for the cook-shops of the future, as the wizard explains that, even if the "good" side is victorious in the War of the Ring, that does not mean that the future is secure: "it is not our part to master all the tides of the world, but to do what is in us for the succours of those years wherein we are set, uprooting the evil in the fields that we know, so that those who live after may have clean earth to till. What weather they shall have is not ours to rule."[41] This pragmatic view also shows the degree to which one cannot maintain an absolute sense of good *versus* evil, notwithstanding Gandalf's use of those terms, since we who are situated in the present moment cannot know for sure what, given the vagaries of their own time's soil and weather, the future generations would find beneficial or not.

Hence, Gandalf's "even the very wise cannot see all ends" comment may be connected to Tolkien's and Jameson's different, yet functionally similar philosophical perspectives, the former concerning the larger sense of chance, fate, or divine providence, and the latter dealing with a Marxist philosophy of history and, more specifically, the role of the dialectical reversal in it. In Tolkien, the idea of "chance" is implied and subsumed in the Christian idea of divine providence, God's will, or the ineffable plan. Mere mortals cannot possible know God's plan—the Lord moves in mysterious ways, as the saying goes—but they can have "faith" in its ultimate wisdom and goodness. This is why losing hope, while understandable during times of crisis, is ultimately a great sin, for the truly despondent persons are effectively asserting that they know better than God, which is in effect the sin of pride. Tolkien takes care to keep openly Christian themes far in the background of his mythology, which takes place in a non- or pre-Christian world, but by having Gandalf repeatedly insist on keeping hope alive (and by emphasizing the concept of hope throughout *The Lord of the Rings*, where even Aragorn bears "hope" [*Estel*] as one of his monikers), Tolkien underscores this faith in a larger vision of fate or history. Gandalf recognizes "more than one power at work. [...] I can put it no plainer than by saying that Bilbo was *meant* to find the Ring, and *not* by its maker. In which case you [Frodo] were also meant to have it. And that may be an encouraging thought."[42]

Such *amor fati* pays off in the *eucatastrophe* of the scene at Mount Doom, after all. Frodo had long before told Gandalf that he wished Bilbo had killed Gollum back when he had the chance, which elicits a stern rebuke from the wizard:

> Many that live deserve death. And some that die deserve life. Can you give it to them? Then do not be too eager to deal out death in judgement. For even the very wise cannot see all ends. [...] My heart tells me that he has some part to play yet, for good or for ill, before the end; and when that time comes, the pity of Bilbo may rule the fate of many.[43]

Of course, it is Gollum, not Frodo, who eventually destroys the ring, bringing to a successful conclusion the great adventure of Frodo and of the Fellowship of the Ring, and Gollum is able to do so thanks to the pity shown by Bilbo, Frodo, and others along the way. He is also able to do so because some five centuries earlier he murdered Déagol, an "evil" act that, through the elaborate vicissitudes of history, can now be seen to have helped to "save the world." Amid even the most terrible circumstances, a utopian element persists. As with Ernst Bloch's principle, *hope* is fundamentally utopian, not in the sense that it involves pie-eyed optimism or looking on the "bright side," but in the fundamental recognition that our present situation is essentially and inexorably *changeable*.

This is a good example of the dialectical reversal, which in Jameson's view is precisely what ought to prevent Marxists from moralizing about this or that phenomenon in its given moment. As Jameson has put it elsewhere, "[t]he dialectic is an injunction to think the negative and the positive together and at the same time, in the unity of a single thought, there where moralizing wants to have the luxury of condemning this evil without particularly imagining anything else in its place."[44] In this sense,

Tolkien's message through Gandalf comports well with a Marxian perspective, and it insists that history be viewed outside of the simplistic morality of those who imagine an absolute good *versus* evil.

The Fantastic Is Good to Think With

Just as the simplistic good-*versus*-evil binary is not an apt model for Tolkien's ethics in Middle-earth, so too it seems that the fantasy-*versus*-utopia opposition does not hold. The misplaced proposition misleadingly opposes two discursive formations whose defining territories often overlap. The real value of utopia lies not in its presentation of a blueprint for an ideal society, but in the ways that it enables us to imagine radical alternatives to the present society. In other words, utopia is a critical practice, and I agree with China Miéville, who sees utopia or science fiction as a subset of fantasy.[45] Hence, fantasy is also a critical practice. In a world made mystified and false by ideology and alienation, the fantastic might actually be a better way to gain access to the "real" world, which can no longer be simply read off the page of realistic fiction. That is, with Miéville's assertion that "the fantastic, particularly because 'reality' is a grotesque 'fantastic form,' is *good to think with*," the old slogan from the May 1968 militants of Paris, *L'imagination au pouvoir* ("power to the imagination"), finds a new lease on life in a different historical moment, one in which the imagination requires empowerment, perhaps more than ever before.

The interrelations of fantasy and utopia in Tolkien's world serve to establish a sense of radical difference from our own everyday world which is nevertheless also a ground upon which we may reflect upon real-world conditions. The distinction between fantasy and realism itself might be blurred, since both modes interact in various ways to open up our perspectives on our world, including of course the world made visible through acts of the imagination. In the words of Eric Rabkin,

> Fantasy represents a basic mode of human knowing; its polar opposite is Reality. Reality is that collection of perspectives and expectations that we learn in order to survive in the here and now. But the here and now becomes tomorrow; a child grows, a culture develops, a person dreams. In every area of human thought, civilization has evolved a functioning reality, but the universe has suffered no reality to maintain itself unchanged. The glory of man is that he is not bound by reality. Man travels in fantastic worlds.[46]

Fantasy, like both the most meticulous realism and the most speculative science fiction, helps to shape our sense of this world and fosters our imaginings of alternatives. In that manner, the genre or mode shares with utopia a fundamentally critical vocation. In the end, the real question is not whether a sober realism, a critical utopianism, or a creative fantasy offers the best mode in which to engage artistically with the world, but rather how we are to engage at all. Otherworldliness may indeed be the best way of seeing our own world with fresh eyes, and, in an age which seems to have forgotten how to think critically, historically, or speculatively, the sort of literary work accomplished by a Tolkien in Middle-earth—be it labeled fantasy, utopia, or other—is all the more valuable.

As Shippey observes, the scholarly opposition to fantasy often corresponds to the poverty of one's imagination. Speaking of Nokes, a character in Tolkien's "Smith of Wootton Major," Shippey writes: "He has only a weak [...] notion of fantasy himself, but assumes that this is all there can ever be; and since he is well aware of the feebleness of his own imagination, he assumes all images of the fantastic, of Faerie, must be feeble too."[47] Ironically, perhaps, Jameson has said something similar about our own postmodern condition, in which for many it is easier to envision the end of the world than an end to the present economic system: "perhaps that is due to some weakness in our imaginations."[48] With empowered imaginations, the utopian impulse may indeed find realization in the form of fantasy, and we may again look upon our own world with fresh eyes, having visited places where the stars are strange.

Conclusion

"We should not neglect the red dragons"

In his Afterword to *Red Planets: Marxism and Science Fiction*, China Miéville offers an insightful defense of fantasy as an inherently political mode or genre, while criticizing the apparent hegemony of science fiction in such discussions, and arguing for a more nuanced understanding of both genres, which are part of a larger category of what might be called the *literature of estrangement*.[1] Observing the ways in which prominent Marxist literary critics have largely dismissed, if not outright attacked, fantasy while promoting the utopian and critical prospects of science fiction, Miéville laments the "generic common-sense that has allowed generations of readers and writers to treat, say, faster-than-light drives as science-fictional in a way that dragons are not, despite repeated assurances from the great majority of physicists that the former are no less impossible than the latter."[2] Miéville then shows how science fiction and fantasy perform similar cultural and critical activities in their function as literatures of estrangement. Moreover, Miéville insists, even where the generic differences between them are to be maintained, these need not be couched in the language of cognition or rationality *versus* that of metaphysics or irrationality, for (as he had stated in a previous essay) fantasy, not unlike science fiction, "is good to think with."[3] The critical study of fantasy is thus as valuable, politically and artistically, as that of any other field of literature. In making sense of the ways that writers make sense of the world—that is, the task of the critic, which is all the more urgent in the case of socially engaged literature and criticism—we would do well to pay attention to the manifold effects that such fantastic literary productions can produce. As Miéville concludes: "*Red Planets* we have. We should not neglect the red dragons."[4]

Representing Middle-earth: Tolkien, Form, and Ideology could be viewed as my modest attempt, as a literary critic and as a fan, to give their due to the figurative "red dragons" that may be discovered in Tolkien's work. As with my notorious sympathy for orcs, about which a book-length study is currently in the works,[5] part of this project involves a revisionist and revisionary perspective on Tolkien's Middle-earth and the narratives that emerge from that world. But this is not a simple reversal or inversion, whereby one simply swaps one's emotional allegiances and cheers for the "bad guys." Rather, my goal has been to highlight the complexity and diversity of perspectives made possible by Tolkien's fantasy writings, which have their own sort of political unconscious and geopolitical aesthetic, to cite expressions made famous by Fredric Jameson, who in addition to being the greatest Marxist critic of our era is a supremely sensitive, generous, and creative reader of literature. In the spirit of Jameson's theory and criticism, I have not so much tried to perform an explicitly Marxist "reading" of Tolkien's works—for example, merely applying one theory or one interpretative model among many other available ones to a given text—as hoped to draw upon Marxism broadly in order to open up new vantages from which to see Middle-earth and its inhabitants anew. For, as Jameson has put it, one goal of his work has been "to enlarge the conception of the literary text itself, so that its political, psychoanalytic, ideological, philosophical, and social resonances might become audible (and describable) *within* that experience of literary language and aesthetic form to which I remain committed."[6] Far from somehow being "reduced" to this or that political message, when viewed from this expansive Marxist perspective Tolkien's writings are thus made richer in their hermeneutic plenitude. Vast as it already is, Middle-earth is enlarged by such readings.

Another part of this involves a defense of the fantasy genre or mode itself, as I have endeavored to reclaim Tolkien in particular, and fantasy more generally, for Marxist criticism, while also urging those in Tolkien Studies, fantasy studies, and related areas to engage with, if not embrace Marxism, which I believe offers a particularly rich and compelling approach to these materials, ideas, and cultural contexts. As I have argued, especially in the opening chapters but also implicitly throughout this book, Tolkien's principal project was to give life to a sense of history in an age that had either forgotten how to think historically or, worse, actively misrepresented and abused history. That he would do so using myth, fairy story, heroic romance, fantasy, and the form of the novel—in short, to employ imaginative literature instead of more straightforward history or historical fiction—reflects the conviction that the imagination, above all, needed kindling in the dark times in which he composed these narratives. Contrary to popular opinion and most scholarly treatment of his work, Tolkien's was in many respects a modernist aesthetic, and his overall project in what he referred to as the "Saga of the Jewels and the Rings" (i.e., the materials that would become *The Silmarillion* and related writings, plus *The Hobbit* and *The Lord of the Rings*) was conceived in response to a modern condition in which "all that is solid melts into air, all that is holy is profaned," in the famous words of Marx and Engels.[7] Like other major modernists, Tolkien attempted to resuscitate history through narrative, shoring his fragments against the ruins of modernity and shaping them into a cognizable whole via "the seamless web of story," as he called it.[8]

Accordingly and notwithstanding the yawning gulf separating the personal socio-political views of these writers, there are powerful resonances between Tolkien's artistic, literary, and philosophical project in *The Silmarillion*, *The Hobbit*, and *The Lord of the Rings* and the ideas of Marx or Engels, later Lukács, even Brecht, and Jameson, among others. Many of Tolkien's personal beliefs and convictions would be abhorrent to those on the political left, just as Tolkien would find many of their views objectionable if not also horrifying. But Marxism maintains its own fantastic historical project, not all that dissimilar in its overall aims to what can be found in a creative interpretation of Tolkien's legendarium. For this reason, a Marxist approach to Tolkien's work and their effects in twentieth and twenty-first-century popular and literary cultures is particularly apt. From a critical standpoint, as Jameson has put it in language well attuned to the fantastic mode associated with myth and romance, "only Marxism can give us an adequate account of the essential *mystery* of the cultural past, which, like Tiresias drinking the blood, is momentarily returned to life and warmth and allowed once more to speak, and to deliver its long-forgotten message in surroundings utterly alien to it."[9] Tolkien's work, read in this light, offers a similar prospect.

Tolkien and Lukács make for strange bedfellows, to be sure, and yet the two intellectuals shared more in common than one might initially suppose. Born near the end of the nineteenth century, their lifetimes more-or-less overlapped, and both men were utterly devoted to the study of language and literature. Each was shaped, in rather different ways, in the crucible of the Great War, in the aftermath of which each scholar formulated distinctive responses and reimagined the relationship between storytelling and social life. In their meticulously crafted writings, Tolkien and Lukács developed unique, but also generalizable and influential interventions into the critical discourse of modernity, each demonstrating the power of literary language and narrative form to reflect, and perhaps shape, our engagement with the world, its historical past, and its prospects for the future. Jameson has referred to Lukács's work "as a continuous and lifelong meditation on narrative, on its basic structures, its relationship to the reality it expresses, and its epistemological value when compared with other, more abstract and philosophical modes of understanding."[10]

It strikes me that Tolkien's project, taken as a whole, might be described along similar lines, with only slight but meaningful modifications to account for his interests in languages and, of course, in the Perilous Realm of *Faërie*. The English fantasist and the Hungarian Marxist critic both maintained a profound sense of how stories shaped the all-too-real worlds in which they were produced and disseminated.

That said, however, it is not my contention that Tolkien and Lukács, or any other Marxist critic for that matter, are somehow kindred spirits. Nor do I intend to argue that, if we can only read his work in a certain light, Tolkien will turn out to have been a "fellow traveler" after all. Rather, less ambitiously perhaps, I have hoped to show how Marxist criticism, and more specifically the Marxist approach to the theory of the novel and the study of narrative, can illuminate Tolkien's work in interesting ways, which in turn may help us to see his world, and our own, in a different light. This also goes for the broader circulation of Tolkien's legendarium in the culture at large, for instance, through the popular film adaptations (some of which I have discussed), video games (which I have not), or other media. In reading Tolkien's writing *with* Marxism, we may descry in the distance those red dragons whose presence defamiliarizes our own world while disclosing the possibilities of other spaces beyond.

A nuanced, dialectical Marxist reading of Tolkien discloses political and social content to be found in his remarkable artistic achievement, the grand literary cartography and history of Middle-earth. Such a reading highlights both ideological and the utopian aspects of Tolkien's legendarium, thereby enabling productive interpretations and extensions of the narratives. Ultimately, Tolkien's work evokes a "history from below," to use a phrase made popular by E.P. Thompson, by which we see that, as Elrond puts it in *The Lord of the Rings*, the "deeds that move the wheels of the world" are performed by "small hands." As he goes on, "small hands do them because they must, while the eyes of the great are elsewhere," but as with the orcs who complain about serving "big bosses," along with those who desire not to serve the powers that be at all, the collective actions of many small hands may lead to the overthrow of "the great" and with their preferred preoccupations. Even the very wise cannot see all ends, as Gandalf observes, and all we have to decide is what to do in the time that is given us.[11] The red dragons to be found in both the fine details and panoramic vistas of Tolkien's Middle-earth might guide us in imaginatively comprehending and transforming the spaces of our own all-too-real, but also fantastic and strange world system in the twenty-first century.

Notes

Introduction

1. In letters from the 1950s, Tolkien used the term *legendarium* to refer to his unpublished "Silmarillion" materials, and some Tolkien scholars (e.g., John D. Rateliff) have suggested that the term be used to refer only to a select group of materials. But in part because Tolkien himself lobbied to include the "Silmarillion" with *The Lord of the Rings* (itself the sequel to *The Hobbit*) and in part for the sake of convenience, I use "Tolkien's legendarium" to refer to all these writings, although not to works set outside this world (e.g., *The Father Christmas Letters*, *Farmer Giles of Ham*, or *Smith of Wootton Major*).

2. On the concept of cognitive mapping in relation to Jameson's overall career, see my *Fredric Jameson: The Project of Dialectic Criticism* (London: Pluto, 2014).

3. Throughout the text, I try to follow the conventional distinction within Tolkien Studies between *The Silmarillion* (i.e., a book-length work first published in 1977) and the "Silmarillion" (i.e., the legendary stories connected with the Silmarils that Tolkien labored to produce over his lifetime, along with related materials published posthumously in *Unfinished Tales* and the 12-volume *History of Middle-earth* series).

4. See my *J.R.R. Tolkien's The Hobbit: Realizing History Through Fantasy* (New York: Palgrave Macmillan, 2022).

5. See my "In the File Drawer Labelled 'Science Fiction': Genre after the Age of the Novel," in Robert T. Tally Jr., *The Critical Situation: Vexed Perspectives in Postmodern Literary Studies* (London: Anthem Press, 2023), 71–86.

6. China Miéville, "Editorial Introduction: Marxism and Fantasy," *Historical Materialism* 10.4 (2002), 42.

7. Paul Lafargue, "Reminiscences of Marx," in *Marx and Engels on Literature and Art: A Selection of Writings*, eds. Lee Baxandall and Stefan Morawski (St. Louis: Telos Press, 1973), 150.

8. See Jameson, *Fables of Aggression: Wyndham Lewis, or, the Modernist as Fascist* (Berkeley: University of California Press, 1979).

9. Tolkien, *The Letters of J.R.R. Tolkien*, ed. Humphrey Carpenter (Boston: Houghton Mifflin, 1981), 63–64.

10. I do not claim to be the first to do this, naturally. For example, see Ishay Landa, "Slaves of the Ring: Tolkien's Political Unconscious," *Historical Materialism* 10.4 (2002), 113–133, which offers a reading of *The Hobbit* and *The Lord of the Rings* based on Jameson's perceived method of "symptomatic reading" in *The Political Unconscious*. Much as I admire that effort, I disagree with its fundamental premise that Tolkien's novels function as an allegory about the abolition of private property and the resistance to revolutionary social change. See also the brief chapter devoted to Tolkien in Peter Burger's *The Political Unconscious of the Fantasy Sub-Genre of Romance* (Lewiston, NY: The Edwin Mellen Press, 2001), 99–114. For a rather different reading of these politics with respect to *The Hobbit*, see Peter E. Firchow, "The Politics of Fantasy: *The Hobbit* and Fascism," *The Midwest Quarterly* 50.1 (Autumn 2008), 15–33.

11. Verlyn Flieger, "But What Did He Really Mean," in *There Would Always Be a Fairy Tale: More Essays on Tolkien* (Kent: Kent State University Press, 2017), 17.

12. This is not to suggest that I am the first to examine connections between Tolkien and modernism. Far from it. I am in any case indebted to the work of Jane Chance, Janet Brennan Croft, Jason Fisher, Verlyn Flieger, Robin Anne Reid, Tom Shippey, and Christopher Vaccaro, among others who have written on Tolkien's modernism. The two-volume collection edited by Thomas Honegger and Frank Weinreich, *Tolkien and Modernity* (Zollikofen, Switzerland: Walking Tree, 2006) contains valuable essays on this topic as well. And, even though I have elsewhere registered my dissatisfactions with its main arguments, I should mention Theresa Freda Nicolay's *Tolkien and the Modernists* (Jefferson, NC: McFarland, 2014), which might have been more aptly titled "Tolkien *versus* Modernism"; see my review in *Mythlore* 33.2 (Spring/Summer 2015), 171–175.

13. Tolkien, *Letters*, 24, 26.

14. See, e.g., Tolkien, *Letters*, 138, 139.

15. On the idea of "literary cartography," see my *Spatiality* (London: Routledge, 2013), especially 44–78; see also my *Topophrenia: Place, Narrative, and the Spatial Imagination* (Bloomington: Indiana University Press, 2019).

16. See Karen Wynn Fonstad, *The Atlas of Middle-earth* (Boston: Houghton Mifflin, 1991). One might also mention a rather different type of literary geography, rooted primarily in fandom, by which the realms of Tolkien's Middle-earth are somehow inscribed upon the real-world places Tolkien lived and worked, as with John Garth's gloriously illustrated book, *The Worlds of J. R. R. Tolkien: The Places that Inspired Middle-earth* (Princeton: Princeton University Press, 2020). Virginia Woolf famously criticized this practice of trying to turn "a writer's country," which is "a territory in his own brain," into "tangible brick and mortar"; see Woolf, "Literary Geography," in *Books and Portraits: Some Further Selections from the Literary ad Biographical Writings of Virginia Woolf*, ed. Mary Lyon (New York: Harcourt, Brace, and Jovanovich, 1977), 161.

17. Tom Shippey, *The Road to Middle-earth: How J.R.R. Tolkien Created a New Mythology* (Boston: Houghton Mifflin, 2003), 94–134.

18. Tolkien, "On Fairy-Stories," *The Monsters and the Critics and Other Essays*, ed. Christopher Tolkien (New York: HarperCollins, 2006), 113–114.

19. Erich Auerbach, "Philology and *Weltliteratur*," trans. M. and E.W. Said, *Centennial Review* 13.1 (1969), 17.

20. See Tolkien, *Letters*, 65.

21. See, e.g., T.A. Shippey, *J.R.R. Tolkien: Author of the Century* (Boston: Houghton Mifflin, 2000), vii–viii: "The dominant literary mode of the twentieth century has been the fantastic. [...] By the end of the century, even authors deeply committed to the realist novel have often found themselves unable to resist the gravitational pull of the fantastic as a literary mode."

22. Herbert Marcuse, "The End of Utopia," *Five Lectures: Psychoanalysis, Politics, and Utopia*, trans. J. Shapiro and S. Weber (Boston: Beacon Press, 1970), 69.

23. See China Miéville, "Cognition as Ideology: A Dialectic of SF," *Red Planets: Marxism and Science Fiction*, eds. Marc Bould and China Miéville (Middletown, CT: Wesleyan University Press, 2009), 234.

Chapter 1

1. J. R. R. Tolkien, *The Two Towers* (New York: Del Rey, 2012), IV.viii.363.

2. As Tolkien observes, "[a] love of learning (other than genealogical lore) was far from general among them, but there remained still a few in the older families who studied their own books, and even gathered reports of old times and distant lands from Elves, Dwarves, and Men." See Tolkien, "Prologue," *The Fellowship of the Ring* (New York: Del Rey, 2012), 3.

3. Although it was published in three volumes for commercial reasons, *The Lord of the Rings* was always understood by Tolkien to be a single novel; indeed, he desperately wished to publish the materials from his "Silmarillion" project along with it, as he believed together it formed a single "Saga of the Jewels and the Rings," as I discuss further in Chapter 3. See Tolkien, *The Letters of J.R.R. Tolkien*, ed. Humphrey Carpenter (Boston: Houghton Mifflin, 1981), 138–139.

4. Tolkien, "*Beowulf*: The Monsters and the Critics," in *The Monsters and the Critics and Other Essays*, ed. Christopher Tolkien (New York: HarperCollins, 1983, 33–34.

5. Tolkien, *Letters*, 288.
6. Karl Marx, and Friedrich Engels, *The Communist Manifesto*, trans. Samuel Moore (New York: Signet, 1998), 54.
7. See Tolkien, *Letters*, 288: "I was born in 1892 and lived for my early years in 'the Shire' in a pre-mechanical age."
8. Marx and Engels, *The Communist Manifesto*, 54.
9. Marshall Berman, *All That is Solid Melts into Air: The Experience of Modernity* (New York: Penguin, 1988), 15–16.
10. On "antiquarian" history, as distinct from "monumental" and "critical" approaches, see Friedrich Nietzsche, "On the Uses and Disadvantages of History for Life," *Untimely Meditations*, ed. Daniel Breazeale, trans. R.J. Hollingdale (Cambridge: Cambridge University Press, 1997), 57–124.
11. See, e.g., Verlyn Flieger, "A Postmodern Medievalist?" in *Tolkien's Modern Middle Ages*, eds. Jane Chance and Alfred K. Siewers (New York: Palgrave Macmillan, 2005) 17–28.
12. Tolkien, "Foreword," *Fellowship of the Ring*, x–xi.
13. Tolkien, *Letters*, 239.
14. *Ibid.*, 245.
15. In what must be a fun coincidence for fans of *Dracula*, one map overlay developed by UCLA geography professor Peter Bird locates The Shire in England's West Midlands, the Grey Havens in Ireland, Edoras in Bavaria, and Mordor in Transylvania. See Ian Bogost's blog post, "Where in the World is Middle Earth [sic]?" (June 20, 2007): https://bogost.com/writing/blog/where_in_the_world_was_middle/.
16. See, e.g., John Garth, *The Worlds of J. R. R. Tolkien: The Places That Inspired Middle-earth* (Princeton: Princeton University Press, 2020).
17. Tolkien, *Letters*, 24.
18. See Fredric Jameson, *The Political Unconscious: Narrative as a Socially Symbolic Act* (Ithaca: Cornell University Press, 1981), 291.
19. Marx, *The Eighteenth Brumaire of Louis Bonaparte*, trans. anon. (New York: International Publishers, 1963), 15.
20. Tolkien, *Letters*, 110. See also my *J.R.R. Tolkien's The Hobbit: Realizing History Through Fantasy* (New York: Palgrave Macmillan, 2022), 41–45.
21. Tolkien, *Fellowship of the Ring*, I.ii.65.
22. Tolkien, *The Hobbit* (New York: Del Rey, 1982), 305.
23. Georg Lukács, *The Historical Novel*, trans. Hannah and Stanley Mitchell (Lincoln: University of Nebraska Press, 1983), 34.
24. On this transition in Tolkien's overall project, see Dimitra Fimi's *Tolkien, Race, and Cultural History: From Fairies to Hobbits* (New York: Palgrave Macmillan, 2009).
25. See, e.g., François Hartog's discussion of the poet-historian as *rhapsode* in *The Mirror of Herodotus: The Representation of the Other in the Writing of History*, trans. Janet Lloyd (Berkeley: University of California Press, 2009).
26. Frank Kermode, *The Sense of an Ending: Studies in the Theory of Fiction* (Oxford: Oxford University Press, 1967), 7.
27. Jameson, "Introduction," *The Ideologies of Theory, Volume 1: Situations of Theory* (Minneapolis: University of Minnesota Press, 1988), xxxviii.
28. *Ibid.*
29. Jameson, *The Political Unconscious*, 285.
30. Tom Bombadil refers to himself as "the Eldest," and Celeborn addresses Treebeard as "Eldest." See Tolkien, *Fellowship of the Ring*, I.vii.148 and *Return of the King*, VI.vi.281.
31. See *infra*, Chapter 5; see also my "Galadriel, Witch-queen of Lórien." *Los Angeles Review of Books* (May 7, 2015): https://lareviewofbooks.org/article/galadriel-witch-queen-of-lorien/.
32. Tolkien, *Letters*, 153.
33. Tolkien, *Fellowship of the Ring*, II.i.261.
34. Jameson, *Archaeologies of the Future: The Desire Called Utopia and Other Science Fictions* (London: Verso, 2005), 263.
35. See Tolkien, *Letters*, 279: "it is of course a mythical feature, even though the world of the tales is conceived in more or less historical terms."
36. Tolkien, *Letters*, 26, 192, 178–179.
37. See Tolkien, *Letters*, 238.
38. Tom Shippey, *The Road to Middle-earth: How J. R. R. Tolkien Created a New Mythology* (Boston: Houghton Mifflin, 2003), 228–229.

39. Tolkien, *Letters*, 333. See also Peter Grybauskas, *A Sense of Tales Untold: Exploring the Edges of Tolkien's Literary Canvas* (Kent: Kent State University Press, 2021).
40. Tolkien, *Fellowship of the Ring*, 370, 349.
41. See Tolkien, *Return of the King*, Appendix B, 415–416.
42. Tolkien, *Letters*, 110–111.
43. Victor Serge, *Memoires of the Revolutionary*, trans. Peter Sedgwick and George Paizis (New York: New York Review of Books, 2012), 439.

Chapter 2

1. I refer to the "Silmarillion" (in quotation marks, rather than italicized) in order to distinguish Tolkien's vast, lifelong, and unfinished work—later collected, organized, and published in various forms by Christopher Tolkien in the 12-volume *History of Middle-earth* (1983–1996), *Unfinished Tales* (1980), and other posthumously published works—from *The Silmarillion*, published as a seemingly complete work, without much visible editorial apparatus, and as if "by" J. R. R. Tolkien in 1977. Christopher Tolkien later lamented the decision to release *The Silmarillion*, which misleadingly presented a much more coherent and consistent narrative than the original "Silmarillion" materials offer.
2. Tolkien, *The Letters of J.R.R. Tolkien*, ed. Humphrey Carpenter (Boston: Houghton Mifflin, 1981), 26, 24, 38.
3. *Ibid.*, 24.
4. See Joseph Pearce, *Tolkien, Man and Myth: A Literary Life* (London: HarperCollins, 1998), 1–10; see also Tom Shippey, *J. R. R. Tolkien: Author of the Century* (Boston: Houghton Mifflin, 2000), xx–xxiv. Both authors reflect on the poll, commissioned by Waterstone's (a British bookseller) and BBC Channel 4, and its aftermath, during which many famous writers and critics—unwilling or unable to hide their disdain for Tolkien in particular and fantasy more generally—bemoaned the results as a sign of cultural infantilism or cretinism.
5. See Tolkien, *Letters*, 139. Tolkien's desire to publish the "Silmarillion" materials together with *The Lord of Rings* is evident in several letters, but here he refers to them as "one long Saga of the Jewels and the Rings," noting that he was resolved "to treat them as one thing, however they might formally be issued" (*Letters* 139). In another letter, he refers to this "whole" work as the "Saga of the Three Jewels and the Rings of Power"; see *Letters*, 138.
6. In its earliest inception, the story of the hobbit was written for his own children (as Christopher Tolkien has noted from his own memories), and Tolkien likely had a child audience in mind when he wrote *The Hobbit*. This is evident in the text itself by the frequent avuncular "asides," for instance, but Tolkien lamented this aspect of the narrative later. For example, in a 1955 letter, Tolkien asserted that "The so-called 'children's story' [*The Hobbit*] was a fragment, torn out of an already existing mythology. In so far as it was *dressed up* as 'for children,' in style and manner, I regret it. So do the children"; see *Letters*, 218, emphasis supplied.
7. Tolkien, *Letters*, 23–24.
8. See *Ibid.*, 414.
9. Franco Moretti, *Modern Epic: The World System from Goethe to García Márquez*, trans. Quintin Hoare (London: Verso, 1996), 2.
10. Mikhail Bakhtin, "Discourse in the Novel," in *The Dialogic Imagination: Four Essays*, ed. and trans. Caryl Emerson and Michael Holquist (Austin: University of Texas Press, 1981), 262.
11. Fredric Jameson, *The Political Unconscious: Narrative as a Socially Symbolic Act* (Ithaca: Cornell University Press, 1981), 143–144.
12. See Nathaniel Hawthorne, *The House of the Seven Gables*, ed. Milton R. Stern (New York: Penguin, 1986), 1.
13. On Tolkien's use of medieval genres, see John D. Rateliff, "Inside Literature: Tolkien's Exploration of Medieval Genres," in *Tolkien in the New Century: Essays in Honor of Tom Shippey*, eds. John Wm. Houghton, Janet Brennan Croft, Nancy Martsch, John D. Rateliff, and Robin Anne Reid (Jefferson, NC: McFarland, 2014), 133–152.
14. Tolkien, "On Fairy-Stories," *The Monsters and the Critics and Other Essays*, ed. Christopher Tolkien (New York: HarperCollins, 2006), 113.

15. *Ibid.*, 114.
16. See Tolkien, *Letters*, 144–145.
17. Moretti, *The Modern Epic*, 50.
18. Tolkien, *Letters*, 150.
19. Georg Lukács, *Theory of the Novel*, trans. Anna Bostock (Cambridge: MIT Press, 1971), 29.
20. See Christopher Tolkien, "Foreword," in J. R. R. Tolkien, *The Book of Lost Tales: Part 1*, ed. Christopher Tolkien (New York: Del Rey, 1983), xvii.
21. Lukács, *Theory of the Novel*, 88.
22. Christopher Tolkien, "Foreword," *The Book of Lost Tales: Part 1*, xii.
23. Christopher Tolkien, "Introduction," in J. R. R. Tolkien, *Unfinished Tales of Númenor and Middle-earth*, ed. Christopher Tolkien (New York: Del Rey, 1988), 1.
24. *Ibid.*
25. For a meticulously researched and helpful account of how the materials from the entire *History of Middle-earth*, among other resources, became *The Silmarillion*, see Douglas Charles Kane's *Arda Reconstructed: The Creation of the Published Silmarillion* (Bethlehem, PA: Lehigh University Press, 2011).
26. See Karl Marx, *Grundrisse: Foundations of the Political Economy*, trans. Martin Nicolaus (New York: Penguin, 1973), 111.
27. As the "national" epic of Finland, created in the nineteenth-century from oral and folkloric tradition, the *Kalevala* is arguably quite different from the ancient epic, and imbued with the sort of nationalist political aims associated with its modern era. Indeed, Tolkien's desire to create an "English mythology" that was influenced by the *Kalevala*, among other works, initially had its own nationalist and arguably racialist (and racist) motives and ends.
28. Tolkien, *The Silmarillion* (New York: Del Rey, 1977), 306.
29. The "Prologue" to *The Lord of the Rings* establishes the marvelous metafiction that the narrative "comes to us" via the Red Book of Westmarch, which was initially Bilbo's "private diary" taken to Rivendell, returned to the Shire by Frodo, who along with Sam and later Merry and Pippin contributed to its pages; see Tolkien, *The Fellowship of the Ring* (New York: Del Rey, 1965), 16. In the Appendices to the novel, we learn that that information was also from the Red Book, even noting that "section A III, *Durin's Folk*, was probably derived from Gimli the Dwarf," along with other "realistic" details to explain the transmission of the historical narratives to our own present day; see Tolkien, *The Return of the King* (New York: Del Rey, 2012), App. A., 341.
30. In earlier versions of the "Silmarillion," Tolkien imagined other scenarios in which the "Silmarillion" narratives would be transmitted to the present, including one with the possibility of time-travel, an oddly science-fictional device for Tolkien's otherwise "fantasy" writings.
31. I discuss the ideas of this section and the next in more detail in my *J.R.R. Tolkien's* The Hobbit: *Realizing History Through Fantasy* (New York: Palgrave Macmillan, 2022), especially 26–35.
32. Dimitra Fimi, *Tolkien, Race, and Cultural History: From Fairies to Hobbits* (New York: Palgrave Macmillan, 2009), 120.
33. *Ibid.*, 118, 119, 120.
34. Quoted in Humphrey Carpenter, *The Inklings: C. S. Lewis, J. R. R. Tolkien, Charles Williams, and Their Friends* (Boston: Houghton Mifflin, 1979), 43. Carpenter there discusses the original scene, circa 1931, in which Lewis and Tolkien debated the value and morality of myths, which led Tolkien to write "Mythopoeia" as a response.
35. Tolkien, "Mythopoeia," in *Tree and Leaf* (New York: Harper Collins, 2001), 85.
36. *Ibid.*, 87.
37. *Ibid.*
38. Fimi, *Tolkien, Race, and Cultural History*, 119.
39. For example, Fimi pays particular attention to Tolkien's transformation of his mythical geography from a flat to a round world, which *in nuce* itself represents the shift from myth to history in the "Silmarillion" materials as they began to incorporate this events of the Third Age; see Fimi, *Tolkien, Race, and Cultural History*, 123–125.
40. Fimi, *Tolkien, Race, and Cultural History*, 128.
41. See Terry Pratchett, "Why Gandalf Never Married" (1985), available online: http://www.ansible.co.uk/misc/tpspeech.html.
42. Walter Scott, "On the Supernatural

in Fictitious Composition," in *Sir Walter Scott on Novelists and Fiction*, ed. Ioan Williams (London: Routledge, 1968), 247. The phrase "extra mœnia flammantia mundi" (i.e., beyond the flaming walls of the world) comes from Lucretius's *De Rerum Natura*, where he had used the phrase in praise of the unforeseen directions taken by Epicurus's philosophy.

43. Tolkien, *Letters*, 26.
44. Fimi, *Tolkien, Race, and Cultural History*, 5–6.
45. Tolkien, *The Hobbit* (New York: Del Rey, 1982), 110.
46. Tolkien, *Letters*, 26.
47. *Ibid.*, 64.
48. Jameson, *The Political Unconscious*, 102.
49. Jerome de Groot, *The Historical Novel* (London: Routledge, 2009), 3.
50. Lukács, *The Historical Novel*, trans. Hannah and Stanley Mitchell (Lincoln: University of Nebraska Press, 1983), 33.
51. Tolkien, "On Fairy-Stories," 144.
52. *Ibid.*, 113.
53. Tolkien, *The Hobbit*, 301, 305.
54. Fimi, *Tolkien, Race, and Cultural History*, 120.
55. Tolkien, *Letters*, 158.
56. As Moretti observes, the very word *comfort* takes on new meanings in the nineteenth century that connect it with a national character of English as well as a class character associated with the bourgeoisie: "The bourgeois home—the *English bourgeois home*—as the embodiment of comfort." See Moretti, *The Bourgeois: Between History and Literature* (London: Verso, 2013), 45.
57. Lukács, *The Historical Novel*, 61; see also Sebastian Mitchell, *Utopia and Its Discontents: Plato to Atwood* (London: Bloomsbury 2020), 175.
58. Tolkien, *Letters*, 279.
59. Tolkien, "On Fairy-Stories," 127.
60. *Ibid.*, 127–128.
61. Tolkien, *The Two Towers* (New York: Del Rey, 2012), III.v.97.

Chapter 3

1. In the United States, publication was delayed even further, with the three volumes appearing on October 21, 1954, April 21, 1955, and January 5, 1956, respectively.
2. Ralph Bakshi's incomplete animated adaptation of the novel (1978) was also to have comprised two films.
3. In fact, Tolkien altered the original text of *The Hobbit*, rewriting the "Riddles in the Dark" chapter to bring Gollum and the Ring more into line with their characteristics as they appear in *The Lord of the Rings*; see Doulas A. Anderson, ed, *The Annotated Hobbit*. 2nd ed. (Boston: Houghton Mifflin, 2002), 128; see also John D. Rateliff, *The History of* The Hobbit (Boston: Houghton Mifflin, 2007). In an unpublished note, "The Quest for Erebor," Tolkien depicts Gandalf's reasoning behind helping to launch Thorin and Company's quest, in part because he anticipated the return of Sauron and knew that the existence of the dragon in the north would have affected various strategies in what would become the War of the Ring; see Tolkien, *Unfinished Tales*, ed. Christopher Tolkien (New York: Del Rey, 1988), 335–351.
4. J. R. R. Tolkien, *The Letters of J.R.R. Tolkien*, ed. Humphrey Carpenter (Boston: Houghton Mifflin, 1981), 221.
5. The franchise now seems to be moving toward a more James Bond-style interminability. These future installments may be organized into trilogies, as with *The Force Awakens* (2015), *The Last Jedi* (2017), and *The Rise of Skywalker* (2019), even as it produces adjuncts, such as *Rogue One* (2016) and *Solo* (2019), which can be featured as standalone films within the same narrative universe. In Hollywood, such a marketing and production strategy has also been taken up with respect to comic book franchises and other properties, to the point that in the decade 2010–2019, not a single one of the Top 20 highest grossing films in the United States was not either a sequel or part of a move-franchise, and 18 of those were produced by a single corporation, The Walt Disney Company, which owns Lucasfilm, Pixar, and Marvel Studios. See Gerry Canavan, "Disney's Endgame: How the Franchise Came to Rule Cinema," *Frieze* (December 6, 2019): https://frieze.com/article/disneys-endgame-how-franchise-came-rule-cinema. As Canvan notes, with the exception of the *Star Wars* prequel film *The Phantom Menace* (1999), none of the Top 20 films of the 1990s had been either

sequels or part of a "franchise," which suggests that much indeed had changed about the film industry, viewers' inclinations, and mass culture more generally in those few decades.

6. Another marvelous literary trilogy for children or young adults, Philip Pullman's *His Dark Materials*, did not meet with similar success at the box office when adapted to the screen, and thus did not become a "film trilogy." The movie version of *The Golden Compass* was cut in such a way that it could conceivably stand alone, and when it failed to take in enough money, the planned adaptations of *The Subtle Knife* and *The Amber Spyglass* were never produced. A similar thing happened to the Susan Cooper series of novels known as *The Dark Is Rising* sequence; after an unsuccessful movie, *The Seeker* (2007), plans to produce film adaptations of the other novels in the series were scrapped. In retrospect and by contrast, the success of eight Harry Potter movies, based on a seven-book series—the seventh book was turned into two films—seems almost miraculous.

7. Apparently, Jackson had originally intended each adaptation to comprise two films. In a well-known story, Jackson "pitched" his *Lord of the Rings* to the studios as a two-film project, but received the "green light" to make three. *The Hobbit* was reportedly shot with it in mind to make two movies, but then Jackson and company expanded or recut it in such a way to have three films, thus making the entire Tolkien project a six-film saga divided into two trilogies. (The decision to transform an already completed adaptation of *The Hobbit* from two to three films was arguably motivated by desire for greater revenues, but it may also say something about the power of the *trilogy* form in contemporary mass culture.)

8. Tolkien, *Letters*, 270.

9. Farah Mendlesohn and Edward James, *A Short History of Fantasy* (London: Middlesex University Press, 2009), 144.

10. Tolkien, *Letters*, 24.

11. *Ibid.*, 26.

12. Quoted in Tolkien, *Letters*, 23.

13. Tolkien, *Letters*, 24.

14. See Dimitra Fimi, *Tolkien, Race, and Cultural History: From Fairies to Hobbits* (New York: Palgrave Macmillan, 2009) and Tom Shippey, *The Road to Middle-earth*, rev. and expanded ed. (Boston: Houghton Mifflin, 2003).

15. Tolkien, *Letters*, 138.

16. *Ibid.*, 163.

17. Tolkien, *The Two Towers* (New York: Del Rey, 2012), IV.viii.363.

18. Tolkien, *Letters*, 167.

19. *Ibid.*, *Letters*, 170

20. *Ibid.*

21. *Ibid.*, 173, 444. In Peter Jackson's film adaption, Saruman speaks of the "union of the two towers," clearly indicating his own Orthanc at Isengard and Sauron's Barad-dûr in Mordor.

22. Tolkien, *Letters*, 184.

23. Tolkien, *The Return of the King* (New York: Del Rey, 2012), VI.ii.208.

24. Tolkien, *Letters*, 178.

25. On this point in relation to the many changes made in Jackson's adaptation of *The Hobbit* to film, please see Janet Brennan Croft, "Barrel-Rides and She-Elves: Audience and Anticipation in Peter Jackson's *Hobbit* Trilogy," guest lecture, Marquette University Libraries Special Collections (March 26, 2015): available at https://www.academia.edu/13050712/Barrel_rides_and_She_elves_Audience_and_Anticipation_in_Peter_Jacksons_Hobbit_Trilogy.

26. On the alterations later made by Tolkien to the original 1937 edition of *The Hobbit*, see Douglas Anderson, *The Annotated Hobbit* and John D. Rateliff, *The History of the Hobbit*, each of which provides details of even minor changes made by the author in both the revised 1951 edition and the 1966 emendations, part of his reassertion of U.S. copyright. As Rateliff points out, Tolkien around 1960 had considered rewriting *The Hobbit* entirely so as to match the style and tone of *The Lord of the Rings*, but he "wisely abandoned the new draft"; see Rateliff, *The History of the Hobbit* (Boston: Houghton Mifflin, 2007), xxvi.

27. During the filming of *The Hobbit*, tantalizing rumors spread of a "bridge film" that might depict the adventures of a younger Aragorn, alluded to in Tolkien's work, but never formally represented in any detail.

28. But see Croft, "Mithril Coats and Tin Ears: 'Anticipation' and 'Flattening' in

Peter Jackson's *The Lord of the Rings* Trilogy," in *Tolkien on Film: Essays on Peter Jackson's The Lord of the Rings*, ed. Janet Brennan Croft (Altadena, CA: Mythopoeic Press, 2004), 63–80, on the effects of the many changes made by Jackson's film to the story of *The Lord of the Rings*.

29. Among the dragon's many epithets is "Smaug the Golden," as is mentioned in Appendix A of *The Lord of the Rings* (see Tolkien, *The Return of the King*, 389).

30. By contrast, one thinks of the never-ending story of the soap opera or other series without a known end-point.

31. Alberto Toscano and Jeff Kinkle, *Cartographies of the Absolute* (Winchester: Zero Books, 2014), 25.

Chapter 4

1. See J. R. R. Tolkien, *The Letters of J. R. R. Tolkien*, ed. Humphrey Carpenter (Boston: Houghton Mifflin, 1981), 266. The mistakes identified by Tolkien are so numerous that Carpenter, the editor of Tolkien's *Letters*, limited himself to "some extracts from Tolkien's lengthy commentary on the Story Line," rather than reprinting the letter in full. The errors are illuminating, as are Tolkien's "corrections." For example, referring to the writer (Morton Grady Zimmerman) as "Z," Tolkien asks, "Why does Z put beaks and feathers on Orcs!? (*Orcs* is not a form of *Auks*.) The Orcs are definitely stated to be corruptions of the 'human' form seen in Elves and Men. They are (or were) squat, broad, flat-nosed, sallow-skinned, with wide mouths and slant eyes: in fact degraded and repulsive versions of the (to Europeans) least lovely Mongol-types" (*Letters* 274). As I have pointed out in "Let Us Now Praise Famous Orcs" (Chapter 6 *infra*), this is Tolkien's most explicit description of the appearance of orcs and his definitive statement on the physical nature of this "race."

2. Tolkien, *Letters*, 270.

3. See Janet Brennan Croft, "Mithril Coats and Tin Ears: 'Anticipation' and 'Flattening' in Peter Jackson's *The Lord of the Rings* Trilogy," in *Tolkien on Film: Essays on Peter Jackson's* The Lord of the Rings, ed. Janet Brennan Croft (Altadena, CA: Mythopoeic Press, 2004), 63–80.

4. Filmmaking is a vast, collaborative endeavor, and even in the case of the great *auteurs*, it is probably misleading to name the director as the "author" of the film. However, for the purposes of this chapter, I will use "Peter Jackson" as the code-word or sign that indicates the collective creators of *The Lord of the Rings* movies, understanding always that screenplay writers (including Jackson himself), cinematographers, special effects wizards, producers, actors, and others have also stamped their subjectivity upon the final product under consideration.

5. Tolkien, *The Fellowship of the Ring* (New York: Del Rey, 2012), I.ii.65. Unless otherwise noted, all direct quotations of language from *The Lord of the Rings* come from Tolkien's novel, not from the films.

6. Of course, another reason to limit myself to *The Lord of the Rings* is that *The Hobbit* trilogy, as was made perfectly clear in the second film (*The Desolation of Smaug*), is not really a film adaptation of Tolkien's work, but rather a form of "fan fiction" in which the persons, events, and places depicted are only loosely tied to the imaginary world described in Tolkien's writings. Although critical readers may question the choices of the filmmakers in adapting *The Lord of the Rings* for the big screen, by the time they have seen *The Hobbit* films they will have understood that the purported source material is not really relevant to the movies at all, so they may as well sit back and enjoy the show. Fan fiction is often marvelous, and I am certainly not opposed to it at all, but it is quite different in intent and effects from what are generally understood to be "adaptations" of a text. That said, the term *adaptation* is itself quite capacious, and may include many things that deviate markedly from the purported sources.

7. Tom Shippey, *The Road to Middle-earth: How J. R. R. Tolkien Created a New Mythology* (Boston: Houghton Mifflin, 2003), 94–134.

8. *Ibid.*, 100.

9. Tolkien, *Fellowship of the Ring*, II.viii.419.

10. Shippey, *Road to Middle-earth*, 103.

11. Tolkien, *Letters*, 177.

12. Tolkien, *The Two Towers* (New York: Del Rey, 2012), III.iii.52.

13. Tolkien, *The Silmarillion* (New York: Del Rey, 2002), 139.

14. This thesis cannot be elaborated here, but see my "Tolkien's Geopolitical Fantasy: Spatial Narrative in *The Lord of the Rings*" in Lisa Fletcher, ed., *Popular Fiction and Spatiality: Reading Genre Settings* (New York: Palgrave Macmillan, 2016), 125–140.

15. For example, there is a remarkable body of geographical work that has been inspired by Tolkien, including the beautiful *Atlas of Middle-earth* by Karen Wynn Fonstad, first published in 1981, which uses state of the art cartographic techniques, lovely drawing, and finely attuned reading to map Tolkien's world.

16. Tolkien, *Two Towers*, IV.iii.278.

17. Tolkien, *Letters*, 332.

18. For example, the "Mouth of Sauron" scene was cut from the theatrical release of *The Lord of the Rings: The Return of the King*, but a version of it appeared on the extended special edition DVD. There the filmmakers designed a bizarre, masked demonic figure whose razor-tooth mouth was the only facial feature visible, but in Tolkien's text, the "Mouth of Sauron" was simply a man, a human spokesperson for Sauron, who had been sent as an envoy to "treat with" the armies of Gondor. Jackson's apparent inability to tell whether a character is merely incorrect without also being inherently "evil," along with Jackson's desire to effectively demonize any character that is not predetermined to be a "good guy," leads to many flaws in the films, including the disgraceful representation of the deeply depressed, despondent, and pathetic Denethor.

19. Michel de Certeau, *The Practice of Everyday Life*, trans. Steven Rendall (Berkeley: University of California Press, 1984), 92.

20. Ibid., 92–93.

21. Ibid., 93.

22. Ibid., 93, 96, 97.

23. Tolkien, *Fellowship of the Ring*, II.vii.407.

24. Tolkien, *Fellowship of the Ring*, II.ii.302.

25. In Appendix B of *The Return of the King*, we learn that Galadriel, Celeborn and a company of elf warriors did engage in battle, overthrowing the forces of Dol Guldur in southern Mirkwood. This is one of apparently many battle-scenes to remain "off-camera" in *The Lord of the Rings*, as the dwarves of Erebor, elves of Thranduil's kingdom, and men of Dale also fought in the North (see Tolkien, *The Return of the King*, 415–416).

26. See, e.g., Tolkien, *Letters*, 271.

27. Tom Conley, "*The Lord of the Rings* and the Fellowship of the Map," in *From Hobbits to Hollywood: Essays on Peter Jackson's Lord of the Rings*, eds. Earnest Mathijs and Murray Pomerance (Amsterdam: Rodopi, 2006), 218.

28. I refer especially to Foucault's analysis of power in *Discipline and Punish*, in which he insists: "We must cease once and for all to describe the effects of power in negative terms: it 'excludes,' it 'represses,' it 'censors,' it 'abstracts,' it 'masks,' it 'conceals.' In fact, power produces; it produces reality; it produces domains of objects and rituals of truth." See Michel Foucault, *Discipline and Punish*, trans. Alan Sheridan (New York: Vintage, 1977), 194.

29. See, e.g., Joseph Frank, "Spatial Form in Modern Literature," in *The Idea of Spatial Form* (New Brunswick: Rutgers University Press, 1991), 31–66.

30. See Kevin Lynch, *The Image of the City* (Cambridge: MIT Press, 1960).

31. Tolkien, *Fellowship of the Ring*, II.iii.321.

32. Jameson, *Postmodernism, or, the Cultural Logic of Late Capitalism* (Durham: Duke University Press, 1991), 51.

33. Jameson, "Cognitive Mapping," in *Marxism and the Interpretation of Culture*, eds. Cary Nelson and Lawrence Grossberg (Urbana: University of Illinois Press, 1988), 356.

34. Jameson, *The Geopolitical Aesthetic: Cinema and Space in the World System* (Bloomington and London: Indiana University Press and the British Film Institute, 1992), 9.

35. Tolkien, *The Return of the King* (New York: Del Rey, 2012), V.x.173.

36. One other, as baffling as it is egregious, is the decision to make Denethor an evil person, so much so that Gandalf actually murders him. In the book, this would have been unthinkable, as Denethor is a figure of great pity, someone driven mad with remorse and sadness, not to mention that he is also preyed upon by Sauron using the *palantír*. In the novel, Gandalf desperately tries to save him, and expresses genuine sadness over the terrible loss of such a

good and noble man. The films' depiction of Denethor is insulting—inasmuch as the filmmakers clearly believe that an audience cannot understand emotional complexity—and outrageous.

37. Tolkien, *Two Towers*, III.iii.44.

38. In the films, Saruman's "magic," such that it is, is also strangely literalized. Although Gandalf in the books makes clear that immense power of "the voice of Saruman" lies in its seductive rhetoric, Jackson chooses to depict this as either hypnotism or demonic possession. The absurd "possession" of Théoden, for example, clearly obviates the need for a Wormtongue character. If Saruman literally controls the king's mind, then why would a fraudulent counselor be needed? As Tolkien once explained, "Saruman's voice is not hypnotic but persuasive. Those who listened to him were not in danger of falling into a trance, but of agreeing with his arguments" (*Letters*, 276-277). Especially when delivered in Christopher Lee's *basso profondo*, coming from one of the wisest and subtlest beings in Middle-earth, Saruman's arguments are likely quite convincing.

39. Tolkien, *Silmarillion*, 90; Tolkien, *Letters*, 151.

40. Wielding a ring of power herself, Galadriel does rule a realm of silvan elves, a realm that she is able to maintain in a state of unnatural changelessness, effectively staunching the flow of time itself within her borders. Depending on one's point of view, she too could seem to be dangerous leader. See, e.g., Chapter 5 *infra*.

41. Tolkien, *Letters*, 146.

42. Tolkien, *Letters*, 279.

43. Douglas Kellner, "*The Lord of the Rings* as Allegory: A Multiperspectivist Reading," in *From Hobbits to Hollywood: Essays on Peter Jackson's Lord of the Rings*, eds. Earnest Mathijs and Murray Pomerance (Amsterdam: Rodopi, 2006), 20.

44. In 2022, such rhetoric reemerged with the Russian invasion of Ukraine, in which Russian solders have been actively likened to orcs in at attempt to literally demonize the enemy while nominally also paying homage to Tolkien's writings (or, more likely, to Jackson's films, which lack the political nuances of those writings).

45. Shippey, *J.R.R. Tolkien: Author of the Century* (Boston: Houghton Mifflin, 2000), 1.

46. For example, throughout *The Lord of the Rings: The Two Towers*, various characters call for or despair at the end of the "world of men," as if Jackson (who personally appears in a cameo as one of the "wild men" loyal to Saruman!) had not also included multiple scenes as incontestable evidence that both Saruman and Sauron have men willingly, indeed eagerly, fighting on their behalf.

47. China Miéville, "Editorial Introduction," *Historical Materialism* 10.4 (2002), 48.

Chapter 5

1. Quoted in Humphrey Carpenter, *J. R. R. Tolkien: A Biography* (Boston: Houghton Mifflin, 2000), 223.

2. Edmund Wilson, "Oo, Those Awful Orcs!" *The Bit Between My Teeth: Literary Chronicles, 1950-1965* (New York: Farrar, Strauss, and Giroux, 1965), 329.

3. J. R. R. Tolkien, *The Fellowship of the Ring* (New York: Del Rey, 2012), II.vii.400.

4. *Ibid.*, II.ii.291.

5. Tolkien, *The Silmarillion*, ed. Christopher Tolkien (New York: Del Rey, 2002), 23-24.

6. See Tolkien, *Morgoth's Ring*, ed. Christopher Tolkien (Boston: Houghton Mifflin, 1993), 394-398.

7. Tolkien, *The Fellowship of the Ring*, II.ii.300.

8. Tolkien, *The Silmarillion*, 23.

9. *Ibid.*, 18.

10. Tolkien, "Words, Phrases and Passages in Various Tongues in *The Lord of the Rings*," ed. Christopher Gilson, *Parma Eldalamberon* 17 (2007), 183.

11. Tolkien, *Morgoth's Ring*, 396-397.

12. *Ibid.*, 394-395, 400.

13. Tolkien, *The Silmarillion*, 303.

14. Tolkien, *The Letters of J.R.R. Tolkien*, ed. Humphrey Carpenter (Boston: Houghton Mifflin, 1981), 151.

15. Tolkien, *The Silmarillion*, 310.

16. Tolkien, *Letters*, 151, 243.

17. *Ibid.*, 152.

18. Tolkien, *The Silmarillion*, 310. One might argue that the unhappy lot was the fault of Morgoth and Sauron, who had created many of the monsters plaguing Middle-earth, but by the same token, one could say that this is all the more reason for

the Valar to wish to protect the remaining Children of Ilúvatar from such dangers.
19. Tolkien, *The Silmarillion*, 311.
20. *Ibid.*
21. *Ibid.*, 343.
22. Tolkien, *Letters*, 151, the reference to "words missing" in the original.
23. *Ibid.*, 243.
24. Tolkien, *The Silmarillion*, 343–344.
25. Tolkien, *Letters*, 276–277.
26. Tolkien, *The Silmarillion*, 90; Tolkien, *Letters*, 407.
27. Tolkien, "The Tale of Years," Appendix B, in *The Return of the King* (New York: Del Rey, 2012), 401; Tolkien, *The Silmarillion*, 358.
28. Galadriel's limited appearances in *The Silmarillion* tell only part of the story, and Tolkien revised her biography several times during the 1960s. For an excellent analysis of the various versions of the Galadriel story, see Romuald I. Lakowski, "The Fall and Repentance of Galadriel," in *Perilous and Fair: Women in the Works and Life of J. R. R. Tolkien*, eds. Janet Brennan Croft and Leslie A. Donovan (Altadena, CA: Mythopoeic Press, 2015), 153–167.
29. Tolkien, *The Silmarillion*, 90.
30. Tolkien, *Unfinished Tales of Númenor and Middle-earth*, ed. Christopher Tolkien (New York: Del Rey, 1988), 241.
31. Tolkien, *Letters*, 407.
32. On the "hierarchical" world of Tolkien's Middle-earth, see Dimitra Fimi, *Tolkien, Race, and Cultural History: From Fairies to Hobbits* (New York: Palgrave Macmillan, 2009), 131–159; see also Helen Young, *Race and Popular Fantasy Literature: Habits of Whiteness* (London: Routledge, 2016), 15–36.
33. Intriguingly, it is possible that the Witch-king was a very distant relative of Galadriel and Elrond. In "The Akallabêth," Tolkien writes, "it is said that among those whom [Sauron] ensnared with the Nine Rings three were great lords of Númenorean race" (Tolkien, *The Silmarillion*, 320).
34. See Tolkien, *The Return of the King* (New York: Del Rey, 2012), App. B, 415. In the final film of Jackson's *Hobbit* trilogy, *The Battle of the Five Armies*, Galadriel even gets to display some of her magical martial arts, as she defeats the Ringwraiths in a showdown at Dol Guldur.
35. Tolkien, *Letters*, 236.
36. Tolkien, *The Fellowship of the Ring*, II.vii.410.
37. *Ibid.*, II.vii.406.
38. Tolkien, *Letters*, 145–146.
39. Tolkien, *The Fellowship of the Ring*, II.vii.405–406.
40. *Ibid.*, II.vii.407.
41. *Ibid.*, II.vii.410.
42. Tolkien, *The Fellowship of the Ring*, II.vii.400.
43. Tolkien, *Letters*, 65.
44. Tolkien, *The Two Towers* (New York: Del Rey, 1965) IV.x.393–394.
45. *Ibid.*, *The Fellowship of the Ring*, II.ii.291.
46. See Tolkien, *The Silmarillion*, 360–361.
47. Tolkien, *The Two Towers*, III.v.102.
48. In the "Valaquenta," for instance, Tolkien writes that Aulë "in thought and powers" was most like Melkor, and "[b]oth, also, desired to make things of their own that should be new and unthought of by others, and delighted in the praise of their skill" (*The Silmarillion*, 18).
49. Tolkien, *Letters*, 145–146.
50. Tolkien, *Letters*, 274.
51. Tolkien, *The Two Towers*, III.v.105.
52. Tolkien, *Letters*, 279.
53. Tolkien, *The Fellowship of the Ring*, II.vii.411. Galadriel's test-passing demonstrates that she realized the degree that her desires were more-or-less identical to Sauron's, and that she had the wisdom to deny herself such power.
54. Tolkien, *The Two Towers*, III.v.102.
55. Tolkien, *Letters*, 243; in a footnote on the same page, Tolkien explains, "[w]hen he [Sauron] found how greatly his knowledge was admired by all other rational creatures and how easy it was to influence them, his pride became boundless." Notably, "pride" is often mentioned as a characteristic of Galadriel as well, not to mention of other "good" characters.
56. Tolkien, *The Fellowship of the Ring*, II.vii.411.
57. Tolkien, *Letters*, 242.

Chapter 6

1. See also my forthcoming study on Tolkien's Orcs, to be published by McFarland in 2024.

2. As Tolkien notes, his use of the term "orc" comes from the Old English *orc*, meaning "demon"; see Tolkien, *The Letters of J.R.R. Tolkien*, ed. Humphrey Carpenter (Boston: Houghton Mifflin, 1981), 177–178. The word *orcnéas* appears in *Beowulf*, in fact, where Tolkien translates it as "haunting shapes of hell"; see Tolkien, *Beowulf: A Translation and Commentary*, ed. Christopher Tolkien (Boston: Houghton Mifflin, 2014), 161–162.

3. Tolkien, *The Silmarillion*, ed. Christopher Tolkien (New York: Del Rey, 2002), 47.

4. Tolkien, *The Two Towers* (New York: Del Rey, 2012), III.iv.91.

5. Tolkien, *The Silmarillion*, 103–104.

6. Dimitra Fimi, *Tolkien, Race, and Cultural History: From Fairies to Hobbits* (New York: Palgrave Macmillan, 2009), 155.

7. See Tolkien, *Morgoth's Ring*, ed. Christopher Tolkien (Boston: Houghton Mifflin, 1993), 408–425.

8. Tolkien, *Unfinished Tales of Númenor and Middle-earth*, ed. Christopher Tolkien (New York: Del Rey, 1988), 401–402.

9. Tolkien, *Morgoth's Ring*, 421.

10. Tolkien, *The Return of the King* (New York: Del Rey, 2012), VI.i.201.

11. Tolkien, *The Silmarillion*, 37–38. In a letter, Tolkien refers to this moment: "The One rebuked Aulë, saying that he had tried to usurp the Creator's power; but he could not give independent *life* to his makings" (*Letters*, 287).

12. Tolkien, *Letters*, 195.

13. Tom Shippey, "Orcs, Wraiths, Wights: Tolkien's Images of Evil," in *J.R.R. Tolkien and his Literary Resonances*, eds. George Clark and Daniel Timmons (Westport, CT: Greenwood, 2000), 186.

14. Tolkien, *The Silmarillion*, 47.

15. Tolkien, *Two Towers*, III.vii.152. Given that orcs are sentient beings who have communities and families and who reproduce sexually, the notion that Morgoth, Sauron, or Saruman "breeds" orcs can only be understood as ideological propagandizing, with little basis in the truth of how orc populations arise and grow. It would be akin to a Soviet commentator asserting that U.S. Presidents Truman and Eisenhower "bred" Americans—it was called the "baby boom," after all—in the late 1940s and 1950s in order to swell the ranks of U.S. soldiery during the Cold War. Orcs are no more "bred" than elves, men, or dwarves, but by rhetorically positioning orcs as livestock or worse, the elvish ideology facilitates the demonizing of the enemy, which in turn makes their genocidal annihilation all the more acceptable. As Charles Mills has put it, "[t]he pen here prepares the way for the sword"; established as "people without history," orcs are excluded from the legitimate spaces of the world, relegated to being mere "slaves" of the dark powers, a term used with opprobrium and without pity. Hence, "[t]he literal genocide of the orcs with which the book concludes is in a sense of secondary importance to the cultural genocide that their creation signified in the first place." The orcs are a racialized underclass used to reinforce racist social hierarchies. See Charles Mills, "The Wretched of Middle-earth: An Orkish Manifesto," *The Southern Journal of Philosophy* 60(Suppl. 1).S1 (September 2022), 128, 135.

16. Shippey, *The Road to Middle-earth* (Boston: Houghton Mifflin, 2003), 233.

17. Tolkien, *The Hobbit* (New York: Del Rey, 1982), 281; Tolkien, *Return of the King*, 392. In the Peter Jackson–directed films comprising *The Hobbit*, both Azog and Bolg are characters who menace and fight Thorin and his company.

18. Tolkien, *Letters*, 195.

19. Tolkien, *Letters*, 274. Tolkien's use of the parenthetical "(to Europeans)" suggests cultural relativism in this regard, as what Europeans find "least lovely" may differ from the aesthetic standards of peoples from other continents.

20. See Fimi, *Tolkien, Race, and Cultural History*, 131–159.

21. See Peter E. Firchow, "The Politics of Fantasy: *The Hobbit* and Fascism," *Midwest Quarterly* 51.1 (Autumn 2008): 15–27.

22. See Robert Stuart, *Tolkien, Race, and Racism in Middle-earth* (New York: Palgrave Macmillan, 2022); see also my book review in *Mythlore* 41.1 (Fall/Winter 2022): 256–261.

23. See Erik Sofge, "Orc Holocaust: The Reprehensible Moral Universe of Gary Gygax's *Dungeons & Dragons*," *Slate Magazine* (posted Monday, March 10, 2008): http://www.slate.com/id/2186203.

24. Tolkien, *Two Towers*, IV.iv.301.

25. Tolkien, *Return of the King*, VI.iv.243.

26. See Tolkien, *Return of the King*, VI.v.266–267.

27. Interestingly, such a possibility of sympathizing with orcs as victims is at least raised briefly in Season 1 of the Amazon Prime series *The Lord of the Rings: The Rings of Power* (2022), particularly through the invented character Adar, who appears to be the first (or one of the first) elves-transformed-into-orcs. See my "Uruk ... We prefer 'Uruk': The Representation of the Orc in *The Rings of Power*," in *Race, Racisms, and Racists: Essays on J.R.R. Tolkien's Legendarium, Adaptation, and Readers*, ed. Robin Anne Reid (Jefferson, NC: McFarland, forthcoming 2024).

28. Tolkien, *Two Towers*, IV.x.391–393.

29. *Ibid.*, IV.x.393.

30. Needless to say, perhaps, but various visions of the "American Dream" have been made possible through the direct conquest, mass killings, and territorial conquest of indigenous populations, not to mention other brutal forms of primitive accumulations, so the seeming barbarism of the orcs' dreams are not that far removed from more putatively "civilized" variants of the same.

31. Tolkien, *Two Towers*, III.iii.42–43. The multilingual cosmopolitanism of the orcs is here in direct contrast to the monolingual parochialism of the hobbit, but few credit the orcs for their worldliness and multicultural sensibilities, of course.

32. *Ibid.*, III.iii.43.

33. *Ibid.*, III.iii.44.

34. *Ibid.*, IV.x.398.

35. Shippey, *J. R. R. Tolkien: Author of the Century* (Boston: Houghton Mifflin, 2000), 133.

36. Tolkien, *Two Towers*, III.iii.51, 60.

37. Tolkien, *Return of the King*, VI.i.201.

38. Tolkien, *Two Towers*, III.iii.46.

39. There is only one reference in all of Tolkien's legendarium to an orc being taken captive. In *The Hobbit*, Beorn reveals that he had caught a goblin and a warg, "forced" them to talk, then brutally killed them, beheading the goblin and skinning the warg, before posted the head and skin outside his house. See *The Hobbit* (New York: Del Rey, 1982), 131. The Peter Jackson film, *The Hobbit: The Desolation of Smaug*, includes a scene in which Thranduil (a.k.a. Elvenking) interrogate a captive orc, who is summarily executed even before the interrogation can be completed, as Legolas points out to his father. Before decapitating his prisoner, Thranduil employed an "elvish trick" by promising the orc freedom in exchange for information, but upon receiving the orc's testimony, as he smugly announces, Thranduil "freed his wretched head from his miserable shoulders" instead.

40. Tolkien, *Letters*, 244. Ironically, perhaps, in this same letter Tolkien objects to the use of the term "political," but does so in part by defining it narrowly, meaning in support of "this or that polity," rather than involving a more "humane" concern for the general welfare. He explains that Frodo's quest had as its object "the liberation from evil tyranny of all the 'humane'—including those, such as 'easterlings' and Haradrim, that were still servants of the tyranny" (i.e., political opponents), and he adds in a footnote that the term *humane* "includes of course Elves, and indeed all 'speaking creatures'" (*Letters* 240–241). Hence, despite himself, Tolkien includes—but without mentioning them by name—orcs as "humane" people to be liberated at the successful conclusion of Frodo's quest.

41. Tolkien, *Letters*, 195.

42. *Ibid.*, 330.

43. *Ibid.*, 190, 195.

44. *Ibid.*, 82, 78, 90.

45. Shippey, *Road to Middle-earth*, 234.

46. It is telling, perhaps, that the letter in which Tolkien suggests that orcs are not "irredeemably bad" was not sent, on the grounds that, in his words, "It seemed to be taking myself too importantly"; see Tolkien, *Letters*, 196.

47. To use a Biblical example, it is hard to imagine that the intended audience of the Book of Joshua sympathizes with the Canaanites when Joshua, with God, invades one city after another, killing "all the souls that were therein; he let none remain" (see, e.g., Joshua 10:37).

48. This is essentially the perspective given in Kirill Yeskov's unauthorized and revisionist retelling of the War of the Ring, *The Last Ringbearer*, which features no orcs at all, as what Tolkien's heroes think of as orcs are simply men from Mordor and

other regions, which is arguably consistent with Tolkien's image of orcs as Mongol-types. See Yeskov, *The Last Ringbearer*, trans. Yisroel Markov (Saint Paul, MN: Tenseg Press, 2011).

49. Tolkien, *Letters*, 110.

Chapter 7

1. Paul Fussell, *The Great War and Modern Memory* (Oxford: Oxford University Press, 1975), 75.
2. See Robert Rhodes James, *Gallipoli*. New York: Macmillan, 1965), 86.
3. Fussell, *The Great War*, 79.
4. Tolkien, *The Letters of J.R.R. Tolkien*, ed. Humphrey Carpenter (Boston: Houghton Mifflin, 1981), 8.
5. Tolkien, *The Silmarillion*, ed. Christopher Tolkien (New York: Del Rey, 2002), 47.
6. Tolkien, *Letters*, 78.
7. *Ibid.*
8. See Tolkien, *Letters*, 55–56.
9. John Garth, *Tolkien and the Great War: The Threshold of Middle-Earth* (London: HarperCollins, 2003), 218–219.
10. Tolkien, *Letters*, 93.
11. Tolkien, *Letters*, 82.
12. Janet Brennan Croft, *War in the Works of J. R. R. Tolkien* (Westport, CT: Praeger, 2004), 47–50.
13. Tolkien, *Letters*, 177–178.
14. There is much debate about the nature and origin of dragons among Tolkien fans. Tolkien himself wrote that Morgoth "bred" the first dragons, but given that "evil" cannot create new life (only Eru or God can), there must have been some raw material to work with, just as orcs are thought to have been "corrupted" elves or men. Dragons are sentient and speak languages, which suggests that they are "humane" in Tolkien's use of the term, although there are many animals (eagles, wargs, etc.) in Tolkien's writings who share these faculties. Some have suggested that dragons, like balrogs, are "Maiar" or perhaps are part-Maiar (as with progeny of Ungoliant, a great spider-like spirit that apparently mated with actual spiders to produce such monsters as Shelob or the great spiders of Mirkwood).
15. See Tolkien, *The Fellowship of the Ring* (New York: Del Rey, 2012), II.v.369–370.

16. Tolkien, *The Silmarillion*, ed. Christopher Tolkien (New York: Del Rey, 2002), 47.
17. Tolkien, *The Two Towers* (New York: Del Rey, 2012), III.iv.91.
18. Tolkien, *The Silmarillion*, 103–104.
19. Dimitra Fimi, *Tolkien, Race, and Cultural History: From Fairies to Hobbits* (New York: Palgrave Macmillan, 2009), 155.
20. Tolkien, *The Two Towers*, IV.iv.301.
21. Tolkien, *The Return of the King* (New York: Del Rey, 2012), VI.v.266–267.
22. Tolkien, *The Two Towers*, III.viii.162–163.
23. Tolkien, *The Return of the King*, VI.iv.243–244.
24. Shippey, "Orcs, Wraiths, Wights: Tolkien's Images of Evil," in *J. R. R. Tolkien and His Literary Resonances*, eds. George Clark and Daniel Timmons (Westport, CT: Greenwood, 2000), 186.
25. Shippey, *The Road to Middle-Earth* (Boston: Houghton Mifflin, 2003), 233.
26. Shippey, *J.R.R. Tolkien: Author of the Century* (Boston: Houghton Mifflin, 2000), 133.
27. Tolkien, *The Two Towers*, IV.v.323; see also Virginia Luling, "An Anthropologist in Middle-earth," *Mallorn: The Journal of the Tolkien Society* 33 (1995), 54.
28. Tolkien, *Letters*, 274.
29. See Charles Mills, "The Wretched of Middle-earth: An Orkish Manifesto," *The Southern Journal of Philosophy* 60(Suppl. 1).S1 (September 2022), 105–135.
30. With respect to the racial hierarchies and to racism more generally, it is mentioned that some of the "Men" serving Saruman resembled orcs, including one "great squint-eyed brute like a huge orc" (see Tolkien, *The Return of the King*, VI.viii.321). "Squint-eyed," which is used several times in the novel and often in reference to orcs or to men who looked like orcs or "half an orc," is undoubtedly also a crude, racially biased way of referring to features of east Asian physiognomy.
31. Shippey, *Road to Middle-earth*, 234.
32. See Tolkien, *Letters*, 240–241.
33. Fredric Jameson, *The Political Unconscious: Narrative as a Socially Symbolic Act* (Ithaca: Cornell University Press, 1981), 52–53.
34. Tolkien, *The Two Towers*, IV.v.314.
35. Studs Terkel, *The Good War: An Oral*

History of World War II (New York: New Press, 1984), 117–118.
  36. *Ibid.*, 118.
  37. *Ibid.*, 137–138.
  38. *Ibid.*, 137. The Peter Jackson films even downplay the role of human enemies, making the armies of Saruman and Sauron more orc-heavy than they are in the novel, for instance. Saruman is even made to say that the "world of men" is at an end, even as he then goes to recruit the "Wild Men" to aid in his war effort, and Sauron's armies are filled with "men" from various parts of the world. The filmmakers thus went out of their way to demonize the enemy much further than even Tolkien's own characters could imagine.
  39. Tolkien, *Letters*, 82.
  40. *Ibid.*, 111.

Chapter 8

  1. T.A. Shippey, *J.R.R. Tolkien: Author of a New Century* (Boston: Houghton Mifflin, 2002), vii–viii.
  2. Kathryn Hume, *Fantasy and Mimesis: Responses to Reality in Western Literature* (New York: Methuen, 1984), 195.
  3. See my *Utopia in the Age of Globalization: Space, Representation, and the World System* (New York: Palgrave Macmillan, 2013); see also my *The Fiction of Dread: Dystopia, Monstrosity, and Apocalypse* (New York: Bloomsbury, 2024).
  4. See J.R.R. Tolkien, "On Fairy-stories," *The Monsters and the Critics and Other Essays*, ed. Christopher Tolkien (London: HarperCollins, 1983), 135.
  5. Fredric Jameson, *Archaeologies of the Future: The Desire Called Utopia and Other Science Fictions* (London: Verso, 2005), 56–71.
  6. Darko Suvin, *Metamorphoses of Science Fiction: On the Poetics and History of a Literary Genre* (New Haven: Yale University Press, 1979), 61.
  7. Jameson, *Archaeologies of the Future*, 56.
  8. See Tolkien, "On Fairy-stories," 147–153.
  9. Here it should be acknowledged that there are in fact many practitioners and theorists of fantasy who do not nicely fit into these stereotypes, and one could easily list many liberal, left-wing, or Marxist fantasists, from Mervyn Peake to China Miéville, Alan Moore to Neil Gaiman, and so on. Indeed, Miéville has noted a certain *rapprochement* between Marxism and fantasy, visible in the special issue of *Historical Materialism* devoted to the subject. See also Marc Bould and China Miéville's edited collection, *Red Planets: Marxism and Science Fiction* (Middletown: Wesleyan University Press, 2009). In an afterword to this volume, Miéville notes that many Marxist critics remain skeptical of fantasy and committed to science-fiction or utopia, largely because of the "ideology of cognition" established by Suvin, Jameson, and others, and that these critics have ignored the revolutionary potential of the fantastic. As Miéville concludes, "*Red Planets* we have. We should not neglect the red dragons" ("Cognition as Ideology: A Dialectic of SF Theory," *Red Planets*, 245).
  10. Suvin, *Metamorphoses of Science Fiction*, 4.
  11. See Georg Lukács, *Theory of the Novel*, trans. Anna Bostock (Cambridge: MIT Press, 1971).
  12. Tolkien, "On Fairy-stories," 144.
  13. Michael Moorcock, *Wizardry and Wild Romance: A Study of Epic Fantasy* (London: Victor Gollancz Ltd., 1987), 126.
  14. Tolkien, "On Fairy-stories," 148.
  15. *Ibid.*, 113.
  16. Tolkien, *The Fellowship of the Ring* (New York: Del Rey, 2012), II.ii.278.
  17. Hence, I am not speaking of the "real world" history and geography that Brian Bates has explored in his *The Real Middle-earth: Exploring the Magic and Mystery of the Middle Ages, J.R.R. Tolkien, and The Lord of the Rings* (New York: Palgrave Macmillan, 2003).
  18. Tolkien, "On Fairy-stories," 135.
  19. *Ibid.*, 134.
  20. Jameson, *Archaeologies of the Future*, 63. As Miéville has also observed, however, there is no particularly good reason to treat "faster-than-light drives as science-fictional in a way that dragons are not, despite repeated assurances from the great majority of physicists that the former are no less impossible than the latter"; see Miéville, "Cognition as Ideology," in *Red Planets*, 234.
  21. Tolkien, *The Letters of J.R.R. Tolkien*, ed. Humphrey Carpenter (Boston: Houghton Mifflin, 1981), 145.

22. *Ibid.*, 145–146.
23. *Ibid.*, 146.
24. Tolkien, *Fellowship of the Ring*, II.vii.405.
25. *Ibid.*, II.vii.406.
26. *Ibid.*, II.vii.407.
27. Tolkien, *The Return of the King* (New York: Del Rey, 1965), VI.ix.339, App. B, 403.
28. Tolkien, *Letters*, 145.
29. *Ibid.*, 146.
30. Jameson, *Archaeologies of the Future*, 58.
31. Moorcock, *Wizardry and Wild Romance*, 125.
32. Shippey, *J.R.R. Tolkien*, 148. Shippey quotes Muir's review, "A Boy's World," *Observer* (November 27, 1955), 11.
33. Tolkien, *The Two Towers* (New York: Del Rey, 1965), III.viii.169.
34. Tolkien, *The Fellowship of the Ring*, I.ii.67.
35. Tolkien, *Letters*, 332–333.
36. Tolkien, *The Two Towers*, II.iv.301.
37. Shippey, *J.R.R. Tolkien*, 128–129.
38. Jameson, *Marxism and Form: Twentieth Century Dialectical Theories of Literature* (Princeton: Princeton University Press, 1971), 309.
39. Tolkien, *The Fellowship of the Ring*, I.ii.65.
40. Tolkien, *The Fellowship of the Ring*, I.ii.55–56.
41. Tolkien, *Return of the King*, V.ix.160. Marx's line about the "cook-shops of the future" appears in *Capital, Volume I*, trans. Ben Fowkes (New York: Penguin, 1976), 99.
42. Tolkien, *Fellowship of the Ring*, I.ii.61.
43. *Ibid.*, I.ii.65.
44. Jameson, *Valences of the Dialectic* (London: Verso, 2009), 421.
45. See China Miéville, "Editorial Introduction: Marxism and Fantasy," *Historical Materialism* 10.4 (2002), 43.
46. Eric S. Rabkin, *The Fantastic in Literature* (Princeton: Princeton University Press, 1976), 227.
47. Shippey, *J.R.R. Tolkien*, 299.
48. Jameson, *The Seeds of Time* (New York: Columbia University Press, 1994), xii.

Conclusion

1. Elsewhere, Miéville himself uses this term, when contrasting "the literature of recognition versus that of estrangement," a distinction he finds far more productive than the false binary opposing "literary fiction" to "genre fiction" such as SF or fantasy. See Sarah Crown, "What the Booker Prize Really Excludes," *The Guardian* (October 17, 2011): https://www.theguardian.com/books/booksblog/2011/oct/17/science-fiction-china-mieville.
2. China Miéville, "Cognition as Ideology: A Dialectic of SF," *Red Planets: Marxism and Science Fiction*, eds. Marc Bould and China Miéville (Middletown, CT: Wesleyan University Press, 2009), 234.
3. Miéville, "Editorial Introduction: Marxism and Fantasy," *Historical Materialism* 10.4 (2002), 46.
4. Miéville, "Cognition as Ideology," 245.
5. This work is tentatively titled *Tolkien's Orcs: A Critical Reassessment* (Jefferson, NC: McFarland, forthcoming 2025).
6. Fredric Jameson, "Introduction," *The Ideologies of Theory, Volume 1: The Syntax of History* (Minneapolis: University of Minnesota Press, 1988), xxvii. Following this sentence Jameson adds, parenthetically, "The stereotypical characterization of such enlargement as *reductive* remains a never-ending source of hilarity."
7. Karl Marx and Friedrich Engels, *The Communist Manifesto*, trans. Samuel Moore (New York: Signet, 1998 [1848]), 54.
8. J. R. R. Tolkien, *The Letters of J. R. R. Tolkien*, ed. Humphrey Carpenter (Boston: Houghton Mifflin, 1981), 110.
9. Fredric Jameson, *The Political Unconscious: Narrative as a Socially Symbolic Act* (Ithaca: Cornell University Press, 1981), 19.
10. Jameson, *Marxism and Form: Twentieth-Century Dialectical Theories of Literature* (Princeton: Princeton University Press, 1971), 163.
11. See Tolkien, *The Fellowship of the Ring* (New York: Del Rey, 2012), I.ii.56, 65.

Bibliography

Selected Works by J.R.R. Tolkien

Beowulf: A Translation and Commentary. Ed. Christopher Tolkien. Houghton Mifflin, 2014.

"*Beowulf*: The Monsters and the Critics." *The Monsters and the Critics and Other Essays*. Ed. Christopher Tolkien. HarperCollins, 1983. 5–48.

The Book of Lost Tales, Part I. Ed. Christopher Tolkien. *The History of Middle-earth*: Vol. 1. George Allen and Unwin, 1983.

The Book of Lost Tales, Part II. Ed. Christopher Tolkien. *The History of Middle-earth*: Vol. 2. George Allen and Unwin, 1984.

The Fellowship of the Ring. Del Rey, 2012.

The History of Middle-earth (12 volumes).

The Hobbit. Del Rey, 1982.

The Lays of Beleriand. Ed. Christopher Tolkien. *The History of Middle-earth*: Vol. 3. George Allen and Unwin, 1985.

"Leaf By Niggle." *The Tolkien Reader*. Del Rey, 1966. 100–120.

The Letters of J.R.R. Tolkien. Ed. Humphrey Carpenter. Houghton Mifflin, 1981.

The Lord of the Rings (three volumes).

The Lost Road and Other Writings. Ed. Christopher Tolkien. *The History of Middle-earth*: Vol. 5. Unwin Hyman, 1987.

Morgoth's Ring. Ed. Christopher Tolkien. *The History of Middle-earth*: Vol. 10. HarperCollins, 1993.

"Mythopoiea." *Tree and Leaf*. HarperCollins, 2001. 85–90.

"On Fairy-Stories." *The Monsters and the Critics and Other Essays*. Ed. Christopher Tolkien. HarperCollins, 1983. 109–161.

The Peoples of Middle-earth. Ed. Christopher Tolkien. *The History of Middle-earth*: Vol. 12. HarperCollins, 1996.

The Return of the King. Del Rey, 2012.

The Return of the Shadow. Ed. Christopher Tolkien. *The History of Middle-earth*: Vol. 6. Unwin Hyman, 1988.

Sauron Defeated. Ed. Christopher Tolkien. *The History of Middle-earth*: Vol. 9. HarperCollins, 1992.

The Shaping of Middle-earth. Ed. Christopher Tolkien. *The History of Middle-earth*: Vol. 4. George Allen and Unwin, 1986.

The Silmarillion. Del Rey, 2002.

The Treason of Isengard. Ed. Christopher Tolkien. *The History of Middle-earth*: Vol. 7. Unwin Hyman, 1989.

The Two Towers. Del Rey, 2012.

Unfinished Tales of Númenor and Middle-earth. Ed. Christopher Tolkien. Del Rey, 1988.

The War of the Jewels. Ed. Christopher Tolkien. *The History of Middle-earth*: Vol. 11. HarperCollins, 1994.

The War of the Ring. Ed. Christopher Tolkien. *The History of Middle-earth*: Vol. 8. Unwin Hyman, 1990.

"Words, Phrases and Passages in Various Tongues in *The Lord of the Rings*." Ed. Christopher Gilson. *Parma Eldalamberon* 17 (2007).

Other Works Cited

Althusser, Louis. "Ideology and Ideological State Apparatuses (Notes Toward an Investigation)." *Lenin and Philosophy and Other Essays.* Trans. Ben Brewster. New York: Monthly Review Press, 1971. 127–186.

Anderson, Douglas A., ed. *The Annotated Hobbit.* 2nd ed. Boston: Houghton Mifflin, 2002.

Aristotle. *The Poetics.* Trans. S.H. Butcher. Boston: Hill and Wang, 1961.

Auerbach, Erich. "Philology and *Weltliteratur.*" Trans. M. and E.W. Said. *Centennial Review* 13.1 (1969): 1–17.

Bakhtin, Mikhail. *The Dialogic Imagination: Four Essays.* Ed. and trans. Caryl Emerson and Michael Holquist. Austin: University of Texas Press, 1981.

Bates, Brian. *The Real Middle-earth: Exploring the Magic and Mystery of the Middle Ages, J.R.R. Tolkien, and* The Lord of the Rings. New York: Palgrave Macmillan, 2003.

Berman, Marshall. *All That is Solid Melts into Air: The Experience of Modernity.* New York: Penguin Books, 1988.

Bogost, Ian. "Where in the World is Middle Earth [sic]?" June 20, 2007: https://bogost.com/writing/blog/where_in_the_world_was_middle/.

Burger, Peter. *The Political Unconscious of the Fantasy Sub-Genre of Romance.* Lewiston, NY: The Edwin Mellen Press, 2001.

Canavan, Gerry. "Disney's Endgame: How the Franchise Came to Rule Cinema." *Frieze,* December 6, 2019: https://frieze.com/article/disneys-endgame-how-franchise-came-rule-cinema.

Carpenter, Humphrey. *The Inklings: C.S. Lewis, J.R.R. Tolkien, Charles Williams, and Their Friends.* New York: HarperCollins, 2006.

———. *J.R.R. Tolkien: A Biography.* Houghton Mifflin, 2000.

Certeau, Michel de. *The Practice of Everyday Life.* Trans. Steven Rendall. Berkeley: University of California Press, 1984.

Chance, Jane. "Subversive Fantasist: Tolkien on Class Difference." In *The Lord of the Rings, 1954–2004: Scholarship in Honor of Richard E. Blackwelder.* Eds. Wayne Hammond and Cristina Scull. Milwaukee: Marquette University Press, 2006. 153–168.

Chance, Jane, and Alfred K. Siewers, eds. *Tolkien's Modern Middle Ages.* New York: Palgrave Macmillan, 2005.

Chesterton, G.K. *Charles Dickens: A Critical Study.* New York: Dodd Mead and Co., 1906.

Colebatch, Hal. *Return of the Heroes:* The Lord of the Rings, Star Wars, Harry Potter, *and Social Conflict.* 2nd ed. Christchurch: Cybereditions, 2003.

Conley, Tom. "*The Lord of the Rings* and the Fellowship of the Map." In *From Hobbits to Hollywood: Essays on Peter Jackson's* Lord of the Rings. Eds. Earnest Mathijs and Murray Pomerance. Amsterdam: Rodopi, 2006. 215–229.

Croft, Janet Brennan. "Barrel-Rides and She-Elves: Audience and Anticipation in Peter Jackson's *Hobbit* Trilogy." Guest lecture, Marquette University Libraries Special Collections (March 26, 2015): https://www.academia.edu/13050712/Barrel_rides_and_She_elves_Audience_and_Anticipation_in_Peter_Jacksons_Hobbit_Trilogy.

———. "Mithril Coats and Tin Ears: 'Anticipation' and 'Flattening' in Peter Jackson's *The Lord of the Rings Trilogy.*" In *Tolkien on Film: Essays on Peter Jackson's* The Lord of the Rings. Ed. Janet Brennan Croft. Altadena, CA: Mythopoeic Press, 2004, 63–80.

———. *War in the Works of J.R.R. Tolkien.* Westport, CT: Praeger, 2004.

Croft, Janet Brenan, and Leslie A. Donovan, eds. *Perilous and Fair: Women in the Works and Life of J.R.R. Tolkien.* Altadena, CA: Mythopoeic Press, 2015.

Crown, Sarah. "What the Booker Prize Really Excludes." *The Guardian* (October 17, 2011): https://www.theguardian.com/books/booksblog/2011/oct/17/science-fiction-china-mieville.

Ekman, Stefan. *Here Be Dragons: Exploring Fantasy Maps and Settings.* Middletown, CT: Wesleyan University Press, 2013.

Ellmann, Mary. "Growing Up Hobbitic." *New American Review* 2 (1968): 217–29.

Fimi, Dimitra. *Tolkien, Race, and Cultural History: From Fairies to Hobbits.* London: Palgrave Macmillan, 2009.

Firchow, Peter E. "The Politics of Fantasy: *The Hobbit* and Fascism." *Midwest Quarterly* 51.1 (Autumn 2008): 15–27.

Flieger, Verlyn. "A Postmodern Medievalist?" In *Tolkien's Modern Middle Ages.* Eds. Jane Chance and Alfred K. Siewers. New York: Palgrave Macmillan, 2005. 17–28.

_____. *A Question of Time: J.R.R. Tolkien's Road to Faërie.* Kent: Kent State University Press, 1997.

_____. *There Would Always Be a Fairy Tale: More Essays on Tolkien.* Kent: Kent State University Press, 2017.

Fonstad, Karen Wynn. *The Atlas of Middle-earth.* Rev. ed. Boston: Houghton Mifflin, 1991.

Foucault, Michel. *Discipline and Punish.* Trans. Alan Sheridan. New York: Vintage, 1977.

Frank, Joseph. *The Idea of Spatial Form.* New Brunswick: Rutgers University Press, 1991.

Fussell, Paul. *The Great War and Modern Memory.* 25th Anniversary ed. Oxford: Oxford University Press, 2000.

Garth, John. *Tolkien and the Great War: The Threshold of Middle-Earth.* London: HarperCollins, 2003.

_____. *The Worlds of J.R.R. Tolkien: The Places that Inspired Middle-earth.* Princeton: Princeton University Press, 2020.

Groot, Jerome de. *The Historical Novel.* London: Routledge, 2010.

Grybauskas, Peter. *A Sense of Tales Untold: Exploring the Edges of Tolkien's Literary Canvas.* Kent: Kent State University Press, 2021.

Hartog, François. *The Mirror of Herodotus: The Representation of the Other in the Writing of History.* Trans. Janet Lloyd. Berkeley: University of California Press, 2009.

Hawthorne, Nathaniel. *The House of the Seven Gables.* Ed. Milton R. Stern. New York: Penguin, 1986.

Honegger, Thomas, and Frank Weinreich, eds. *Tolkien and Modernity.* Zollikofen, Switzerland: Walking Tree, 2006.

Houghton, John Wm., Janet Brennan Croft, Nancy Martsch, John D. Rateliff, and Robin Anne Reid, eds. *Tolkien in the New Century: Essays in Honor of Tom Shippey.* Jefferson, NC: McFarland, 2014.

Hume, Kathryn. *Fantasy and Mimesis: Responses to Reality in Western Literature.* London: Methuen, 1984.

James, Robert Rhodes. *Gallipoli.* New York: Macmillan, 1965.

Jameson, Fredric. *Archaeologies of the Future: The Desire Called Utopia and Other Science Fictions.* London: Verso, 2005.

_____. "Cognitive Mapping." In *Marxism and the Interpretation of Culture.* Eds. Cary Nelson and Lawrence Grossberg. Urbana: University of Illinois Press, 1988. 347–358.

_____. *Fables of Aggression: Wyndham Lewis, or, the Modernist as Fascist.* Berkeley: University of California Press, 1979.

_____. *The Geopolitical Aesthetic: Cinema and Space in the World System.* London and Bloomington: The British Film Institute and Indiana University Press, 1992.

_____. "Introduction." *The Ideologies of Theory, Volume 1: Situations of Theory.* Minneapolis: University of Minnesota Press, 1988. xxv–xxix.

_____. *Marxism and Form: Twentieth-Century Dialectical Theories of Literature.* Princeton: Princeton University Press, 1971.

_____. *The Political Unconscious: Narrative as a Socially Symbolic Act.* Ithaca: Cornell University Press, 1981.

_____. *Postmodernism, or, the Cultural Logic of Late Capitalism.* Durham: Duke University Press, 1991.

_____. *The Seeds of Time.* New York: Columbia University Press, 1994.

_____. *Valences of the Dialectic.* London: Verso, 2009.

Kane, Douglass Charles. *Arda Reconstructed: The Creation of the Published Silmarillion.* Bethlehem, PA: Lehigh University Press, 2011.

Kellner, Douglas. "*The Lord of the Rings* as Allegory: A Multiperspectivist Reading." In *From Hobbits to Hollywood: Essays on Peter Jackson's* Lord of the Rings. Eds. Earnest Mathijs and Murray Pomerance. Amsterdam: Rodopi, 2006. 17–39.

Kermode, Frank. *The Sense of an Ending: Studies in the Theory of Fiction.* Oxford: Oxford University Press, 1967.

Kisor, Yvette. "'Poor Sméagol': Gollum as Exile in Middle-earth." In *Tolkien in the New Century: Essays in Honor of Tom Shippey.* Eds. John Wm. Houghton, Janet Brennan Croft, Nancy Martsch, John D. Rateliff, and Robin Anne Reid. Jefferson, NC: McFarland, 2014. 153–168.

Lafargue, Paul. "Reminiscences of Marx." In *Marx and Engels on Literature and Art: A Selection of Writings.* Eds. Lee

Baxandall and Stefan Morawski. London: Telos Press, 1973. 150–151.

Lakowski, Romuald I. "The Fall and Repentance of Galadriel." In *Perilous and Fair: Women in the Works and Life of J.R.R. Tolkien*. Eds. Janet Brennan Croft and Leslie A. Donovan. Altadena, CA: Mythopoeic Press, 2015. 153–167.

Landa, Ishay. "Slaves of the Ring: Tolkien's Political Unconscious." *Historical Materialism* 10.4 (2002): 113–133.

The Lord of the Rings: The Fellowship of the Ring. Dir. Peter Jackson. New Line, 2001.

The Lord of the Rings: The Return of the King. Dir. Peter Jackson. New Line, 2003.

The Lord of the Rings: The Two Towers. Dir. Peter Jackson. New Line, 2002.

Lukács, Georg. *The Historical Novel*. Trans. Hannah and Stanley Mitchell. Lincoln: University of Nebraska Press, 1983.

_____. *The Theory of the Novel*. Trans. Anna Bostock. Cambridge: MIT Press, 1971.

Luling, Virginia. "An Anthropologist in Middle-earth." *Mallorn: The Journal of the Tolkien Society* 33 (1995): 53–57.

Lynch, Kevin. *The Image of the City*. Cambridge: MIT Press, 1960.

Marcuse, Herbert. "The End of Utopia." *Five Lectures: Psychoanalysis, Politics, and Utopia*. Trans. J. Shapiro and S. Weber. Boston: Beacon Press, 1970. 62–82.

Marx, Karl. *Capital, Volume I*. Trans. Ben Fowkes. New York: Penguin, 1976.

_____. *The Eighteenth Brumaire of Louis Bonaparte*. Trans. anon. New York: International Publishers, 1963.

_____. *Grundrisse: Foundations of the Political Economy*. Trans. Martin Nicolaus. New York: Penguin, 1973.

Marx, Karl, and Friedrich Engels. *The Communist Manifesto*. Trans. Samuel Moore. New York: Signet, 1998.

Mendlesohn, Farah, and Edward James. *A Short History of Fantasy*. London: Middlesex University Press, 2009.

Miéville, China. "Cognition as Ideology: A Dialectic of SF." In *Red Planets: Marxism and Science Fiction*. Eds. Marc Bould and China Miéville. Middletown, CT: Wesleyan University Press, 2009. 231–248.

_____. "Editorial Introduction: Marxism and Fantasy." *Historical Materialism* 10.4 (2002): 39–49.

Mills, Charles. "The Wretched of Middle-earth: An Orkish Manifesto," *The Southern Journal of Philosophy* 60(Suppl. 1).S1 (September 2022), 105–135.

Mitchell, Sebastian. *Utopia and Its Discontents: Plato to Atwood*. New York: Bloomsbury 2020.

Moorcock, Michael. *Wizardry and Wild Romance: A Study of Epic Fantasy*. London: Victor Gollancz Ltd., 1987.

Moretti, Franco. *The Modern Epic: The World System from Goethe to Garcia-Márquez*. London: Verso, 1994.

Nicolay, Theresa Freda. *Tolkien and the Modernists*. Jefferson, NC: McFarland, 2014.

Nietzsche, Friedrich. "On the Uses and Disadvantages of History for Life." *Untimely Meditations*. Ed. Daniel Breazeale. Trans. R.J. Hollingdale. Cambridge: Cambridge University Press, 1997. 57–124.

Pearce, Joseph. *Tolkien, Man and Myth: A Literary Life*. New York: HarperCollins, 1998.

Pratchett, Terry. *The Color of Magic*. New York: Harper, 1989.

_____. "Why Gandalf Never Married" (1985): http://www.ansible.co.uk/misc/tpspeech.html.

Rabkin, Eric S. *The Fantastic in Literature*. Princeton: Princeton University Press, 1976.

Rateliff, John D. *The History of the Hobbit*. 2 vols. Boston: Houghton Mifflin, 2007.

_____. "Inside Literature: Tolkien's Exploration of Medieval Genres." In *Tolkien in the New Century: Essays in Honor of Tom Shippey*. Eds. John Wm. Houghton, Janet Brennan Croft, Nancy Martsch, John D. Rateliff, and Robin Anne Reid. Jefferson, NC: McFarland, 2014. 133–152.

Reid, Robin Anne. "Race in Tolkien Studies: A Bibliographic Essay." In *Tolkien and Alterity*. Eds. Christopher Vaccaro and Yvette Kisor. New York: Palgrave Macmillan, 2017. 33–74.

Rosebury, Brian. *Tolkien: A Cultural Phenomenon*. New York: Palgrave, 2003.

Serge, Victor. *Memoires of the Revolutionary*. Trans. Peter Sedgwick and George Paizis. New York: New York Review of Books, 2012.

Shippey, Tom. *J.R.R. Tolkien: Author of the Century*. Boston: Houghton Mifflin, 2000.

_____. "Orcs, Wraiths, Wights: Tolkien's Images of Evil." In *J.R.R. Tolkien and his Literary Resonances*. Ed. George Clark and Daniel Timmons. Westport, CT: Greenwood, 2000. 183–98.

_____. *The Road to Middle-earth: How J.R.R. Tolkien Created a New Mythology*. Boston: Houghton Mifflin, 2003.

Sofge, Erik. "Orc Holocaust: The Reprehensible Moral Universe of Gary Gygax's Dungeons & Dragons." *Slate Magazine*. Posted Monday, March 10, 2008: http://www.slate.com/id/2186203.

Stanton, Michael N. *Hobbits, Elves, and Wizards: Exploring the Wonders and Worlds of J.R.R. Tolkien's* The Lord of the Rings. New York: Palgrave, 2001.

Stuart, Robert. *Tolkien, Race, and Racism in Middle-earth*. New York: Palgrave Macmillan, 2022.

Suvin, Darko. *Metamorphoses of Science Fiction: On the Poetics and History of a Literary Genre*. New Haven: Yale University Press, 1979.

Tally, Robert T., Jr. *The Critical Situation: Vexed Perspectives in Postmodern Literary Studies*. London: Anthem, 2023.

_____. *Fredric Jameson: The Project of Dialectic Criticism*. London: Pluto, 2014.

_____. *J.R.R. Tolkien's* The Hobbit: *Realizing History Through Fantasy*. New York: Palgrave Macmillan, 2022.

_____. *Spatiality*. London: Routledge, 2013.

_____. "Tolkien's Geopolitical Fantasy: Spatial Narrative in *The Lord of the Rings*." In *Popular Fiction and Spatiality: Reading Genre Settings*. Ed. Lisa Fletcher. New York: Palgrave Macmillan, 2016. 125–140.

_____. *Topophrenia: Place, Narrative, and the Spatial Imagination*. Bloomington: Indiana University Press, 2019.

_____. "'Uruk ... We prefer *Uruk*': Representing the Orc in *The Rings of Power*." In *Tolkien, Race, and Racism*. Ed. Robin Anne Reid. Jefferson, NC: McFarland, forthcoming.

_____. *Utopia in the Age of Globalization: Space, Representation, and the World System*. New York: Palgrave Macmillan, 2013.

Terkel, Studs. *The Good War: An Oral History of World War II*. New York: New Press, 1984.

Thomas, Paul Edmund. "Some of Tolkien's Narrators." In *Tolkien's "Legendarium": Essays on "The History of Middle-earth."* Eds. Verlyn Flieger and Carl F. Hostetter. Westport, CT: Greenwood Press, 2000. 161–181.

Toscano, Alberto, and Jeff Kinkle. *Cartographies of the Absolute*. Winchester: Zero Books, 2014.

Vaccaro, Christopher, and Yvette Kisor, eds. *Tolkien and Alterity*. New York: Palgrave Macmillan, 2017.

Wilson, Edmund. "Oo, Those Awful Orcs!" *The Bit Between My Teeth: Literary Chronicles, 1950-1965*. New York: Farrar, Strauss, and Giroux, 1965. 326–332.

Wise, Dennis Wilson. "On Ways of Studying Tolkien: Notes Toward a Better (Epic) Fantasy Criticism." *Journal of Tolkien Research* 9.1 (2020): https://scholar.valpo.edu/journalofTolkienresearch/vol9/iss1/2.

Woolf, Virginia. "Literary Geography," *Books and Portraits: Some Further Selections from the Literary ad Biographical Writings of Virginia Woolf*. Ed. Mary Lyon. New York: Harcourt, Brace, and Jovanovich, 1977.

Yeskov, Kirill. *The Last Ringbearer*. Trans. Yisroel Markov. Minneapolis: Tenseg Press, 2011.

Young, Helen. *Race and Popular Fantasy Literature: Habits of Whiteness*. London: Routledge, 2016.

Index

Agee, James 20–21
Aldiss, Brian 35
Anderson, Douglas A. 172n3, 173n26
Aristotle 19, 39, 47–48, 50, 117
Auden, W.H. 28
Auerbach, Erich 20

Bakhtin, Mikhail 15, 43, 170n10
Balzac, Honoré de 13, 15
Barthes, Roland 16
Bates, Brian 181n17
Brecht, Bertolt 14, 24, 61, 165

Canavan, Gerry 172n5
Carpenter, Humphrey 171n34, 174n1, 176n1
Certeau, Michel de 86–89, 90, 175n19
Clausewitz, Carl von 133
Collins, Suzanne 67
Conley, Tom 89, 175n27
Conrad, Joseph 13
Croft, Janet Brennan 80, 133, 168n12, 173n25, 173n28, 174n3, 180n12

Dante 50
Delaney, Samuel R. 111, 114
Dostoevsky, Fyodor 15

Eliot, T.S. 51
Engels, Friedrich 2, 26, 150, 165, 169n6, 182n7
Evans, Walker 20–21

Fimi, Dimitra 52–57, 60, 71, 119, 121 136, 169n24, 171n39, 172n44, 173n14, 177n32, 178n6, 180n19
Firchow, Peter E. 121, 167n10, 178n21
Flieger, Verlyn 16, 167n11, 168n12, 169n11
Fonstad, Karen Wynn 19, 168n16, 175n15
Foucault, Michel 16, 87, 89, 116, 175n28
Frank, Joseph 90, 175n29
Fussell, Paul 131–132, 133, 180n1

García-Márquez, Gabriel 42, 145
Garth, John 132–133, 168n16, 169n16, 180n9
Gissing, George 13
Goethe, Johann Wolfgang von 42
Golding, William 145
Groot, Jerome de 58, 172n49

Hawthorne, Nathaniel 44
Hegel, G.W.F. 45, 59
Hoffmann, E.T.A. 56
Homer 47, 50
Honegger, Thomas 168n12
Hume, Kathryn 145, 181n2

Ishiguro, Kazuo 42

Jackson, Peter 4, 64–65, 67–70, 74–78, 79–81, 84–86, 89, 92–94, 99, 105, 111–112, 173n7, 173n21, 173n25, 174n4, 175n18, 176n38, 176n46, 177n34, 178n17, 179n39, 181n38
James, Edward 69, 173n9
James, Robert Rhodes 131, 180n2
Jameson, Fredric 2, 4, 6, 12, 13–15, 19, 27, 31–32, 35–36, 39, 41, 43–44, 51, 58,62, 80–81, 90–91, 96, 111, 141, 146–148, 151, 155, 157–160, 162, 164–165, 167n2, 167n10, 181n9, 182n6
Joyce, James 28, 35, 42, 47, 145

Kane, Douglass Charles 171n25
Kellner, Douglas 95–97, 176n43
Kermode, Frank 31, 169n26
Kinkle, Jeff 78, 174n31

Lafargue, Paul 167n7
Lakowski, Romuald I. 177n28
Lefebvre, Henri 19
Le Guin, Ursula 111, 145
Lewis, C.S. 53, 171n34

Index

Lewis, Wyndham 13, 15
Lukács, Georg 12, 15, 30, 47–49, 56, 59, 61–62, 149, 165–166, 172n57, 181n11
Luling, Virginia 139
Lynch, Kevin 90, 92, 175n30
Lyotard, Jean-François 2, 23, 31

Manzoni, Alessandro 43–44
Marcuse, Herbert 21, 96, 168n22
Marx, Karl 2, 15, 26, 29, 31–32, 49, 150, 165
McCarthy, Cormac 42
Mendlesohn, Farah 69, 173n9
Melville, Herman 42, 66
Miéville, China 6, 14, 66, 97, 111, 161, 167n6, 181n9, 181n20, 182n1
Mitchell, Sebastian 172n57
Moorcock, Michael 150, 155–156, 181n13
Moretti, Franco 42–43, 46–47, 170n9, 172n56
Morris, William 25
Morrison, Toni 42
Muir, Edwin 98

Nietzsche, Friedrich 114, 116, 128, 129, 157, 169n10

Orwell, George 145

Pearce, Joseph 170n4
Polanski, Roman 66
Pound, Ezra 50
Pratchett, Terry 55–56
Pynchon, Thomas 42, 145

Rabkin, Eric S. 161
Rateliff, John D. 167n1, 170n13, 172n3, 173n26
Reid, Robin Anne 16, 168n12

Scott, Walter 15, 56, 59, 171n42
Serge, Victor 39
Shippey, Tom 19, 36–37, 71, 80, 82–83, 96, 120, 125, 128, 138–139, 141, 145, 156–157, 162, 168n12, 170n4, 173n14, 178n13, 182n32
Sofge, Erik 178n23
Sophocles 66
Suvin, Darko 14, 96, 111, 146, 148–149, 151, 181n9

Terkel, Studs 142–143
Thompson, E.P. 21, 166
Tolkien, Christopher 15, 17–19, 20, 29, 37, 38, 48–49, 51, 58, 70, 71, 84, 109, 119, 128, 134, 144, 170n1, 170n6
Tolkien, J.R.R. *passim*
Toscano, Alberto 78, 174n31

Unwin, Rayner 71, 72–73
Unwin, Stanley 28, 40, 70, 72

Vaccaro, Christopher 168n12
Vertov, Dziga 88
Virgil 47
Vonnegut, Kurt 141, 145

Wagner, Richard 42
Wells, H.G. 145
Williams, Charles 45
Wilson, Edmund 98
Woolf, Virginia 168n16

Yeats, W.B. 145
Yeskov, Kirill 21, 114, 179n48
Young, Helen 177n32

www.ingramcontent.com/pod-product-compliance
Lightning Source LLC
Chambersburg PA
CBHW032102300426
44116CB00007B/853